BULLIES & ALLIES: BOOK 2

THE GOAT DRIVER

A Story of Trust That Bonds Friendships and Saves Lives

By JAMES F. JOHNSON

The Goat Driver: A Story of Trust That Bonds Friendships and Saves Lives
Bullies & Allies: Book 2
Copyright © 2018 by James F. Johnson. All rights reserved.

Published by:
Aviva Publishing
Lake Placid, NY
(518) 523-1320
www.AvivaPubs.com

All Rights Reserved. No part of this book may be used or reproduced in any manner whatsoever without the expressed written permission of the author. Address all inquiries to:

James F. Johnson
james@jamesfjohnson.com
jamesfjohnson.com

ISBN: 978-1-944335-90-8
Library of Congress Control Number: 2017916368

Editing: Tyler Tichelaar, Superior Book Productions
Cover Designer: Nicole Gabriel, AngelDog Productions
Interior Book Layout: James F Johnson
Author Photo: Robin L. Nellist

Every attempt has been made to source all quotes properly.
Printed in the United States of America
First Edition
2 4 6 8 10 12

The GOAT DRIVE

For my family, Colette, Stephen, Casey, & Corrine, Joey, Ben and Yvonne, and for Trip

Your faith in me has taught me that I can trust those who love me.

JAMES F JOHNSON

The GOAT DRIVE

*People feel alone on a planet filled with people who feel alone.
But, in truth, we're together.*

*If we learn the proper way to trust and be trusted,
then we're strong together.*

JAMES F JOHNSON

The GOAT DRIVE

All the characters in the Bullies & Allies series are fictional

Torano Island, along with all its street names, businesses, schools and churches, is fictional

Norton Hill, Minnesota is also fictional

JAMES F JOHNSON

PART 1

TO FIND AND ACCEPT TRUST

JAMES F JOHNSON

NORTHERN MINNESOTA RURAL HIGHWAY

Late Afternoon, Friday, August 2, 1974

JAMES F JOHNSON

The GOAT DRIVE

1

Rescue For a Rescue

My name is Kyle Rickett. I was fourteen when I met and befriended Tuck Taylor. He was twenty-one. We became inseparable after only a few, somewhat rocky days. We soon learned that to explain our intense bond and our age difference, we were wise to introduce ourselves as brothers.

Officer Schuman, now retired, has never forgotten the day he met us in August of 1974. He proudly wrote Chapter 1 for me.

By Minnesota State Police Officer, Rick Schuman

My lazy Friday afternoon patrol was ruined by another punk kid in another fast car. For nearly a year, most chases had been with slower, smaller cars, but now that the 1973-1974 oil crisis was over, some surviving old, big, fast hotrods were coming out of mothballs with a vengeance.

"God damn it!" I blurted out. The old GTO flew past me like Highway 6 was an airport runway. "God-damned kids!"

I spun the patrol car around with a nasty screech of rubber on road, hit the gas and sirens, and called it in. "Beth, this is Schuman. I'm in pursuit of a mid-1960s Pontiac GTO, gold in color. He's flying fast and low northbound on Highway 6, about fifteen miles north of Deer River."

"Roger that, Rick. Do you need backup?"

"Na. I got it. Looks like Texas plates, but I can't read them yet. I'll call it in when I catch up…if he doesn't kill himself first!"

"Good luck. Sounds like a fast car."

"Don't you worry, young lady. I can catch this one. There's nowhere for him to go on this stretch of highway."

The chase turned out to be a snoozer. Once I got up to about ninety, the driver gave up. My favorite kind of chase. My guess was that it was a kid. The way they gave up quick, I figured there'd be no trouble.

White-haired boy

I coasted to a stop behind the now quiet hotrod.

"Beth, this is Schuman.…" I gave her the license plate and the exact mile marker where we'd stopped. She told me my deputy, Anders, was heading in my direction and that she would let him know where I was.

I looked toward the car to see the driver doing something I hated. He or she was getting out of the car. That's when my adrenaline started pumping. I jumped out of mine as fast as I could with one hand up and the other hovering over my holster.

"Just stay in the car!"

The driver's hands went up quick. He or she was tiny. Shorter than the roof of the car, and with the whitest hair I'd ever seen. Was it a little old man? A short-haired, bleached-blonde woman? He or she was wearing a filthy white tank top, yellow gym shorts, and some kind of hiking boots. "Jesus!" I questioned. "Is that a little *kid*?"

"Help!" he screamed, not getting back in the car. "Please help! Officer, it's an emergency. Can you help us find a hospital *please*?"

Knowing this could be a trick, I unsnapped my gun holster.

"Just step away from the car and keep your hands up, young man."

The kid's voice hadn't changed yet. No way should he have been driving that car. He followed my orders better now, but at the same time, I saw no other head through the back window. So, who was "us," why was he so covered in dirt and leaves, but driving such a nicely kept hotrod, and why were "they" going in the opposite direction of a hospital? Unless this was a kid who stole his neighbor's car, nothing was adding up yet, so I carefully walked toward him, maintaining an always important authoritative swagger.

"My brother's hurt."

"Is he in the car?"

The boy nodded politely and pointed through the open driver's door.

"How did he get hurt?"

"A tree fell on him." He pointed again, but more frantically into the car. His polite voice began to rise in panic. "We were cutting wood for our grandpa. Please hurry."

I finally made it to the driver's door with one eye on him and another on the passenger's seat. I wasn't ready for what I saw.

"Oh, Mother of *God*," I gasped.

One hell of a lot of blood

In the passenger's seat lay a young man, early twenties maybe, passed out cold—or dead. His thick light brown hair definitely looked like it had been professionally styled before it got messed up. That told me he wasn't a backwoods hick or a 1970s hippy. His jeans were torn at the knee, and his right leg was covered in blood from waist to boot. His white tank top was spattered with a blend of blood, mud, and more tree pieces.

"When did this happen?" I bellowed.

"About an hour ago. He isn't bleeding as bad as it looks; it's just soaked into his pants."

I glanced disbelievingly back at the boy, then at his injured brother. Obviously, reality wasn't setting in with this kid at the moment.

"I'd say he's bleeding pretty bad, son." I should have been less blunt with the poor kid. "This is as God-damned *serious* as it gets!"

The boy was so small. I don't know how he drove that big car as fast as he did. The top of his head barely reached my chin. He looked more panicked after I said what I said. I snagged his elbow before he could pass out.

"What's your name, son?"

"Kyle…Taylor." He tried holding it together and politely answering the questions he knew I had for him next. "That's my brother, Tuck. It's his car." He burst into bawling, "He can't die! He can't die! *Please*, don't let him die! He's all I have left!"

"Shh-shh-shh. I'll do everything I can, Kyle. Come with me." I pulled him by his shoulders toward the back of his car to get him off the highway before someone ran him over. I'd been a cop for two decades and cleaned up plenty of roadside bloodbaths, but this kid was choking me up. His voice had a sadness to it that I have never since been able to forget. "Will you stay right here for me, Kyle?"

The kid nodded, but I wasn't sure how coherent he was.

"I'm calling for an ambulance. Okay? Don't move from that spot!"

"I was trying to get him to a hospital!" He nodded more frantically and kept craning his neck toward his brother in the car. "Please hurry!"

"Deer River Hospital's the other way, son!" I shouted back as I grabbed my open driver's door and faced him again.

He snapped his head toward both directions like he was trying to figure out where he was, but his eyes were glossing over. His expression, though panicked, was also turning vacant. He'd held it together pretty well to get his brother this far, but now that I was here to help, I think he was starting to fall apart. I've seen it before in bloody accidents. Shock. But this Kyle kid went into it deeper and quicker than any kid that age had done before. I think the poor youngster was dropping into his own private hell just then.

"Beth, get me an ambulance as fast as you can."

"Roger that Rick. I'll get Anders there also. What's going on?"

The GOAT DRIVE

"The passenger's been hurt. His little brother, looks to be no more than twelve, was trying to drive him to a hospital. It looks bad, Beth. Some sort of an accident in the woods. Get someone here fast." I looked up at Kyle again. He was starting to shiver and turn gray. He was becoming more and more frazzled by the second. "Beth, I think the driver's going in to a bad case of shock and I can't deal with both these boys. Call a second ambulance. And Anders needs to get here *now*!"

"He's three minutes out."

"Tell him to *speed it up*! I need him *now*!" I threw the mike onto the seat and ran back to the car to see if I could stop any bleeding while we waited for backup and an ambulance, which I knew would be a while. Kyle had handled himself well, but he hadn't seemed to realize that he was headed fast in the wrong direction

JAMES F JOHNSON

ONE WEEK PRIOR

Duluth Union Depot Train Station

Almost Noon, Saturday July 27, 1974

JAMES F JOHNSON

2

Meet My Destiny

I arrived in the Duluth Union Depot Train Station on Saturday morning, fully expecting my grandpa, Papa Louie, to pick me up. I'd been sent without notice from my home in Washington State and was in the worst mood of my life. When Papa didn't show, my bad mood morphed into downright enraged infuriation.

Rather than pick me up, the old coot sent his neighbor's grandson to get me. Some guy I didn't know named Tuck Taylor. This is hard to admit, but my life was such a train wreck that when I saw Tuck staring at me, I honestly thought he wanted to pay me for sex—can you believe that? It definitely shows what a mess I was that summer. As embarrassing as it is to say now, I had actually planned to take him into the men's room to do whatever I thought he wanted in exchange for enough money to buy a steak dinner. I'd barely eaten in days and I was starving. But when he introduced himself, he seemed kind. So I kept that messed-up first impression to myself.

Now that you know of my mistake that Tuck wanted to purchase sex from me, I assume you can see just how bad my *summer was turning out to be—surreal bad. I was not a street kid—yet. Up until only one day earlier, I didn't even know boys did that for money. I was a normal, sheltered, American teenage 1970s boy, viewing the world from a new and abnormal angle.*

What nice-guy-Tuck didn't know was that I'd recently been educated in the real world, molested by my father's best friend, Dr. Krieg, and then sent away by my family who was too dysfunctional to deal with my emotional withdrawals and chronic nightmares. Papa Louie had apparently agreed to care for me for a few weeks as if this were a standard summer visit. I didn't know what Papa had been told, but I was pretty sure my family members back home were giving themselves time to sweep my mess under the rug.

The way I saw things, I had been abandoned by my trusted family for being molested by their trusted friend, which meant I had no idea how to trust anyone at all, including some kind, gentle, "trusted" friend of my grandfather's. But he was my only ride offer, and because I was confused about who I did and didn't trust anymore, I didn't know if I should go home with him or not.

By Kyle Rickett

"Yeah...home. I'm here to take you home." Tuck's concerned eyes drilled downward into mine. Adult to child. I didn't trust adults. But he had a young face. He was about six inches taller than me, but I was small for my age. He was probably 5' 9" or so. Time briefly slowed as I sorted through my memories, trying to remember if I'd ever met him before. He seemed so familiar. "Kyle? Are you okay?"

"Um." I cleared my throat, shook my head once quickly and forced a smile. "I'm fine." I shrugged to at least *look* confident, "Why *wouldn't* I be?"

He paused for a second. "You seem kind of...." He broke the gaze and lifted his tone. "never mind. Louie asked me to give you a ride."

"A ride?" That was a trigger word, which only added more confusion. I was still trying to process whether I even remembered having ever met Tuck before, which, in turn meant that he was technically a *stranger who wanted to give me a ride*.

"Yeah…um." Tuck tipped his head in an exaggerated look of curiosity. "You know…in a *car*?" He chuckled once at his own question.

Old Kyle doesn't accept rides from strangers!

I know this is going to sound silly, especially after I'd spent a couple of recent weeks privately rehearsing hitchhiking moves on the highway that led off my hometown of Torano Island, Washington State. I'd planned to snag a trucker who would help me escape my messed-up family—whom I loved desperately, but I couldn't trust. But this surprisingly discombobulated moment of accepting or rejecting a ride wasn't practice; it was real. An *actual stranger* offered me an *actual ride*. As crazy as it sounds, there were two Kyles fighting for the helm in my head that morning. New Kyle had been learning to hitch rides and how to offer to take potential customers into men's bathrooms. But without warning, all my childhood training kicked in, and from out of nowhere, Old Kyle stepped up to try to stop me.

"Uh." I pretended to laugh at his comment, to look like I was still in control of my brain. Was this a trap? The problem was that more voices than just mine were in my head. My controlling mother and my condescending older sister were always in my head, judging me. Always. If I accepted a ride from a stranger, *would Mom find out*? I wasn't so afraid of this stranger killing me, but I was terrified that if he did, Fran would get her ultimate chance to roll her eyes and laugh at my headstone, saying, "I always knew he'd do something stupid like that." I was never, *ever* to get into cars with strangers. My survival was dependent on not being that outrageous story Mom used to tell about the boy who'd hitchhiked with the wrong guy and got his arms cut off.

"I should call my grandpa and ask if he knows you."

"Oh. Gotcha." He winked at me like I had just teased him.

"No, really."

"You're…you're not kidding?" He sounded surprised and looked down at himself like he couldn't figure out what I was afraid of. "*Really?*"

"Yeah, really." I didn't want to look him in the eye now. So I glanced over toward the payphone and tapped my pocket for coins. "I'm supposed to call—"

"Says who?"

"I…" His question surprised me. Everyone knows a kid isn't supposed to accept rides from strangers. "I'm just…I'm *supposed* to."

"But…there's no one to call. He's *not* home." Still not taking me seriously, he leaned forward and quietly shared, "Otherwise, he'd have come himself."

"Oh." I froze. Calling home was where the training always ended. No one ever said what I was supposed to do if no one was home.

"Kyle, relax…I'm unarmed." He comically patted himself down and grinned with only half a mouth. With his fairly long, thick light brown hair, he reminded me a lot of my best friend back home, Conner Mason. In fact, his joking smile was a near perfect Connor-like expression.

I laughed ever so slightly, in part from nerves, but also because he was the first person to talk with me for this long in over a week. I may not have been happy about the situation, but talking with anyone who would joke around with me was almost like getting a big, warm hug. Tuck was funny. I admit I *liked* his attention. And his humor, and his boyish expression—a lot.

"I'm pretty trustworthy," he added.

To trust or not to trust

My relational brain went to work making mental comparisons with things I already knew. For one thing, he looked like Connor, and Connor would never tattle on me for getting in a car, so maybe Tuck wouldn't either. That was good. I wanted to trust him so I took his looking like Connor as sound proof that I could. Then I searched his face for more reasons.

The GOAT DRIVE

Smiling stretched his upper lip, which exposed a well-healed three-quarter-inch scar, like from a childhood playground accident. It added interest to an otherwise ordinary, but nice, face. He was flawed, like me. I liked that. He wasn't intimidating, or perfect. Perhaps, like me, he knew the sting of being treated like shit for not being perfect, which would be another reason to trust him. Right? Like kindred spirits. Two peas in a pod. Brothers of the playground war zone.

I envied his thick, sandy-colored "normal" hair because of how self-conscious I was of my odd, almost pure white albino mop. His was longer than mine, thick, parted just off-center and feathered. I best liked the way his heavy bangs draped lazily across an eye. While waiting for my answer, he did that classic four-fingertip move of trailing it back behind an ear. Hair like that would have made me look good. How could I not trust someone who had hair like what I wanted?

"Uh." He had something else I wanted—a ride home. But what would he want from me in return? In my family, it seemed like there would eventually be something I'd have to give up for making my brother or sister drive a half hour each way for me. What would Tuck want? And when? I didn't like the mix of feelings. I was being hurried into trusting a stranger who seemed nice. It was a Catch-22. He claimed family had sent him for me, but that same family had rules against it. Old Kyle wanted to obey his mother's cautious voice in his head, and let this stranger just turn and leave. But for some complicated reason, New Kyle wanted to go with him, *no matter where he was going.*

"Well?" He exaggerated a shrug by lifting both shoulders and eyebrows. Again, acting like a kid.

I tried not to laugh, but I couldn't hold back. I liked him. Something about him felt so comfortable. But this was only more confusing. My mind started racing. For crying out loud—*I'd just planned to offer a bathroom encounter with him in exchange for a steak dinner!* On the other hand, I wasn't ready for an on-the-spot decision about an actual family law. *What if Mom finds out?* I looked toward the front door and angrily asked in my head, *Why did Papa have to go and send a stranger?* This wasn't *fair*. Frustration and anger welled as I knew I could be punished for either choice.

"God!" I blurted out, irritated.

"What?" He shrugged again, but his eyes widened, still confused.

Then, as the pressure started pounding, I looked at his unthreatening body and heard another in a series of snapping sounds in my head. All the pressure vanished, as it had with that same snapping sound the night before when I stepped off the train in St. Paul and wandered carefree into the night for an hour.

"You want a ride home or not?" he asked.

"You know what?" My shoulders dropped in relief. With a new smile of my own, I nodded. "*Fuck it.*" New Kyle had fully returned, and just like the night before, he had made me ready to wander into the unknown without a care in the world.

"Fuck it?" Still trying to figure me out, he looked at the door, "So…" then he looked again at me "…we're *cool?*"

New Kyle to the rescue

"We're cool." Anxiety had vanished. Old Kyle was *gone*. So were the ghosts of Mom and Fran. Somehow or other, no one was left in my head to argue with. Louie wasn't coming. I didn't have another ride. The train was gone and I couldn't go home. The decision had just gotten super-easy. In fact, I thought it was ironic that *Mom* was the one who had sent me into this stupid mess and Mom would be the one most worried about me getting into a stranger's car.

I almost hoped that getting into this sexy-haired, scarred stranger's car was the wrong choice. I smirked while imagining Mom screaming for me to tell him *no*! Then I envisioned her guiltily sobbing at my armless funeral. That'd teach her to send me away.

But as hot tension vented off, cold sarcasm settled in.

"You know what? If you've got ten minutes, Tuck Taylor," I boldly asked, "you want to go to the bathroom first?" There! *Take that, Mom.*

"Uh." He cocked his head back, then looked over at the restroom door. "Uh."

While he faced away, I slowly shook my head in disbelief at what I'd just asked him. There was no doubt now that there really were *two* Kyles in my body.

"Um, no. I, um…I went before I left the house. I'll watch your bags if you need to go." He looked back at me with a confused furl to his brow.

"Tsahhh," I sighed kind of arrogantly.

"What?" He started to sound irritated.

"Let's just get in your car." I picked up the duffle bag, momentarily straightening my middle finger, safely flipping Mom the bird where only God would see it.

"Wow…you're a little hard to figure out." He paused and blinked several times. *That* turned out to be an easy sell after all."

"Got any pot?" I firmly changed gears on him.

"Pot?" He questioningly glared into my eyes.

I shrugged.

"Why?" he grunted, unable to restrain a laugh. "Are you a *cop*?"

"No!" I bolted back. "A *cop*?" I looked down at my dirty little body, my filthy white T-shirt, child-size blue suitcase, and duffel bag. "Of course I'm not a *cop*!"

"Then why'd you ask for pot?"

"I was just…wondering."

"Okay, well…" He looked at the ceiling and shook his head, "it doesn't matter either way; I don't have any pot."

"Too bad."

"I don't have any liquor either," he sarcastically joked.

"That's fine," I replied. "I don't drink anyway."

"I don't have any hookers, or dice, or tickets to a basement cock fight either."

"Okay. Okay!" I angrily answered. "I get it. I was just *asking*."

"All right, I'm glad we got that cleared up."

"Whatever," I mumbled.

"Yeah. *Whatever*." He contemptuously pointed to the parking lot. "Car's outside. I'll carry something." Then he mumbled something too, but just under his breath. I was pretty sure it was, *"so we can get this over with and I can be done with you."*

"Na, I got it." I nodded for him to lead. A moment of dizziness returned—I assumed from the two Kyles inside my head fighting for control of my mouth. With the place emptied and his back turned, I was free to look up and down the mysterious Tuck Taylor. He was dressed like anyone in 1974 might have been, in tight dark blue jeans tucked into cowboy boots, and a loose red tank top. Around his neck, a thin leather strap trailed into his shirt, pulled taught by something heavy. His athletic arms were bare, but a tan line showed he used to wear a watch. He wasn't a tie-dyed hippy, but more like a naturalist. Probably played guitar and sang "Kumbaya." Not, in any way who I had anticipated leaving the station with.

In a crowd, I'd have never noticed him. He didn't look threatening. He certainly wasn't ugly, but neither was he strikingly handsome. He was John Q. Public. A wallflower whose great hair, flawless skin, and warm smile elevated his plain-ness to not-bad-looking status. Having an unusual name, Tuck seemed out of place. I'd never met anyone with that name before. He should have been a John or a Dan or a Mike.

He cordially held the station door and watched me pass. I glanced at his mouth and speculated about the scar. It trailed from the left side of his upper lip almost all the way to the nose. Sort of a colorless crease that added a hint of uniqueness to his smile. Once past, the hot sun beat down, forcing me to squint. I focused all my attention on a flash in the parking lot. That's when things became *truly* surreal.

"Holy shit," I whispered quietly.

"What?" He'd heard me.

"That's not *yours,* is it?"

Meeting the Goat

It was the only car in the lot, so it had to be his. Parked facing us was the most beautiful—no, the most *gorgeous*—shimmering gold 1967 Pontiac GTO I'd ever laid eyes on. I drew a slow breath in awe. As the sun's reflection flickered in the chrome and glass, chills permeated my back, shoulders, arms, and fingers. It was the exact car I'd been trying to find for my Hot Wheels collection. It was perfectly outfitted with my favorite Cragar Mag wheels. The rear was slightly lifted to make room for the large hotrod tires. It was a hunting cat—a cougar—ready to chase down a deer. There was nothing I'd change if it were mine. I'd dreamt of owning a real version of this exact car for years. In fact, another in a long string of dizzy spells made me question if I was even awake.

"You all right?" Tuck caught up with me from behind.

"Uh...yeah." I stopped gawking for a moment to glance at him on my right. I flatly moaned, "Nice car, man."

"Thanks." He proudly smiled, stepped over the yellow parking curb, and tapped the fender.

He opened the passenger door as if being polite to a date. But instead of holding it for me, he crawled in head-first and reached across the dashboard. I heard keys jingling. He backed out holding the ring, then stepped to the trunk and inserted one of them. The lid squeaked and ascended.

I continued to spin into the dream-state. This couldn't be real. But in case it was, I followed carefully and lifted the bags high over the taillights, being respectful not to touch the car and risk a scratch. Tuck slammed the lid shut, which sent a warm blast of air against my chest and allowed my eyes to fall onto the GTO emblem, which then sent shivers through me. I couldn't believe this car was real. And it was rescuing me from being alone in the train station. I returned to the open passenger door and got in. All the windows were open. It was warm but not scorching inside.

"This *is* your car, right?" I mumbled barely audibly. My moods were all over the charts. I was relieved that he was taking me to Papa's, suspicious about being tattled on, angry about being in Minnesota at all, and confused about sitting in the car from my dreams.

"What the hell's *that* supposed to mean?"

"The keys were in it. You're not just taking it?" I showed no expression.

"It's mine." He smirked like he wasn't sure that I was joking.

"Don't you like the car?"

"What?" He squinted his eyes like he was really trying hard to figure out what I was yacking about.

"You take the keys so no one steals it."

"But I left the keys and no one stole it."

"You got lucky."

He didn't answer this time. Maybe he could see my point.

"You're a trusting guy to leave them in the ignition like that." I ran with it.

"I do it all the time, Kyle."

"But it's a GTO."

"*But it's a GTO,*" he mocked in a cartoony voice. "We car guys call it a—"

"A '*Goat.*' I know what *we car guys call it.*" I taunted back. "But how can you leave the keys in it like that?"

"Are you *scolding* me?" he challenged.

I huffed and rolled my eyes.

"I'm a big boy, Kyle. I don't need a 'talkin'-to.' This is Duluth. No one's touched it. And *I* should be the one scolding *you.*" Tuck put the key in, but he didn't turn it.

"This isn't the best part of Duluth, Tuck. You're not on your grandpa's farm now. A car like this needs to be protected better."

"Okay!" He put up a hand to stop me from saying more. "Maybe you're right. Maybe I should be more careful when I'm in town like this. But don't scold me. You know, *I'm* the adult here!" He smirked again and spun the conversation against me. "You're the dumb little kid who got into a car with a stranger—didn't your mama teach you that you're never supposed to do that?"

Rocky start

"I'm not afraid," I lied.

The GOAT DRIVE

"Why not? You don't even know me."

"You look safe." I shrugged sarcastically, and thought *fuck it*. If this was a trap, I was already caught.

"We always do…." Then he twisted at the waist toward me, lifted his hands above his head, and waved them crazily, "BLAAAAH!"

Unamused, I rolled my eyes again.

"Blah," he teasingly whispered.

I sat still, too angry at Mom for putting me into this situation to enjoy Tuck.

"Blah, blah, blah." If not for his mouth, no other muscle moved. "Blah." He stared for a second longer before dropping his hands and untwisting into the driver's seat. "Yeah, you're definitely not in any danger." He bounced to get comfortable. "Nobody's going to hurt *you*."

"Why's that?"

"Because you smell." He laughed again. I could tell my attitude was pissing him off. "No one'll get close to you right now—unless they use a ten-foot pole."

That comment embarrassed me. Bad. He was right. I smelled. How could I have tried to look cool when I was such a real-life mess? Back home, my adult sister, Fran, and even my former Catholic school classmate/best-friend-turned-enemy, Andreo, would have had a field-day if they could have seen how far into the dumps I'd sunk. How vulnerable I'd become. One more reason for both to point and laugh and abuse. Being smaller than average, I figured the dirty shirt alone made me look like a three-year-old. I could hear Fran's voice in my head calling me disgusting and making sure I knew that better people didn't stink like me. As I sank deeper into my usual shame, that moment with Tuck had become utterly humiliating. He was probably going to tell both grandpas how disgusting I was. Somehow Fran was going to find out about this and the bullying would begin as soon as I got settled.

"I've had a rough week." I humbly looked down at the stained shirt while running my hand through my itchy white hair. I was starting to hate Tuck Taylor. "I promise I'll clean up when I get to Grandpa's."

"I'm just glad the windows are down," he mumbled. The engine awoke from its slumber with a musical rumble, filling my chest and the passenger compartment the way some crescendos fill a cathedral.

Make it about the car

"Wowwww," I accidentally whispered.

Tuck turned and winked. A nice distraction from my schizophrenic morning. The car slowly backed up. The engine revved once like a growl as Tuck shifted into first and then crept toward the road. He tapped the throttle a second time before pulling out onto the street. It sounded sexy. Now I started liking him again.

"This car's my best friend," he admitted while slowly accelerating onto Michigan Street.

"Then you shouldn't leave your keys in it." I didn't mean that as a dig. I was sincerely worried he was going to lose it.

"I will be more careful in the future." His answer seemed as sincere as my advice had been.

"Well, the engine sounds nice." Talking about any car was always a welcome diversion for me, but talking about this one, at *this* time, was an especially liberating break from focusing on my aroma. I did, however, self-consciously hold my arms tightly down, hoping not to release any extra pit odor. "A four-hundred?"

"Duh. What else is there?"

"Wow." I nodded with a smile. "And a four speed. In signet gold…black buckets." I looked at him, the proud owner. "It's a rare combination for a Goat." Then, in an effort to prove I was smart, I asked, "How about the gear ratio?"

He chuckled once. "The gear *what* with the who now?"

"Ratio. Is it geared quick or fast?" Excellent! I knew something he didn't.

"Quick or…fast? Aren't they the same thing?"

"No." I smiled like I couldn't believe he didn't know.

"Well, it's kind of…both, isn't it?"

"Hmm." I nodded like I was a genius. In reality, I'd listened to my dad talking to truckers my whole life. Gears were a big thing in their world, so I had a rudimentary understanding of gearing in general, plus I had coincidentally recently read an article about Mustangs, Camaros, and GTOs, so I rattled off what I'd learned in that article. "Probably 3.23 to 1. That's the best ratio for a street car." The fact that I'd remembered those exact numbers is what surprised me the most.

"Wow." He chuckled again like I'd surprised him. "I guess I got lucky then."

"Yeah." I'd proven myself to him, so I restated my earlier comment. "It's a perfect combination for a Goat."

He smiled at me like he thought I'd said something cute.

I shrugged back like I was just stating a fact.

"Truth is I kind of stumbled onto it. The three-to-whatever the gears are were in it already."

"You got lucky. This would be a hard car to find on purpose."

"Well, I'll admit, you really know your cars." He nodded approvingly. "So what's your favorite?"

"I dunno. Don't really have one." While being grateful to have proven my smarts on a topic we both had an interest in, I wasn't sure if I liked him or not, and so I wasn't anywhere near ready to give him the satisfaction of knowing that my favorite was *his*. "I like lots of cars."

3

Passenger Assessment

I've talked about what it was like for me to meet Tuck, and he was having a mixed reaction to me in return. When he was asked to pick me up, he remembered my photographs along Papa Louie's walls and assumed, by the fact that I was always smiling on film, that I'd be a bundle of joy in real life.

Surprise!

By Tuck Taylor

I carefully rolled us out onto Michigan Street, disappointed that this kid wasn't as happy and fun-loving as the photos had always made me think he was. I glanced over at him whenever I shifted gears. The photos weren't wrong about one thing; aside from being a road-worn mess, he was an exceptionally cute little dude. But he was small. Real small. Way smaller than I ever imagined, but it made him even cuter. His cheekbones were big and his hair nearly pure white. He was literally the blondest young person I'd ever physically seen. If his eyebrows hadn't been so white also, I'd have assumed he was bleached.

The most disheartening aspect of all this was that I was getting tired of not having any friends at this point in my life. College had taken me to Texas for two years, which separated me from childhood buddies, and my very best friend Trenton, who'd moved to Texas with me, had come out as gay, which was a bigger deal in the '70s than it is now, and even though I was fine with it all, he joined a lifestyle I couldn't keep up with. He'd recently moved to New York to live with others who were more like him than I was, which left me in Texas alone. I couldn't handle that, so during the past two days I'd driven myself and my best friend, The Goat, back up to Northern Minnesota to stay with Grandpa. As of that morning, I had begun to hope Louie's grandson would be someone I could go out for a burger with. Maybe toss the Frisbee around and talk with about baseball, girls, or even about our grandfathers…anything other than the dull, lonely life I'd been reduced to as of late.

Sadly, my car seemed to be the only topic that didn't start an argument between us. I loved my car, but I wasn't the kind of guy who liked to talk about it. I had no idea what kind of gears it had. Didn't really care. I just liked how it looked and sounded. I didn't have much more dialogue to offer Kyle on that topic, so he wasn't proving to be as much fun as I'd hoped.

Shame on me for projecting my personality expectations onto someone without ever meeting him, I guess. As a psychology major, I should have been more self-aware. Kyle was not the new friend I had been planning to make after all. He was apparently just going to be a manic-depressive passenger for a quick half-hour ride home—a favor to my grandfather who gave my cab service as a favor to Kyle's grandfather.

4

First Ride on the Bi-Polar-Coaster

> *I didn't believe I'd know Tuck Taylor for much longer than the duration of a drive to Papa's house. The ride was a roller coaster of emotions, such as I had never before experienced. Gone from my family for the first time ever, I was a free spirit in a conversation with a stranger. As bad as some of the moments were, I also had some moments of fun in my abnormally sarcastic exchanges with Tuck that morning.*

By Kyle Rickett

Traffic was lazy—pretty much non-existent. Michigan Street paralleled the Lake Superior waterfront two blocks from the piers. Our tires clopped in a rhythmic gallop to the equally spaced crevices between its concrete slabs. The warmth of Tuck's introductory handshake still soothed my right wrist like he had a magic touch. And talking about his car had left us in a friendly state. Now safely en route to Papa's, I could relax.

It was comforting to me to know the exact course Tuck would take home. While this was only my fourth trip by train, Dad had driven us cross country too many times to count, so once Tuck and I left the train station, the highway route was the same. Knowing every familiar bump and turn gave me a grounded feeling of control.

We crossed the tracks I'd ridden into town and veered east, up the onramp and onto State Highway I-35. Tuck crossed the tracks faster than Dad usually did, and Tuck's GTO springs were stiffer than the ones on Dad's Oldsmobile, so the tracks rattled us a bit more than I was used to. It was kind of fun. The current speed limit was fifty-five, to which Tuck accelerated firmly, nestling me, like we were on a carnival ride, into the seatback and teasing a faint smile from me. I think he was driving like this to be playful, but having just met him, I didn't know for sure. By the sound of his RPMs and the points where he shifted, I believed my guess to be right. He was running 3.23 gears. Exactly what I would get in my Goat someday. Mentally confirming memorized car facts grounded me with a sense of stability and eased my nerves.

As we sped predictably up the onramp, I closed my eyes and pretended we were taking flight. Warm wind rose up to buffet our hair while a throaty engine vibration massaged my legs through the seat. I knew that if Tuck drove the same speed as Dad and Papa, I-35 would last for eighteen minutes before reaching Big Lake Road, where we'd go another fifteen minutes to reach a canopy of shade trees that would envelop us; then Tuck would downshift for a hard left onto the Carlsson Trunk cut-off. Papa's farm would be eight-tenths of a mile on the left. Technically, Papa's farm wasn't in Duluth, but just outside the city limits of Cloquet, which is twenty miles from Duluth. But my family had always called the whole region Duluth in the same way we called our Torano Island home Seattle. We lived forty miles north of Seattle, but it was so much easier to tell people we were from a city whose name was recognized most anywhere.

About four minutes in, I realized I didn't want to fade into my head, comforting myself by correctly predicting every inch of the trip, because that was making me miss out on the experience that *this* ride wasn't imaginary, like the thousand or so I'd driven in my mind to escape unbearable Catholic school classroom isolation. I cleared my throat and pulled myself back into the present moment so I could *enjoy* the warm, sensory-rich, real-live journey in progress.

"Thanks for picking me up." My eyes remained closed as I contemplated how Tuck had no possible way of knowing how complicated my head was. I'd tried to kill myself only hours earlier, and I was still wrestling with wondering why I had so many detached and bizarre new memories of being hurt in ways a boy should never be hurt by his dad's best friend. These soul-sucking problems were mine to deal with alone. I was doing my best to hide all the new revelations back into the shadows where they used to live so I could just be my naïve, ignorant, happy-go-lucky little self again. It wasn't working too well. Only for short blasts here and there. The anger kept exploding between smiles.

"No biggy," Tuck politely responded.

I opened my eyes and looked over at him, then to my right at the fencing and trees whizzing by. I wrapped my fingers around the door handle to make sure it was real, and inhaled a long, deep helping of the aroma of sundried grass. "Thank God," I whispered to myself, "I'm not at St. Tiberius's right now."

I didn't know what was going through Tuck's mind, but the wind was tossing his hair in ways I'd wished it would mine. In fact, I'd begun to wish I *was* him. *He* was cool. For me, the rustling wind and sense of our speed were sobering; it was helping me forget the whole chain of horrible events that had led to that train station freak-out where I'd asked him for pot and offered to take him to the men's room. I hoped he could forget it too.

"So do you live with your grandfather?" I tapped my knee in four-four time as if the radio were on.

"No. I'm from St. Paul."

"Oh." Then I asked, "So why do you have Texas plates?"

"I went to Texas for a couple of years. College."

"Oh. How long have you had the car?"

"Uh." He winced in thought for a moment. "About three years?" He smiled graciously, checked his mirrors, and then refocused on the road. "Yeah." He answered his own question like he'd just done the math in his head. "Almost exactly three years."

"How come it's not rusty?"

"Huh?"

"If you're originally from here, how come the car's not rusty?" I pestered like a little kid. "From the winter road salt?"

"Oh. Um…" he stammered like I'd interrupted a daydream. "You really *do* know shit about cars." He gave me a little nicer smile. "I drove it all year-round in Texas, but it's a summer ride when I'm in the northern states. No winter salt's eatin' *my* car. I'm keepin' it for life."

"Good plan." I nodded. "It's definitely a keeper."

He returned the nod.

"How old are you?" I asked.

"Twenty-one."

"How many more years you got?"

"Eighty, I hope."

"What?" I tipped my head.

"Eighty…years…I *hope*."

"No." I accidentally laughed out loud when I realized how dumb my question sounded. "I mean in *college*."

"Oh!" Tuck laughed too. "Gotcha. I thought you meant…." He laughed again. "Never mind. I'm done. I quit."

"Why?"

"I was getting a degree to be a psychiatrist, but I discovered I hated it."

"Why did you start in the first place?"

"Gads, you ask a lot of questions."

"What made you hate it?"

He playfully chuckled.

"*C'mon;* what made you hate it?"

"Okay, okay." He teasingly shook his head. "If you absolutely *must* know, I found my passion…photography. So I switched plans."

"Oh. Passion." My parents had taught that passion was for dreamers, and that a real man gets a job and pays his bills. I pictured Tuck's awesome hair hovering behind the cold, prying lens of a camera. I saw his gentle, warm fingers press the shutter and advance the film, "passionately," photographing me without my permission, the way Dr. Krieg apparently used to do in secret when I was seven—if my mysterious new memories were based on real events, that is. From out of nowhere, my stomach and wrists began to ache. My heart became a rock. Just my luck. This interesting stranger had to be a fucking photographer. I know that Dr. Krieg was the person I truly owed this hatred to—the reason for my sour gut—my hatred for photographers, but the entanglement of long-standing family values dictated that I wasn't allowed to hate Dad's only friend openly. The irritation had nowhere else to go but onto poor Tuck. Another fucking photographer.

"What?" he asked, noticing my scornful expression.

"Nothing," I muttered while discretely rubbing the now stinging wrist. "Just wondering what you're going to do about a job."

Good thing he's only a ride

"A *job*?" he repeated, going on the defensive. "Weren't you listening?"

"You have to have a *job*. Don't you?"

"I won a state award last year and I *might* be getting one of my fishing pictures into *National Outdoorsman*." His voice rose. "This isn't a whim. I've wanted this my entire life."

"So you like to take pictures," I commented expressionlessly. "That's cool." Then I mumbled, "It's not a job, but...."

He paused as if to ponder my shifting demeanor.

I looked out the window again, hoping we could change the topic back to cars long enough to get me delivered to Papa's so I could get on with my summer alone.

"Exactly what is wrong with *that*? So I want to be a photographer. I'm not ashamed of my choice, Kyle." He sounded like I might not have been the first person to challenge his decision. "I know what I'm doing—and it's *my* life, by the way."

"I hate getting my picture taken."

"Oh, okay." He turned sarcastic. "I'll give up my life's passion of being a photographer because some kid I'm giving a ride to doesn't like getting his picture taken."

I quietly checked my watch. There were seventeen long minutes of travel left, but apparently, I'd lit a short fuse. Perhaps if I sat still, he'd let it go.

"Okay!" He didn't let it go. "I won't take your picture."

"Good!" I blurted cantankerously. "I'm glad." My heart throbbed with fear of being told off, but also with anger at the image of Krieg photographing me naked on his exam table. Another pain shot through my head like an ice pick and I sort of left my body. Dizzily, my conscious awareness moved outside to peer in safely at the two of us through the windshield. Somehow, I felt like I had done this before; left my body to watch myself with someone—someone who had a camera.

"Yeah. *Good*."

He let the conversation rest for a few miles, but he gave dramatic sighs loud enough for me to hear. We made the turn to Big Lake Road and cruised for a good five minutes, by which time I had calmed down enough to move back into my body and apologize.

"I don't know why I said those things, Tuck…. I'm sorry about how that came out." I cleared my nervous throat. "You shouldn't listen to me. I'm a clumsy dork. I didn't mean you shouldn't be a photographer. I just…really hate getting my picture taken." The open confession cured my headache as if by magic.

He examined my face for a few long seconds. I didn't know yet if he was the kind of guy who'd accept an apology or use it, as would Fran or the nuns, as a chance to attack when my sword was down.

"Your grandfather's excited to see you." His quiet forgiveness sounded forced, but to my relief, proved he was not like Fran.

"Sure he is," I droned in self-pity.

"No—he really is, Kyle."

"So that's why he sent *you?*" Anger swelled.

"C'mon," he said kindly. "Don't be like that."

"Really?" I blurted back. *"Don't be like that?* Now I'm the one who's getting scolded?"

"I'm not *scolding* you."

"Well, it feels like it." Words I'd normally not say flowed uncontrolled—which felt oddly wonderful. My hands numbed and trembled because I was unused to letting anger out. "He's retired, but he's so busy he had to send *a stranger* to pick me up?"

"Hey, that is *not* fair." Tuck's voice wasn't calm anymore. "I'm no *stranger*. He trusts me. And I *like* the guy. He doesn't *deserve* that."

I needed to shut up. He was right. I looked out the window again and defaulted to wishing I'd taken the other path and stayed in St. Paul at the previous night's train transfer, where I'd witnessed two boys my age selling themselves for cash. There'd be no explaining myself. No apologies. No caring what people think. A transaction. My services in exchange for simple money. There was a *lot* of money in that taller kid's hand. I'd be eating a steak dinner right now, compliments of the waterbed salesman who had offered me "some cash," if I'd stayed in St. Paul and gone into the bathroom with him. Ten minutes. That's all he said he needed from me. How simple.

Confronting the eye roll

"Kyle…really." Tuck pulled me out of distraction and back into the conversation. "He didn't know you were coming."

I rolled my eyes a third time.

"Oh!" he angrily bellowed. "You and that fucking *eye roll.* Oh, God! You win! I'm bleeding now." He bunched his tank top into a fist, pulling it a few inches from his heart.

I watched, angry and embarrassed—but faintly amused by his exaggerated, irate clowning.

"I remember doing the *eye roll!*" He let go of his shirt and shook his head. "I was fifteen when I quit doing it. How old are you? Twelve?"

"*Fourteen!*" I wanted to open the door and jump out.

Tuck clenched his jaw and shifted gears. Our heads both tilted backward an inch or so as the Goat heatedly accelerated in ways Dad's Olds couldn't. He passed the car we'd been following and reentered our lane. The Goat relaxed back to fifty-five, but Tuck didn't. He was still mad.

"You look twelve," he mockingly snapped back. "Maybe eleven. Or *nine!*"

I gave a poisonous glare with eyes half-shut, then looked back out the window. We both, wisely, let the conversation rest for a few more miles. Tuck must have been trying pretty hard that day to be the adult because he intentionally calmed himself down and resumed his attempt at an intelligent exchange.

Pretty nice guy, actually

"I'm sorry I called you nine."

"I'm used to it," I mumbled angrily.

I expected him to try to make me feel better with an "Oh, don't say that," but instead, he drove quietly for a few moments.

"But let's give Louie a break." He changed subjects, "You know, he *is* the Grand Marshall for the Ridge-Runner-Railroad-Riding Days events." Then he joked, "He's a real rascal, romping around and riding railroads…really…uh…." He'd run out of 'r' words.

I accidentally laughed through painfully tightened lips.

"Ar, ar, ar." Two of his fingers gently slapped at my shoulder. "Yup. Yourrrr grrrrandfatherrrr's a rrrreal rrrrascal."

I laughed again, but this time, the lips didn't hold it back. Moisture, almost like tears, warmed my eyes. How could he be joking with me after how rude I'd been? I stopped laughing as quickly as I could, and with a fast glance, I saw him smile. Who *was* this guy?

"Seriously, Kyle, you know this is *his* event every year. The show *must go on!*" he chuckled at his own witticism. "He heads up the parade committee and plays music in the gazebo all weekend long. And he was committed before he found out you were coming."

"It's Friday. It's not the weekend yet." I honestly hadn't tried to sound rude, but I think it came out that way.

"Wow. You're a smart one." Tuck's voice deflated and went sour. "Most of us hillbillies here in Duluth think it's Saturday."

My head snapped toward him, genuinely confused.

"You lost a whole day?" His blue eyes stared into mine again, appearing concerned, which gave rise to a warm sensation from my heart. Then he tried to make light of it. "You had a long train ride, I suppose. You must'a lost count is all."

I couldn't let him see that I was vulnerable to him. A guy could do me some real damage if he knew that. I gave an angry glare straight out the windshield like it was his fault I'd missed out on the day.

He saw the glare. I heard a frustrated sigh. "Or else you're rrrrreally stupid."

JAMES F JOHNSON

5

Trying Hard to Like Me

I wasn't the only complicated person in that car. There was a lot more to Tuck Taylor than I could possibly know in my first half-hour with him. The one thing I will always be the most grateful for was that he didn't allow himself to judge me too permanently by our first impression. I was a mess, and if he'd have been like so many other people I've known, he'd have written me off long before giving me a second chance. I'd be dead today if he had.

By Tuck Taylor

Kyle gave me a loathing squint, which I probably deserved, and then he turned away to stare out his window. Angry as he was, I didn't blame him for disengaging. Our age difference gave me an obvious advantage in arguing skills. I've always been a pretty nice guy, but not without a short temper at times. The problem is that he had his own advantage over me. He was a kid. He was allowed to misbehave. I was the adult who had to show some responsibility in my reactions.

I've always had a delicate guilt trigger, which he'd just squeezed. Ever since my cancer scare, where I'd survived but my hospital roommate hadn't, my empathetic connection to people was my Achilles' heel, dragging me into their pain too quickly for my own good. I was the adult, but I felt like a child for having stooped to insults, even though— and to my defense—he was awfully good at making me mad. The devil on my right shoulder approved of my retaliation. Kyle was behaving badly. But the little angel on my left reminded me that if a kid as bright as this one was off by a day, then something may have been very, very wrong in his life. By my irritated banter, I was now part of his problem, not of his cure.

My inner jury returned a verdict: Even as a joke, calling him stupid was way over the line.

To complicate matters, selfishly, I was also disappointed. I hadn't so much as shared a single laugh with a buddy in a long time and had actually left the house *excited* to enjoy a ride home with one of Louie's "cheerful" grandsons. While the little shit sat there sulking, I was tossing a salad of mixed emotions in my head and heart. This was just supposed to be a simple train station pick-up mission, hopefully with a few laughs to make for a light-hearted first morning on a sorely needed vacation.

"Kyle, I'm..." I groveled slightly. My invisibly pierced heart actually *hurt* when I confessed, "I'm *really* sorry I called you stupid."

He ignored me, driving the stake of repentance a bit deeper into my chest.

"I haven't had a good night's sleep all summer," I rambled, "and this day just isn't going exactly how I'd hoped."

I'd grown up around pictures of Kyle all over Louie's house, always sporting a brighter-than-average smile. In fact, I'd always wondered if the images had been enhanced to make his eyes sparkle unnaturally. I had assumed that when I finally got to meet him, I'd like him. Louie'd talked him up for years, and because of the long-term relationship I'd had with his name and photos, this morning with the genuine article was proving to be quite a letdown.

"Yeah?" he mumbled in sad defeat, still facing away. "This whole *summer's* not exactly working out for me either."

"Okay, well...I'm sorry to hear that." I was relieved to have him talking to me again. I accepted his disclosure in hopes it was proof that he was capable of more than sarcasm and car talk. Now I wanted to cheer him up. "For what it's worth, I really like your grandfather."

He nodded. I couldn't see his face to know whether he was happy about that or not, but at least he acknowledged I'd said it.

A glimmer of hope

"He's usually the life of the party, if you know what I mean. The Railroad Days event thing is a big deal to him, you know."

"Glad he's having fun." He sighed cynically.

"C'mon, Kyle; give him a break." I remained calm, but I couldn't identify the heat in my chest. Was I feeling pure compassion on a distraught youngster? Was I filled with remorse over my cynical retorts? Or was I pissed at this angry little twerp for treating Louie and me like we were being mean to him? It had to be a combination of the three. I felt bad for the kid and accountable for my reactions to him, but I was also growing tired of him pushing my buttons. "He feels terrible about this, you know."

He puffed and ignored me.

"God!" I whispered loudly. I'd already exploded at him for eye-rolling me—which apparently didn't change his behaviors. He just wouldn't cut me a break. As a barely beginner psychology student, I grabbed the wheel more tightly, ensuring the back of my hand wouldn't accidentally fly toward his cheek.

He continued to ignore me.

"In fact, he said to my grandpa last night..." I was determined not to let him get to me. Joking with him had worked once, so I tried it again. I shook a finger and impersonated Louie's German-Norwegian hybrid accent, "'If I'd have known my little Q-Tip was a-comin', I'da told 'em all to go to hell." Then I added one of Louie's most common taglines, "Oh, ya-ya. Uh-huh.'"

Kyle turned halfway. His sulking head pointed forward and launched another accidental smile.

"Oh-ho-ho! I saw that," I cheerfully mocked. "You think I'm funny, right?"

His brighter response gave some hope that maybe he would lighten up again—for a few minutes at least.

"Or…maybe you *like* the old guy after all, eh?"

"He really said that? You're not making it up?" He bit his lower lip.

"That's exactly how my grandpa said he said it. Word for word. Cross my heart."

"Because if you're making it up, that's really fucking mean."

"I wouldn't do that to you, Kyle. No way." He wasn't being particularly nice yet, but at least he was engaging in *some* form of conversation. I kept it going. "He was mad that your mom didn't give him more warning. It was too late for him to change his plans."

"Cool." Color washed into his cheeks as he slowly nodded.

"You like being called Q-Tip?"

"No!" He jerked his head toward me. "Please don't." He looked away again like he had other things on his mind. "I only like it when Papa calls me that."

I smiled. I'd never heard anyone call Louie "Papa." Kyle's emotion around the use of nicknames clued me in that he knew Louie loved him.

He quietly stared straight through the windshield. Something was tumbling through his mind. I saw more signs that little Kyle Rickett wasn't a total jerk. The whole interaction: the accidental smile, the question *"He really said that?"*—those were the reactions of a gentler young man than what I'd seen so far. The bitter, angry pothead teen was something Louie had never mentioned—where was it coming from? While I'd heard plenty of hair-raising stories about his sister, from my own sister who'd had a brief summer friendship with Fran many years back, Q-Tip was usually one of those whom Louie proudly boasted about.

The GOAT DRIVE (handwritten)

Time to make the turn

All total, we'd been cruising for about a half hour. Things darkened when we drove beneath a canopy of trees. I began slowing to make my hard left onto the Carlsson Trunk Cutoff. My eye caught the movement of Kyle checking his watch. I made one last intent glance toward him. He appeared angry and dazed, but he also presented an interesting profile.

His protruding cheeks beneath that unusually blond hair would make him a great modeling subject, even though he'd made it quite clear he never wanted me taking his picture. How could a good-looking little shit like that not like being photographed? It's a crime if you ask me.

As I turned on the left blinkers and downshifted to third, the portraits on Louie's walls flashed before my eyes. Kyle's engaging grin, which I hadn't yet seen in all its glory in person, was nice on film.

My temper cooled as I processed about a million thoughts in a split second. I hadn't been too far from his age when I'd found out I had cancer, and as I recall, I'd heaped some pretty wretched bad-mood fury onto my loved ones for at least a few weeks. My family never held any of it against me, and after all I'd done or said, they never gave up on me. Their forgiving support was one of the main reasons I'd survived at all.

I suddenly felt like I knew Kyle better—or at least owed him another chance. There had been a dove fluttering through my dreams all summer. It was the dove I used to dream of when I was battling cancer. It flashed into memory just then for some reason. As far as I knew, I had cancer again, and that's what was bringing the old dreams back to life. I'd been so depressed as of late that I didn't even bother to have a doctor look me over—or maybe I was afraid to hear the truth. Or maybe I'd become complacently ready to accept my fate.

I checked the mirrors, then looked straight over at my passenger again. *Show them love* rang through me from nowhere. Those were the words that dove had said to me the very first time I'd dreamt of it…while nearly dying on the operating table three-and-a-half years before. Me and this wreck of a boy were the same somehow. Deep down I just knew it. My heart needed me to do the kid a favor. I knew it wasn't *me* he needed right then. I dropped into second gear, turned *off* the blinkers, and hit the gas. "Fuck it." I mumbled.

"Hey!" he scolded. "That's where we live!"

"I know, shithead; I live next door, remember?"

"Then why aren't we turning?" His response was animated but not necessarily angry. "You *are* dangerous, aren't you?"

"Yup!" I shifted back to fourth and laughed at the sliver of humor that had leaked out his lips. "You shouldn't've gotten into the car with a stranger, man—*big* mistake."

"Probably going to cut off my arms now."

I glanced over in confusion.

He shrugged and raised his brows high like I was supposed to know what that meant.

"You're kind of odd," I commented.

"Yeah, like you're *real normal*. And, by the way, there are *no shortcuts*." Kyle followed our missed turn with his eyes. "It's on *that* road."

"I know the terrain."

He sat stone still, waiting, or maybe processing all the possibilities of where I might be taking him.

"I just think your 'Papa' needs to see you…that's all."

Kyle didn't say another word, but he relaxed back into his seat. And I think I caught a glimpse of another frail, yet authentic smile.

The GOAT DRIVE

6

Passing Thoughts on a Different Life

I think the magic of travel vacations is that we visit places we are not integrally a part of. Every city in the world has problems: crime, politics, toxicity, anger. Every home town has bullies and enemies. Bills to pay. People to avoid. But when we visit another town for only a short time, we are not aware of the problems. Like visiting a photograph, we see what it shows our eyes: sunshine, buildings, trees, rivers. Vacations are superficial. No depth. No back stories. No enemies. Just a leisurely romp through the simplistic surface of someone else's complex terrain.

By Kyle Rickett

For the next thirteen minutes, the only noise I heard was the hum of Tuck's Goat engine and the wind buffeting in through the open windows.

It was hypnotizing. My mind fell back onto my problems. A whole new look at seven years of confusing abuse and bad luck. None of the good memories came up, even though I had plenty. I wasn't in a good mood.

It had been twelve long hours since I had completely given up on life. I still regretted that the guy in a Twins hat had come out of nowhere at that St. Paul train platform and grabbed and pulled me to the ground as I jumped into that train's path. My head still hurt from the pavement. A few minutes before that, I'd seen an even worse fate. I watched my destiny on display only twenty feet from me as two boys, about my age, sold themselves for cash at a bus station bathroom. That was the moment I discovered that men would pay boys for something my dad's best friend liked to do to me for free.

Only a month before, a bicycle crash had put me in Dr. Krieg's office for stitches. His fingers on my naked body had unleashed horrible memories. Things I had always believed were dreams had suddenly become actual *memories* of actual events of actually being tied down and molested by Krieg and his friends, beginning when I was seven and going on for at least a few years. I had new memories of at least two events: one in his office under a Christmas tree when I was seven, and one in a tent on a campout when I was nine. The memories felt like they were small bites of a larger bag. I had no way of knowing for sure how often or how many times it had happened. But I knew it had been more than once, and it was too horrible to remember in its entirety.

I'd recently quit praying because I'd finally accepted that prayer had never done me any good. In fact, I'd noticed that the people I knew who didn't pray seemed to have better lives than those of us who did. They sort of took care of their own problems and accepted fate better than we prayer warriors did. Most of my last and final prayers from about two weeks prior were for a savior. I had released pleas for help into the ear of an imaginary white dove and sent them to God using the most powerful imaginative visioning I could. I was a dork, I know. However, the freakiest attribute of the imagined savior was that I often pretended he drove me away in a gold GTO. I grabbed the door handle and squeezed again. Was this GTO ride *really* happening? Had anything in my brain ever really happened? Was I fading into my dreams forever?

My stomach began to hurt again as I sat quietly next to Tuck and tried to look like I wasn't a sex toy he'd just purchased. Somehow, out of nowhere, I suddenly believed people could see what I had done with Krieg just by looking at me.

But Tuck was not from Torano Island. If he was from St. Paul, then he probably had never even heard of my home island town, so he didn't know my relatives, Fran, or even my *frenemy* from Catholic school, Andreo. I was safely disconnected from my secrets here.

Back home, my parents acted like they didn't know, but I think they did. Why else would they send me away? Whether Tuck stayed in my life for many days or not, he didn't need to know any of the horrible things I'd done or planned to do. He didn't need to know how ugly my past was, nor how seedy my future just might be. He especially didn't need to know that I'd planned to take him into the bathroom as my first voluntary adult male customer. How embarrassing that thought had become! I couldn't think about it too long or I'd blush in shame.

The movement of the highway felt nice against the backs of my legs. I sighed heavily. The nice thing about suicide was that I could always do it later. It would always be an option. The guy in the Twins hat hadn't taken my one and only chance from me. He had just postponed that one opportunity. No one can ever take it away completely. Death would always be there, waiting for when I was ready.

JAMES F JOHNSON

7
A Drama Unfolds

As you've already guessed, Tuck and I weren't together by accident. Even the GTO was a coincidence too perfect to be an accident. Neither of us had yet figured out the connection with the dreams and the dove, but both of us had seen some sort of empathetic attraction to the other. Neither of us knew the other was feeling it yet. The roller coaster of emotions I was on still had to give him a run for his money.

By Tuck Taylor

Kyle hadn't spoken since we passed Louie's cutoff. He looked pretty haggard and very deeply lost in his mind. He'd thought today was yesterday, so I knew he was confused. But I doubted his life was too terribly complicated. He was just a normal, moody teen coming off a long trip. So I stayed quiet too and let him have his cute little teenage drama, which I'm sure to him seemed like life-or-death hardships.

I slowed the Goat as we approached the town center. I chuckled slightly when I realized that cars were parked on lawns while pedestrians with food wandered the streets. It seemed backwards.

The soon-to-be-blazing heat was still bearable, about 89°.

"There's one. Let's grab it." I rolled us into a makeshift parking spot on a dried lawn with a few other haphazardly parked cars.

"Can you park here? It's a lawn."

"Other people did."

Turning the car shifted the air and I caught another whiff of his body odor. I almost gagged, but I kept quiet. I gave the throttle a couple of my famous sexy taps. Kyle seemed to enjoy the sound as much as I did. Teen boys can smell, but they're fun to impress.

Distant Scandinavian folk music, too loud and crisp to be from 1970s base-rich stereo speakers, filled the scene. The aromas of flame-cooked fish, burgers, bratwursts, and onions wafted through the air. This was summer at its best. Music, food, heat, dry grass, people laughing—truly good times, man.

Of heaven and earth

I was twenty-one, but unlike other men my age, I didn't take life lightly. I am one of the lucky few to have seen firsthand that it can end at any moment and that the true existence of a peace that can't be described is only one accident away. I once walked for three minutes in a place I can't forget. A pasture grassland that seemed to be illuminated from within. As a photographer, I noticed there were no shadows there, as if the light source were everywhere. I'd actually died of cancer but been revived. My out-of-body experience in the grassy field was one of utter peace.

I wasn't sorry it had ended when they revived me, but I also wouldn't have been sorry to stay there. Just as my three minutes ended, a dove flew overhead and told me that I was to return to my life and use it to teach trust. To show love. Somehow or other, in the three-and-a-half years that had transpired since, that message had yet to fade even slightly. What Kyle didn't know is that this summer of '74 had brought a new barrage of recurring dreams about that place without shadows, and they hosted the dove itself. I eventually decided just to call the place heaven.

As I drove the kid around and joked with him, I held to a tiny suspicion that my cancer had returned and was generating the dreams. It bothered me somewhat, but the idea of seeing a doctor was too frightening for me. Not knowing seemed easier. The whole experience of having been to heaven increased my appreciation for the little things—like music, food, heat, dry grass, and…the ability to make Louie's grandson laugh. Yep. Cancer or not, I was having some fun finally.

The dream, as peaceful as it was, had rejuvenated my love for the things I didn't seem to have while I walked there on the shadowless grassy field. I knew I had been given a chance to see it and then return to this life—to a place not only fraught with problems, but also rich with senses: smells, sounds, temperatures, pleasures, and even pain.

My visit to heaven had created within me a calm sense that death wasn't so bad—but also, *neither was life*. Death would always be there, so why not wait for it? Even the undesirable aspects of life here—like headaches, hunger pains, a cough—aren't permanent, so why not enjoy even them for as long as I could? Sometimes when I'd scratch an itch, I'd chuckle to myself over having the gift of a few more years in a human body that could feel the joy of such a simple relief.

My only true complaint was that I was a tad lonely. I looked over at Kyle. Maybe he was lonely too.

I called myself a "second-chancer," and I hoped one day to meet others like me—cohorts I could share a camaraderie with. I'd almost died twice. Having survived a rollover car accident at six and a near-death cancer scare at seventeen had given me both a scar on my lip and a unique and indescribable appreciation for being allowed to participate in such a simplistic, yet sensory-rich event as a summer Railroad Riding Days picnic.

Assessing motives

Even unhappy, Kyle was someone I'd wanted to meet for a long time, and so to enjoy him a little more, I thought that perhaps if we didn't talk too much, we wouldn't get so mad at each other. As a psych student,

I was learning to question my motives around everything I did. I briefly wondered if blowing through the Carlsson Trunk intersection was really because the dove had told me to let Kyle see his papa or if it was so I could be not-so-lonely for a little while longer.

We walked quietly together toward the music, leaving the car unlocked and windows down—but to keep Kyle satisfied, I took the keys with me. The folk dancing polka music was lively but foreign to me. Nevertheless, I found the tempo and locked my step with the down beat. A few people stared. The kid's over-the-top blond hair was an eye-catcher, no doubt. But he was a mess, too. Maybe they thought I'd found him wandering the hills with a pack of albino wolves. I almost shared that with him, but I wasn't sure how he'd take to the albino joke. So I kept it to myself.

We crossed over the sidewalk and onto the grass of Center Park where we navigated through the crowd and kept moving toward the music.

Family matters; an unforgettable reunion

Kyle emerged at the gazebo first to see Louie on a stool, surrounded by five other musicians with horns, a base guitar, and drums; they were all wearing brown shorts, suspenders, and green felt hats, each with a single protruding feather. Louie, the accordion player, was a large, strong man with hair as white as Kyle's. It just hadn't always been that way. I emerged in time to witness their reunion. The scene was pretty amazing actually. The traditionally white-painted gazebo was decorated with a ton of red, white, and blue ribbons. On the railings here and there were a few strategically placed iced beer pitchers and steins…for Louie and the musicians, no doubt. The gazebo was alive with music while a large crowd of mostly older people, probably German and Norwegian, surrounded it, kicking in place and holding up beverages.

Louie saw Kyle. His eyes perked. Kyle's sullen face softened and blushed, and then he shot a brief, but glimmering smile at me. My God, his eyes *did* sparkle. The hairs on the back of my neck stood up. I knew then and there that my idea to bring him here was intentionally given to me by that dove, and that I'd done the right thing by responding. He looked away quickly. Louie finally smiled. Kyle smiled more brightly. I looked back and forth between their faces, admiring the emotion—wishing I'd had my camera.

The song ended. Louie whispered to the guitar player, then let go of the accordion, allowing it to dangle from his shoulders. The crowd immediately started talking and moving away. Louie held his arms out and waved the boy in with both hands. I actually heard Kyle gasp. Louie set the accordion down.

"Papaaaaaa!" Kyle yelled and launched toward him. He ran up the steps into the gazebo and hit Louie's chest hard and fast. He buried his filthy white head into it and burst into violent sobbing. The guitarist quickly retrieved the microphone stand. The speakers squealed. People stared. Louie looked up at me. I had followed Kyle in, but only to halfway up the steps. Louie's look of terror surprised me. I'd never seen it on him before. My eyes must have been as big as pies also. I shrugged, shook my head, and silently mouthed, "I don't know."

"Oh, dear God, Q-Tip." Louie put both his big hands on Kyle's back to tighten his squeeze. "What's the matter?"

His words put more drama into this scene for me. He closed his eyes like he was trying to communicate telepathically. Then he leaned toward the guitarist and said, "I'm taking ten."

"What should we do?" the guitarist asked.

"Play. Don't play. I don't care. But I'll be back in ten. It seems I got a problem here."

Louie may have been late into his seventies, but he was as strong as a horse—maybe stronger. He scooped Kyle up while lifting himself from the stool and carried his sobbing grandson like an oversized baby, with his big right hand across Kyle's bottom and his big left hand between his shoulder blades. Kyle continued to bawl loudly, like a bombing victim, almost unable to breathe. His body shook. Louie's concern didn't fade. People watched as if they were witnessing a car accident. From ten feet away, it felt like the boy was unloading the weight of the whole world onto his grandfather.

Kyle's feet dangled about halfway between Louie's knees and the ground. I tracked them until the two reached a place where they were basically alone. Kyle couldn't catch his breath. It was unnerving to watch, and it was starting to bring tears to my eyes too. Louie lowered himself onto a park bench in the picnic area, and I sat across from them. Kyle wailed a little longer, and Louie finally slid him off onto the bench, but kept him close. He pressed a full-size leg tightly against Kyle's small one. His big, strong right arm drew the little shoulder in so they were still connected, head to chest.

"Q-Tip, what's wrong with you? You look terrible."

Kyle's wailing eventually simmered. When he was able to sit upright on his own, I handed him a napkin from a picnic table. He calmed a bit more and wiped his eyes with trembling hands. His sobbing cooled to sniffles. After maybe a minute, he'd composed himself.

"I'm sorry about that. I didn't mean to cry. I had a bad trip." He inhaled. "That's all." With both hands, he grabbed the top of his stomach as if in pain. His chin wrinkled in an effort to stop from bursting into tears again.

"That's not all." Louie wrapped his strong arm around Kyle's head, pulled it back into his chest, kissed the top of it, and remarked, "I known you your whole life. I never seen you do that before—I never seen *anyone* do that before."

"I'm sorry, Papa." He drew in another shaky breath.

"Don't be." Louie glanced down at Kyle's hands, still pressing against his gut. "What's wrong with your belly?"

Kyle shook his head like he didn't know.

"When did you eat last?"

Kyle didn't say anything again.

"Kyle," I interfered softly, "don't you remember the last time you ate?"

"It's Saturday?"

I nodded as politely as I could. My heart ached a bit.

Kyle did math on the fingers of one hand, while he blew his nose and wiped his eyes with the other. He counted back the two-and-a-half days it takes to get from Seattle to Duluth on the train, plus the morning he'd probably enjoyed a big going-away breakfast with his family.

The GOAT DRIVE

"I had half a sandwich yesterday—kind'a stale. And a little bit of spaghetti three days ago...and half a piece of birthday cake on Sunday." He pushed the fist deeper into his chest and winced.

"Oh, that's no good." Louie turned his attention onto me. He shook a disapproving head and said, "A teenage boy's gotta *eat*!" He dug into a pocket, pulled out his wallet, and handed it to me. "Tuckster, pull out a ten-spot and take this little fella for some brats. And get whatever you want too." He shook Kyle gently. "You eat what he buys you, boy. You hear me?" Then he said to me, "He'll pick bratwurst. Buy him three. This boy here likes extra kraut and *loads* of mustard."

Kyle smiled slightly and gasped to hold back a cry/laugh combination.

"I'm family, boy..." Louie responded to the partial smile. "I know what you like."

"I'm sorry I was mad at you, Papa," more tears flowed from both eyes, "when you weren't at the train station." His chin wrinkled again as he whimpered. He inhaled and readied for another burst of wailing.

"Q-Tip, don't! It don't matter. You said it yourself; you had a bad trip. You're not mad at me now." Louie squeezed the little guy again. "Only *now* matters."

Kyle calmed quickly. He took a deep cleansing breath, wiped his eyes again with the napkin, and gave me a sad smile as he leaned his head onto his papa's shoulder.

My vision was partially blurred from suddenly moistened eyes, but I was able to pull a bill out of the wallet and hand it back to Louie. Then I waved for the kid to follow.

"C'mon, Kyle. Your Grandpa's got music to make."

He got up, but turned to Louie, who smiled back and nodded. Kyle leaned down and kissed him quickly on the mouth. I'd never thought of Louie as a man who'd let a boy do that. This was obviously a special bond.

"I love you so much, Papa." He looked like he was about to cry again. "I shouldn't a' been mad at you."

"Hey, hey, hey, no sad. *No sad!*" Louie commanded. "This is my party. I worked hard to make everyone happy today." With that, he slapped Kyle's butt and pointed toward the food stands. He instructed me to feed him, take him home, and get him cleaned up. He told us that he himself wouldn't be home until after dark because he had meetings that night with the event staff.

On our way

We ordered enough food for four—me and three Kyles. Kyle's exhaustion was obvious, but as we sat together, he managed to scarf down all three brats in relatively no time at all.

"How the heck did you squeeze those into that tiny little stomach of yours?" I asked in a friendly tease.

"I'm hungry."

"Obviously."

"And I'm not that tiny." He'd stopped crying, but his nose was stuffy and eyes still red. "I'm *fourteen!*"

We sat together for about fifteen minutes. I got him a stack of napkins and dipped each into a glass of ice water. He cordially thanked me and wiped his face clean. We heard the music playing some more, and so before we left for the car, we went to where Louie could see us for a wave goodbye.

In another display of closeness, Kyle tapped his thumb to his chest, then crossed both arms over his heart, then pointed at Louie. I knew it was sign language, and I easily interpreted it as "I love you." I knew that Louie had taken some classes in signing at the Senior Center, but I didn't realize he'd taught it to any of his grandkids. When Louie could free a hand off the accordion, he silently nodded his fist; then he pointed back at Kyle and bumped his forefingers together in what I assume was the sign for "I love you also."

I studied their faces as they signed, and I attempted to absorb the affection the boy and his papa projected into each other. I now knew why Louie loved the kid so much. On the way to the car, I mentioned it.

"It's cute how you and Louie talk to each other."

"You think I'm cute?" he asked in a cold tone. Apparently, his *mood* had returned.

And here we go again

"I'll say it again." I sighed. I couldn't believe how quickly he'd toggled back on me. "*I think it's cute how you and your papa communicate.* But I think *you're* kind of a jerk." I immediately regretted having said that. But gosh-darn it, why couldn't he just stay nice?

He puffed an air of arrogance.

"Okay—*that's it!*" I stopped.

He stopped. We faced off, me looking slightly downward at him.

"What the *fuck* are you so pissed off at *me* for?" I flailed my right arm toward the Goat still parked on the lawn down the street. "All I fucking did was *pick you up* because my friend asked me to!"

He reddened with embarrassment.

"Huh?" I poked at his chest. "Is there something you need to say to me?"

"No," he muttered and looked toward his feet. His face blanked out like his very spirit had somehow *abandoned* him there right in front of me.

"Then *please* don't ever put words into my mouth again." I admonished, but I calmed myself as maturely as I could.

Kyle reestablished eye contact but with eyebrows dipped. The comment appeared to confuse him. I hoped it was making him think about showing me some respect. I didn't know if I would see much of this little twerp again, but if he was going to be here for the rest of the summer, then I'd at least bump into him from time to time as our grandfathers played out their tight friendship.

In yet another shift of his emotional roller coaster, Kyle's spirit seemed to reenter his body. His reddened face appeared to warm and soften. What he said next showed that he'd caught the gist of my comment. If his tone and demeanor were genuine, then down deep, he meant what he was about to say. His face found even more healthy color.

"I'm sorry, Tuck. I didn't mean to do that."

"Do what?" I wanted to hear him say it so I'd know he'd gotten my message.

"I twisted what you said."

"Okay." I turned toward the car. "Thank you."

"I don't know why I did it. But I'm sorry."

"Don't fret too much. Just don't do it again. Lots of people play that game." We started walking. "They just don't play it with me. Not *twice* anyway."

The boy looked intently at the side of my head as we walked. I hoped I could keep him showing me at least some respect until I could drop him off at Louie's and finally be done with him.

8

He Took Me home

All this time, I've been complaining about how hard it was for me to learn to trust other people. But when I look back at that first day, I can't even imagine how difficult it must have been for Tuck to figure out whether or not he could trust me. If trust is the ability to predict someone's reactions, I wasn't giving him any solid patterns to follow. I'd laugh at some of his jokes, get offended at others, even turn and insult him every now and then. I guess learning how to trust includes learning how to be someone who can be trusted. Giving a person a history of steady, repeatable, consistent responses makes it a lot easier for him to predict a future response out of me too. In a perfect friendship, both people should be allowed to trust each other equally.

By Kyle Rickett

The ride home with Tuck went really fast. Less than fourteen minutes. I had so much anger in me I could hardly control it, so I tried not to talk much. This time we really did turn down the Carlsson Trunk

Cutoff—thank goodness. My head itched, and now that I'd been welcomed and loved by Papa, I wanted to clean up with a shower. I hoped Tuck would drop me off and go.

We went another quarter mile and turned left into Papa's driveway, which was a gravel road that climbed uphill for about thirty feet. It leveled off in a circle with a small green colored house to the right, an old darker green shop/garage to the left, and white-painted horse fences straight ahead.

I loved that place so much that I began to feel a burst of excitement at just being there. Maybe my problems were gone now—all left behind in Washington. I looked ahead at the fence. Beyond it was a big place to play, mostly wooded, with a creek-side trail leading to a now-abandoned horse pasture behind the house. The hot afternoon air smelled like dry grass. Tuck eased the GTO to a quiet, peaceful stop. The gravel beneath his tires went silent first. Then, after one quick throttle pump, the beautiful rhythmic rumble of the hot rod engine also went silent. Once we'd slammed our doors shut behind ourselves, the clicking and tapping of a cooling engine from beneath the hood, combined with our steps in the gravel, sounded like an orchestra was exiting the pit. The rest of the rural world around the three of us, Tuck, myself and the Goat, was quiet, hot, and still. So peaceful. A lot more peaceful than what was happening inside my head. I was still kind of on edge.

"Let me come in to make sure you get settled okay."

"You don't need to," I dismissed. "Papa doesn't lock his door. I know where my room is."

"Let me do it. I'll feel better. You're in my care right now."

"I'm four*teen*! I'm not in your *care*! I don't need a babysitter."

"Kyle…I'm coming in."

"Fine!" Maybe this wasn't over yet. Not being able to get this guy to leave was making me mad and nervous at the same time. A whole summer of distrusting adults just wasn't going to go away in one morning. As much as I loved it there at Papa's farm, I couldn't get my exile from Washington off my mind. I was humiliated. Let down. Abandoned. Sent away. I was there because of being attacked and mistreated by a trusted adult, while not being protected by my own family. That kind of trauma stays in a guy's head all day and all night, for quite some time.

Tuck might have been small, but I was even smaller. Something new was happening in my over-worked brain. Ever since Krieg had been allowed into my room with me unconscious to remove the stitches and fondle me one more time under my mother's nose, I had begun to suspect everyone. I seemed to be normal for *men* in general to want me. I didn't trust *anyone* anymore…except Papa. I recalled a vague, hazy memory of going into the train bathroom once to check myself and see if the attendant, who had innocently asked me how I was doing a few times, had been *in my pants* while I was asleep. Where would this obsessive insanity finally lead me? I hated this new fear, but it was real, and it was *consuming* me.

"Suit yourself." I used the same words on him that the waterbed salesman had used on me when I didn't go into the bathroom with him.

"Suit myself? Kyle, why are you so hard on me? I'm your grandfather's friend."

Tuck's reasoning wasn't sound. Doc Krieg was *Dad's friend*. I tried to think of the mean things Tuck had done, but I couldn't remember any. On the other hand, I was used to having my mind twisted by people so as to confuse me into giving them whatever they wanted. My adult sister was a sociopath who did it to me constantly. But, believe it or not, ever since Tuck had yelled at me and clearly instructed me never to put words in his mouth, I'd started to sort of…*like* him. He'd set a boundary and I liked it. I felt bad for my distrusting thoughts. I drew back one side of my mouth so I would at least *appear* apologetic.

"Sorry, Tuck. I'm having a really bad summer. Come in with me. Papa keeps sodas in a cooler. You can have one."

"I know about that cooler. He's a generous old guy."

I smiled at the kind words. Tuck met me at the trunk to snatch the duffel before I could. He refused to give it up.

"Just…*let* me!" he commanded.

I rolled my eyes.

He rolled his back.

I rolled mine a second time, but I shook my head no along with it.

Tuck quietly laughed.

I started to hate him again.

We each carried one bag to the house. I felt as if he'd taken it from me and wouldn't give it back. Something the kids at Catholic school did a lot after my former best friend told them all some set of lies I didn't know how to defend myself against. At least Tuck was doing it for kinder reasons. The wooden steps creaked under our weight. The house was unlocked and uncomfortably warm, but not miserable, so we left the door open behind us.

"I love it here," I confessed. I'd spent many Thanksgivings, Christmases, and summer vacations running through this house, my mom yelling at me to slow down and walk. I got treats from Papa and Gramma when she was alive. The house was mostly kitchen with white-painted, plywood cabinets. The countertops were pale yellow Formica with a once-shiny aluminum edging. There was a small TV area that Papa called his living room, three small bedrooms, and one bath. The attic was an open room with angled walls and six mismatched beds, but it was only used as a sleeping hall when too many grandkids came at once.

The whole place smelled old, and it needed decorating. But this little unassuming house was always the same—year after year after year. And it could be home to a lot of lucky grandchildren during some summer and holiday seasons.

The walls were so lined with photos that even Papa probably couldn't always remember who was who in each one. A lot of us kids mostly looked alike, and from year to year, it was easy to forget which of us was which. My light hair kept me pretty easy to spot, but the McBride boys all looked the same. Scooter McBride was my absolute favorite. He lived in Portland, Oregon, and for some reason, my family had recently put a ban on us talking to each other—another reason I now hated my life.

There were even pictures of Tuck Taylor at various stages of his life. In one, he looked to be about ten years old, using all the strength he had to hoist an extraordinarily large fish with Papa's help, both smiling like proud sportsmen. At fourteen, looking at a picture of Tuck when he was

The GOAT DRIVE

only ten, I was able to see that he had been a cute little kid once. A genuine but mischievous smile—and that scar over his lip was there then too.

"I didn't realize this was you." I tapped on the photo and looked back and forth between it and him. "Now I have the connection."

"Yup. That's me. In the flesh." He patted his chest playfully. "Tucker James Taylor. And that's the biggest fish I ever caught." He smiled with pride. "Louie's known me my whole life."

"Hmm."

"Hmm, what?"

"Your middle name," I said.

"You like it?"

"Yeah." I patted my own chest like he did. "It's a great name. It's mine too. James. I'm Kyle James Rickett."

"Wow. That's kind of cool, huh?" He leaned forward like he was going to tell me a secret. "I just have to deal with some people calling me James Taylor. After the singer."

"Yeah." I chuckled slightly. "I thought of him when you said your name out loud."

"Let's just say it was funny the first hundred times I heard it."

I laughed a little more freely as I kept getting more and more comfortable with him.

"Well then, Kyle James Rickett, should we put the bags in your room?" He lifted the duffel. "You're his only visitor right now, so I'm guessing you'll stay in the kid's room down the hall?"

Terror in the bedroom

A chill ran between my shoulder blades. Why did he already know which room was mine? Was he just trying to make me feel comfortable with him so he could trick me? My eyes quickly glanced at his belt as if I needed to know how hard it would be to undo for him—wait—*Oh, my God*, this was so unfair to him. Especially now that I'd seen his picture with Papa, I truly thought that he seemed like a nice guy. And he had my middle name. But my suspicions were too restless for me to control. The man I'd just met, who wouldn't give back the bag, now wanted to go into the bedroom with me? My thoughts started leaving my head like they were escaping and then turning back to yell, "Don't trust him!" at me. I accidentally pictured Dr. Krieg in my bedroom at home last month. The chill reached my fingertips. I wanted to get this over with. On a conscious level I knew this was an irrational fear. I knew Tuck was a good person. But the thing about trauma is…*it's not rational*. Like acrophobia, knowing you aren't going to fall doesn't stop the physical panic attack. My inner dialogue said Tuck was safe. But my heart and nerves were throbbing anyway. I was trying to look calm on the outside, even though uncontrolled panic was ravaging all my inner organs.

"Sure, let's go into my room." I waited for Tuck to go first. I couldn't stand the thought of him walking behind me. I didn't believe he'd really do much more than set things down and leave, but at the same time, he could wedge himself between me *and the door,* and that was against my constant need to have an escape route in place.

Unfortunately, Tuck used his manners and waited for me to move on ahead. He was the adult, so I gave in and led the way, now feeling more disconnected, as if my body traveled on its own to wherever he pointed. I walked in first, but I wished I could run…. My imagination made the door look like the restroom door at the train station. I could just *feel* him grabbing me from behind. I wouldn't look back, but I sensed his eerie presence between myself and freedom. My muscles were rigid and ready for the attack that I hoped was a crazy fear. We got through the door. I was inside now, almost wanting to vomit. Bunk beds stood like a tree house against the wall to the right, and a series of three small mismatched dressers sat in a row under the already-open window, stacked with various toys for boys and girls both. I saw the window as a possible escape route into open pasture. I knew it was young Tuck Taylor occupying the space behind me, but my brain kept picturing old Dr. Krieg. I could almost smell his cigarette breath. My chest chilled as if a winter storm had blown in.

In the bedroom, more pictures hung on the walls. One set of photos by the closet door was obviously devoted to my family. We looked happy and in love with each other. And in so many ways, we were. But in so many others, those photos were mocking me. I was always the little one in the center surrounded by my parents and two older siblings with their hands on my shoulders. Everyone looked so innocent.

My fears of being trapped in the room were slowly changing now from frustration to anger. Tuck wasn't dropping and leaving...he was hanging around. Touching things. Irritating my nerve endings. The longer my panic festered inside me, the more crazily I wondered about his motives. He may still have wanted a quick—you-know-what. And behind me was a selection of beds, upper and lower. I started to wish he'd attack and get it over with. If he gave me the choice, I'd go for the top bunk so I wouldn't feel so claustrophobic with him on top of me. I surely wouldn't fight him. In fact, I'd obviously proven to myself that I would never tell on anyone who would do that to me. No matter how this played out, it was going to be a win for him—unless I finally started charging. I looked around at the photos of my happy family and thought, *You sent me here, you creeps. You can all watch me earn twenty bucks now!* Insane as it seemed, that thought felt empowering.

"KYLE!"

"Huh?" I came to. Tuck was staring at me like he'd been trying to get my attention for a while.

"Are you okay?" He walked around me to the bunk beds, with a concerned eye on my expression.

I nodded yes, but the room was spinning and I had to shake my head once to come back into the real world.

"You kind of spaced out there for a minute."

"Yeah. I got lost in thought." I shook my head again. "Sorry about that."

"I guess you're pretty tired, huh? Long trip?"

"Definitely." Grateful for his explanation that I only had to agree with, I still offered a deeper answer, "I had a long night in St. Paul." I spoke softly and did my best to come back fully into reality with him. "Almost...jumped...onto the...wrong train."

"Okay...it's just that...you look a little gray all of a sudden." He *finally* put the duffel bag down and asked, "How often do you smoke pot?"

"Huh?" I silently looked at the floor, not knowing how to answer. "Um."

"How does it affect you?" Tuck's eyes brightened like he thought something was funny all of a sudden.

"You know. Like it does everyone." I shrugged. "It makes me see snakes and bugs and then I forget everything I said."

He cracked up.

"What?"

"Snakes and bugs?" He laughed again. "You've never touched the stuff, have you?"

I rubbed the floor with the bottom of one foot. I shrugged sheepishly.

"Do me a favor." His smile appeared to be one of both joy and relief. "Don't try it until you're a little older, okay?"

I shrugged again, but this time to acknowledge that I would obey.

"Knucklehead." He chuckled some more as he walked toward the Rickett photos. "I'll admit it's cool to actually meet you finally."

Photos never lie

"Really?" I asked. The gentleness of Tuck's voice comforted me a bit. "You know about me?"

"Sure. Louie talks about you all the time. I know some of your family by name, but haven't met most. My sister spent a summer with your sister once. But that was like…twenty years ago."

"Tell your sister I'm sorry."

"For what?" He looked confused.

"For anything Fran may have said or done that still needs an apology." Zing! My anger was still present, but my sense of humor was returning.

Tuck laughed. He looked so friendly when he did that he drew a laugh out of me too. It was a nice distraction from the fear I'd been dealing with.

"Ronnie said Fran was a…tough person to like…. Kind of 'churchy'…and…evil…at the same time." He pointed at the Rickett wall. "But all in all, your family looks happy."

I huffed.

"Don't they?"

"I guess they do—*look*—happy."

"I thought photos never lied."

I huffed again.

"Sorry." He tried to change the mood politely. "They definitely told the truth about your hair. I had no idea you were called Q-Tip because your hair was this white. I figured the pictures were making it look blonder than it really is."

"Let's not talk about my hair," I said slowly.

His head tilted.

I tried not to sound rude that time. I was genuinely asking my guest not to talk about the white hair I hated so badly and that Dr. Krieg loved so much.

"Okay. That's cool." He looked around the room like he was wondering what else needed to be done.

"Want a soda?" I had a clear shot at the door now, which helped me to feel somewhat relaxed.

"Yeah. I think he keeps root beer for me." He turned and walked out the bedroom door. I breathed a sigh of relief and followed him out. The chill had left my shoulders and chest, but now my hands were numb. When his back was to me, I smiled. So far, this guy was all right.

"He treats me like I'm his thirteenth grandkid," he said.

We passed through the kitchen into the laundry room, which was a porch Papa had enclosed with used lumber. There he kept boots, overalls, snow shovels, and an old refrigerator full of his grandkids' favorite sodas. Tuck opened the freezer door to look for an ice cream bar.

"*What the fuck?*" He stepped back and slammed the door so hard the refrigerator rattled and the thud echoed.

"What?" I asked with widely opened eyes.

"Holy *shit*!" He grabbed at his chest and panted for a second. "What the *hell* does he have that in there for?"

"What?" I asked a second time. "Come on, Tuck; what did you see?"

Tuck carefully stepped up to it again, and opened it slowly, cautiously. "Good God!" and he closed it again.

I stepped up to where I could see it too.

"Open it up," he dared me. "And tell me what the hell is that thing."

Slightly nervous, I carefully, slowly pulled open the door. But then I relaxed and laughed. "Oh, my God! He still has it!"

"What *is* it?" Tuck asked. "It looks like a—"

"It's a raccoon."

"Is he going to *eat* it?"

"No!" I laughed again, even harder when I looked back at Tuck's shocked face. "He told me about it on the phone. It was in his crawl space. He killed it a few months ago and was waiting for the furrier to come through town so he could sell it."

"The furrier?"

"An old friend of Papa's. He comes through town a couple of times a year, buys furs, and goes back to Illinois where he makes stuff out of them."

"Well, it's disgusting!" he blurted out. "And it's in there with *food*!"

It's wrapped in plastic." I shrugged. "No one's ever gotten sick from his ice cream."

"Yeah, well. From now on, I buy ice cream at the store! I'll stick to pop when I'm here." He pushed the freezer door closed for me. But when he opened the refrigerator portion to grab himself a root beer and me a Pepsi, he did it slowly, and cautiously—peeking in with one eye before the door opened up too wide.

I couldn't stop laughing now at how funny he was. "You think he keeps the live ones in the fridge?"

The GOAT DRIVE

"After what I just saw, who knows what the hell he keeps in the fridge?" he said, also laughing. He grabbed our drinks, popped both caps off, handed me one, and lifted his bottle as a toast.

"Thanks." I had accidentally begun to smile—and laugh—more warmly than I had in weeks.

"I'll take mine to go, though," he said. "You probably want to get cleaned up." He motioned toward the front door to indicate his planned departure. "Maybe even take a nap. My grandfather's phone number is on the chalkboard by Louie's telephone. I go by Tuck; he goes by Tucker. If you need anything, give us a call, 'kay?"

"'Kay." The guy was leaving. I felt the pressure of being trapped lift off of me like a blanket, which then exposed me to the Universe as a first-class heel all of a sudden. It was now like I'd been insulting the Dalai Lama for the last couple of hours. Plus, this guy still kept being nice. I tried to smile to appear apologetic again, and said, "I'm sure I'll be all right, but I'll call if I need anything."

"Cool," he said casually.

Then I lifted my Pepsi to make a toast, and with a strange sense of confusion in my voice, I humbly offered up, "Um...thanks, Tuck...for everything."

"No problemo!" He smiled, clinked his root beer against my Pepsi, and nodded once. We went outside to his car. I stayed at the top of the stairs, wanting to hear it roar to life. Dust rolled out from beneath the engine. Tuck gave it a few extra bonus revs. He slowly rolled forward into the circular drive and turned the wheel. Then when he could see into my eyes, and the rear end was safely pointed toward the woods, he gunned it. The huge Pontiac engine sang. Gravel pelted the fence. The rear slid to the right in a cloud of dust. The front wheels cranked to compensate and *drift* past me sideways. He giggled when he saw my smile. I even laughed out loud once, too. He let off the gas and coasted down the hill to the road with his arm out the window and his thumb pointed to the sky.

"I only know two words in sign language," he yelled back, "and this is the nice one!"

9

His Lost Spark

First impressions are shallow in that we don't usually know the backstories behind the smiling faces we meet. Believing that everyone was having a better life than me, I naturally assumed Tuck was just another lucky bastard with great hair, a great car, a great family, and a great childhood. It would be a few days before I'd begin to delve into the complexity that was the true Tuck Taylor. I'd have respected him sooner if I'd have known of the tragedies that had given him the physical scar and his unusual remorse at any outburst I had driven him to.

I now know that Tuck was having a wonderful life, but not because of good luck. His life was no better than mine, but his family supported him through every tragic and irresponsible thing he had gotten involved in. With their support, he had apparently picked himself up, shaken out the pains, and moved on—several times.

Tuck's connection to his sister Ronnie was his most cherished alliance. He enjoyed a different family dynamic than I had ever believed existed. His sibling was on his side no matter whose fault his problems were. I would one day discover that these two, and their parents, had hearts so big that they actually still had room in them for one more kid. And if I could somehow learn to trust them, that one more kid could be me.

By Tuck Taylor

After dropping Kyle off, I drove back to Center Park to talk with Louie. I couldn't get the old guy's concerned look out of my head. He sat me down over a plate of sauerkraut and frankfurters to tell me that the only other time he'd ever seen a look like Kyle's on someone's face was the day before a friend committed suicide. He was worried enough now that he could hardly keep himself at the event, but because of his trust in me and my promise to check on Kyle, he continued to honor his commitment to play music.

At about four, I stopped off at Louie's house, but the kid was sound asleep, still dressed, on the lower bunk of the room I'd helped carry a bag to. He looked to be okay, so I went on home to Grandpa Tucker's.

At a little after five, I called my sister, Ronnie, in Washington DC. She was the only phone call I'd made when I left Texas on Monday, so I owed her a trip report. I still hadn't told my parents I was quitting school. They wouldn't have punished me, but I didn't want to disappoint them so I found myself doing that thing kids do—I avoided calling them at all. Now, since it was after five *and* a Saturday, the long-distance rates were about as low as they'd go.

Trip report

"Hello?"

"Hi, Sis. I'm at Grandpa's."

"Oh, hi, Tuck! I'm glad you called. I was starting to worry."

"No need. I made it safe."

"So, how is he?"

The GOAT DRIVE

"Ornery!" I chuckled. "He and Louie still keep each other young." I said that as much for Grandpa as for her. He was listening from the kitchen table and nodding in agreement. "Those two are funnier than hell when they're together."

"I know they are," she said, laughing into the phone. "So how was your trip?"

"Awesome! I actually enjoyed the time alone to think."

"Any trouble getting gas?"

"The gas shortage ended months ago, Sis. I told you it'd be fine. The whole trip went off without a hitch. Not even a rock chip in the windshield. Somehow I got here nine hours faster than I'd expected to." I chuckled again. "But you won't believe what I saw when I rolled into Duluth last night. When I stopped at the Circle J to top off the tank, a sign in the Railroad Worker's Credit Union window across the street read, 'We're Strong Together.'"

"Whoa…I'm getting chills."

"I told you on the phone last Monday," I ranted in a teasing but serious voice, "this was the right choice. I'm meant to be here. Those three words came into your dream when I was at my darkest moment."

I was trying to sound cheerful, but my mood wasn't good for talking with her. I was tired and concerned about Louie and Kyle.

Louie's main concern

"You were dead," she laughingly interjected. "That's a pretty dark moment if you ask me."

"I know," I said, politely laughing back. "But that was the exact time when the dove in *my* dream told me to go back. It was my turning point."

"Well, little brother—I'm not so sure you don't still need another one of those."

"Another turning point? Oh, come on, Sis. Give me a break."

"Tuck, that isn't fair. Ever since you called me this week, I've had legitimate reason to worry about you."

"What do you mean?" I lowered my voice as Grandpa moved to the living room to watch the news. I was alone with her now, and we could talk more seriously.

"You've almost died twice. Both times my heart almost couldn't take it. Every time I see that scar on your lip from the windshield.... I don't know how you got through that mess without more injuries. I thank God for that simple scarred smile every time I think of how close I came to losing you altogether." She continued, "And after waking up from the cancer scare nine years later, you became such a deeply introspective and gentle person, so kind—but I have to admit I miss the spark you used to have."

"The 'spark'?"

"You are not the person you were. Some of that is good, but...I miss the spark."

"Some people called it arrogance."

"You were a teenage athlete. Arrogance is part of the package. I still call it a spark."

I twirled the phone cord around my fingers while digesting her admission. She was right. I was happy to be alive, but all in all, life had become heavy.

"Either way, it's gone now, and I miss it."

"In the car," I confessed, "I thought about what you'd said Monday on the phone. About how I need to keep from being too depressed."

"And?"

"Well, something happened today. I saw how...alone...I've become. It's pretty hard to be cheerful after all the people I've lost. Shannon, Micah, Trenton.... Sis, all my friends from high school are in college or in the workforce."

"It's not too late to go back, kiddo. The college might not even realize you're gone yet."

"I refuse to go back."

I heard an angry sigh.

"I don't know how to describe it, but I felt like my guts were on fire when I was sitting on that campus. The homework was sandpaper grinding away at my head. I was starting to skip classes because I couldn't drag myself out of bed. It got way worse when Trenton moved away...the guy was my best friend. Staying there wasn't an option. I realize now that I need a friend, Sis. A real *friend*."

"Tuck, Trenton was on a different path. You are far better off without him. This is not about him. This is depression, pure and simple."

"Noooo. I'm not *depressed*; I'm...forlorn."

"Forlorn?" I heard laughter and pictured her head shaking at my clever descriptor. "I wish I could talk you into seeing someone to get help."

Oh, that irritated me. I was a man now. I was a partial shrink. I didn't need a shrink of my own.

She kept pushing. "You don't stop grieving the losses you've taken in a few short years—especially when Micah was your own child. Some people never get over what you've lost. Please get some help."

"I'll think about it." I drew in a long, thoughtful breath.

"Mom called." Ronnie paused for a moment. "Have you talked with her yet? She's worried about your trip."

"No. I'm calling her next. And how did she know about my trip?"

"Grandpa was so excited for your visit that he tattled on you the morning you left Texas."

"He's a little kid." I laughed.

"She's concerned—but not mad—over you quitting school. So don't worry about what she'll say when you call her; she loves you like crazy, and she's excited to hear from you tonight."

I sighed loudly. I was nervous. I felt like an irresponsible child. I'd let Mom down by quitting school, and I wasn't excited about facing her, even on the phone.

"She also read me a letter you wrote her, word-for-word. I didn't know you'd been winning awards with your photography. Why didn't you tell me that?"

"Slipped my mind. Sorry."

"Well? Tell me now."

Ronnie always loved hearing my stories and about my accomplishments.

"They were both state awards—one for a photo of an old man and a small girl playing patty-cake at a bus-stop with a bakery sign in the background, advertising a gimmick product that they called—of all things—*Patty Cakes*."

"Oh, that sounds cute."

"It was a hit. The other one I took at the zoo—of a white dove taking flight. Its wings are eclipsing the sun, and in the foreground, you can see the crisscross of the chain-link fence that made up part of its cage. The crisis clinic is hoping I'll donate it to them so they can use it in a poster advertising their services. They're working on a slogan that has to do with 'setting the spirit free' or something like that."

"They both sound like great photos."

"I'll tell you this: Winning awards and having people want my work for advertisements is a good feeling—like I might actually have something to contribute to the world."

"Well, you sound excited when you talk about it. I hope it works out for you."

"I do too, Sis. If it doesn't, there's no passion for anything else really left." I suddenly wished I hadn't confessed that part.

"Tuuuuuck—! Please see someone about that. Don't gamble that making a friend or making it as a photographer will magically heal your life. You're not 'forlorn,' young man; you're depressed. That's what it's called. *Depressed*! Having no passion at twenty-one years old is a bad sign—a *really* bad sign. You should be on fire right now. You should still be arrogant and full of yourself like other twenty-one-year-olds. You're way too young to be feeling so defeated."

"Sis." I took another breath to change topics comfortably. "I can't shake the feeling that this trip is going to be important. I'm on the verge of tears all the time, and it's not depression; it's some kind of…I don't know…some kind of compassion. But I don't know why or who for. Maybe it's my next turning point."

She didn't speak a word. But I knew she wanted to tell me again to get help.

"Sis, I can't believe I left a big city to come up here to 'Hicksville,' but maybe…just maybe, I was sent here on purpose, to take the most famous photograph in the world and launch myself onto an amazing life—maybe to relight my fire."

I assumed that the next moment of silence was from worry. "I know you only got there last night," she finally restarted, "but what sorts of things have you been doing?"

"Babysitting! Ugh!"

"Huh?"

"Louie's running the show for the Railroad Days event. Meanwhile, one of his grandkids showed up on the train, so he asked me to go get him. I spent most of today with him."

"Is he your age?"

"No, it's Fran's little brother. The blond. He's a little squirt. Kind of moody." I thought about what I'd said and restated, "Actually, he's really, *really* moody. And he won't be old enough to drive for two more years, so I'm transporting him here and there until Louie's off duty."

"Well, Fran was different, that's for sure. Hopefully, he's not like her and he won't wear on you. I remember a moody teenager sucking the life out of me once."

"Hey! I resemble that remark."

She laughed quietly for a few seconds. "It's part of being fourteen. I didn't let you get to me, so don't you let him get to you."

"Well, I hope he doesn't distract me from finding my mysterious reason for being in Duluth."

"I'm sure you weren't brought all the way up there after a barrage of bizarre dreams only to let a moody teenager trip it up. Have patience. Your premonitions have been right ever since you got better. Your reason will surface. *It has to.*"

"The long drive also gave me a chance to think long and hard about the kids you think I should visit in St. John's Hospital."

She remained quiet.

"You said that they're in those big, cold beds, whether I come by to visit or not—that really got to me."

"I'm sorry I said that, Tuck; I was wrong. Totally wrong. As soon as I suggested it, I knew I'd made a terrible mistake. You do *not* need to spend time in the very place where your son died. You're twenty-one years old. I know you'd be a godsend to those kids, but you're a kid yourself. I was wrong. Wrong. You need something more upbeat going on right now."

"I'd save them all if I could." I sighed deeply.

"God damn it, Tuck—*don't* go there!"

"Sis, I should go. I still need to call Mom."

"I was wrong, Tuck." Her voice had risen higher like she could sense I was about to cut her off from this conversation.

"Sis, don't worry about it, okay?"

"Despite what Bug says, *you're not a superhero.* You're her special uncle and my special little brother. Tuck, no one is expecting more than that. Don't be hard on yourself over not being able to save Micah or any of those kids. Their illnesses are *not* your fault."

"I know." My throat knotted, and I wallowed one more time in my emotion. "I just wish I was man enough—that just once, I could actually somehow save a kid from dying—it would make up for everything."

"No, Tuck! It won't make up for *anything*! You keep saying that making a friend, or selling a photograph, or saving a child will make everything right." She exploded, "Micah's gone! It's nobody's fault." Then she sighed and regrouped. "I know you want to, sweetheart. That's what makes you such a gem. But before you can help someone else, you need to get some—"

"Okay, okay, I will, I will. I'll get some help. I'll start looking for a good shrink."

"Promise?"

"Yes. You always have my back, and I know it. You're trying to take care of me."

"You're darn right I am." A moment of silence ensued.

"I love you for it."

"Okay, well, I love you too…. Tell Grandpa I love him."

"I will, Sis. You give my little Bug a huge Uncle Tuck kiss on the forehead for me.

"I always do."

"And I love you…. Goodbye."

I hung up, but with no intention of looking for a shrink.

JAMES F JOHNSON

10

Unreasonable Anger

Normalizing on Papa's farm was absolutely the vacation I needed. Unfortunately, I hadn't been able to get Tuck out of my mind since having met him. Mostly, I felt horrifically guilty for any distrust or insults I'd lobbed at him. He really did seem like a good guy. Why was I being such an angry jerk?

I didn't realize the stress he was under, but I was soon to see that he could be pretty short-fused too. If, that is, my issues accidentally touched the wrong nerve connected to his issues.

By Kyle Rickett

Papa had already left for the fairgrounds by the time I got my lazy butt out of bed. I'd slept right through my stupid alarm!

"Damn it!" I said into the bathroom mirror. "I *really* wanted to go with him today."

I hadn't been able to sleep for weeks, and now I couldn't wake up on time. Why couldn't he have gotten me out of bed and then let me doze in one of the tents until I woke up like he used to do when I was little? How could he have left me behind?

I guess the three hours of time zone difference and the tiring train ride were both part of why I'd slept in. I made the best of it when I got the chance to soak for an hour in his tub. I couldn't believe how good it felt to wash my hair—three times—brush my teeth, and soap up my whole body after a full week without a shower. The soap smelled so fresh…the washcloth was a massage, and the toothbrush tickled my gums. It was the best bath of my life.

Later, after I had eaten a couple of eggs and a slice of melon, I zoned out the way teens do while washing mine and Papa's morning dishes. I was wearing Grandma's white lacy apron—the cleanest on the hanger. I was pondering the fact that Tuck and I had the same middle name, and since he was sometimes called James Taylor, I was humming "You've Got a Friend," my favorite song sung by the real James Taylor. Over the spray from rinsing the frying pan, I heard gravel rolling under tires, waking me from my trance. I turned off the water and listened to the rev of a sweet four-hundred-cubic-inch muscle-car engine with ram-air.

"*Tuck*!" A surprising burst of excitement overcame me. I rushed to dry the last of the dishes, but I wouldn't leave the kitchen until everything was put away.

Three taps rattled the front door as the apron slid up over my head. In a cool, smooth motion, I hung it on the hook with several others while jogging casually to the door.

When it swung open, I was elated to see him. He looked surprised. I guess I knew why. My hair was washed and fluffy, making it twice as white as yesterday. My face was clean, and I was wearing the bright blue polo shirt my mom always said brought out the shimmering blue of my sparkling eyes. I had on my latest pair of short-cutoffs with tall, blue-striped tube socks pulled up to my knees. Yesterday, I had looked like Raggedy Andy, but today I was stylin' 1974, like a real boy.

"Is Kyle here?" Tuck chuckled.

"I'll go get him—oh wait—that'd be *me*!" I teased back.

We both laughed politely.

The GOAT DRIVE

"Grandpa and I came to see you last night, around six, but you were dead to the world."

"You came by? Really?" I smiled. "I wish I hadn't gone to bed so early."

"No problem. I checked on you. You were breathing. You seemed fine."

"Wow. Thanks." Well, now I knew he'd come into my room while I was sleeping. That was nice of him...and a tad creepy.

"Damn, kid." His eyes moved downward innocently enough so as to see the whole new person. "You clean up good!"

My crazy spell started all over again. What the hell was happening to me? My cheerful moods turned into nightmares almost instantly now. This was a new thing that wouldn't go away. I laughed at his joke and then—bam! I was scared. At first, I knew I looked good—*I'd dressed like this on purpose*, so I *would* look good. But then when he noticed—damn it, I got such a creepy feeling all of a sudden. This guy was sneaking around in my room and now looking down toward my short cutoffs. I didn't mean to do it, but my hands instinctively—and accidentally—crossed in front of my crotch.

First accusation

"What?" he asked. His face looked like I'd just betrayed him.

"Nothing. What do you mean?"

"What the *hell* was that for?" he shouted. The look changed to rage. "What the hell do you think I was looking at?"

"Uh. I'm sorry. Uh. I just..." I turned fire-engine-red.

"Ah, to hell with ya!" He turned away, waved his hand downward, and started back down the staircase. What in the world had made him so mad all of a sudden? "I thought you might want to spend the day with Louie. That's all...but for-*get* it, you prick!"

"Prick? Tuck!" He was halfway to his car. "Tuck! What did I do?"

He got in the car. My heart sank. He revved and gravel flew. He looped the driveway, and on his way past, he sneered at me. I wanted to sneer back, but my heart was broken.

"Please!" I screamed at him in panic. "I'm sorry! I thought my fly was down." I yelled more quietly. "That's all. I just…I thought my zipper was down." I was a liar now—another new thing.

Halfway down the hill, he froze all four tires and slid ten feet to a stop. The engine silenced as his door flew open.

"*Fine!*" he yelled back. "You wanna see Louie today or not?"

"Yes, please!" I shouted and then swallowed hard.

"All right then." But he got mad again. "I'm ready to go *now*, so you god-damn well better hurry!"

"Wait! I'll be right back." I vanished into the house, wondering why he'd gotten so mad so fast. Granted it was rude what my hands had done, but wow. He took it *hard*. To his advantage, my family—my mom, dad, brother, and sister—all had volatile tempers too. They would explode on me without cause, and I would become their servant, doing everything in my power to calm them down and be their best friend. Instinctively, that's what I wanted to do now with Tuck. The angrier he got, the more I wanted to be close to him.

I ran to the community dresser in the grandkids' bedroom. The twelve of us shared clothes when we visited. I threw a few items into a grocery sack, slammed the drawer, and ran back out to the GTO. Tuck had started it and backed it up to the door again, but he was ignoring me. I tossed the sack through the open rear window as I got in through the passenger's door. Tuck started driving off before my door closed.

"I said I was sorry," I muttered.

"You looked like death-warmed-over yesterday. I was complimenting you. That's all." He refused to look anywhere but at the road. "That was really insulting what you did."

"I thought my fly was down," I lied again.

"*I hate* it when people don't trust me." Still looking straight ahead, and shifting gears roughly, he finished, "I'm a *good* person."

I didn't know what to say. I knew I was wrong to have mistrusted him, but I couldn't help myself. My hands moved like that automatically. If he'd known how much this new fear of mine was consuming me with worry that I'd never be normal again, he'd have been a lot more compassionate. What was coming over me? Why couldn't I control it?

"Oh, Jesus." Tuck finally looked over. "Are you crying now?"

"No," I lied again. Actually, it wasn't a lie; it was a mistake. At that moment, I myself hadn't noticed that I was, but as sure as could be, a tear was falling for me to wipe nervously.

Tuck sighed and rolled his eyes.

"I'm really sorry if I hurt your feelings, Tuck." I sucked in a painful breath. My right hand started to shake, so I grabbed it with my left to hold it steady. I stared for a moment and then said it again. "I mean it. I'm really, really sorry."

"Well, shit." He sighed again. "You don't have to *cry* over it. So I got mad. Big fat hairy deal. I hate it when people don't trust me; that's all."

I disconnected and looked back out at the road. My left hand let go of the right to massage gently the top of my stomach. Tuck saw the move, then looked back at the road again. That's when I looked back to try to figure him out. I was confused by the oddity of a man who could get mad so fast and calm down so quickly, and then say honest things, so openly. Normally when I'd stick a foot in my mouth—which I did a lot—people counter-attacked by shouting accusations and lies that heated into wars that lasted for days—wars I always lost.

"Did Papa ask you bring me to see him?"

"No. I thought I'd surprise him. I know *he* likes you…and I like *him*. So…I'm bringing his grandson to him. *That's all.*"

"Are you going to stay too?" I knew I liked him a little, but I realized then how badly I'd suddenly *wanted* him to like me in return.

"Not planning to."

"Why not?"

"You want me to stay?"

"I dunno," I lied again. The truth was that it would have been awesome for him to start to like me. I looked out my passenger window and rubbed my stomach again.

"I'll ask Louie if he wants me to leave you. I'm doing this for him. I'll let *him* decide."

"'Kay," I whispered. I guess I deserved his anger. With a heavy sigh, I stopped talking altogether.

11
Unconventional Talents

I wanted Tuck to like me. Especially after he got so mad. I wanted to fill the void left empty by my dad whom I used to make proud. I wanted to show Tuck my talents so I'd be worth hanging around with. Young men want older men to value them. The feeling in my gut, as I prepared to show off to him, was the same feeling I had whenever I sought praise from my dad for loading more firewood than an average kid could do. For a boy who felt like the world hated me, I had an amazing number of talents that I kept hidden—in part, I suppose, because some of them were strange talents. I wasn't a normal kid who could score the winning points on a ball field. My talents were more prone to bring unwanted teasing from the general public. But they were talents nonetheless, and they were important to me. Over the years, they became part of my identity. To show my talents was to show myself to someone.

That morning, when Tuck offered to take me to the festival, I got an idea that I hoped like hell wouldn't backfire on me. I went to the drawer and pulled out one of my odd skills, but I kept it in a bag in case I chickened out before I could show it to him.

If Papa wouldn't let me do it, or if I couldn't impress Tuck with it, then I didn't even want him to know I had planned to try.

By Tuck Taylor

I spotted another clever grassy-patch parking spot and coasted in, shut off the engine, and let the car roll to a stop. I halted with the parking brake. Rrrrt! The car rocked to and fro for a moment.

"Thanks, Tuck." The kid opened his door.

I didn't respond. I was furious and confused about him. I was also unhappy with my own temper. I hadn't meant to get so angry earlier. I had a slight temper issue, but that explosion had rattled me. Ronnie was right. I was an unhappy twenty-one-year-old. Kyle's accusatory move frightened me more than anything else. How does a guy prove he's *not* a pervert after someone accuses him of it? In 1974, the notion of being gay was far more of an oddity than it is now. Almost everyone was homophobic, and being accused of looking at another man's (or a boy's) body in the wrong way could completely end a guy's life. Also, it wasn't the first time I'd been in that position. The last time I'd been accused of it, my life *was* catastrophically altered. I guess the psychological slang for why I got so angry so fast was because I had baggage from my past.

I had felt vulnerable to Kyle's accusation, so I lashed out. Old baggage came up with it that morning. I didn't respond as well as I could have. It was easy to see that he was an emotional mess. But the way Louie loved him...well, I had to respect that, and I had to trust that he might still be a good kid. But was he worth the frustration of getting too close to?

The makings of forgiveness

I was curious about what Kyle had brought with him. He reached through the window to grab his mysterious sack and walked respectfully toward the music. He either couldn't take the guilt any longer, or my silent treatment had gotten to him. He groveled for me.

"Tuck, *please* don't be mad at me."

The GOAT DRIVE

I looked into his shimmering blue doe eyes, which had a look of pain in them. I stared for a moment, then shook my head and smirked. The truth is that my youthful male temper had a short life. I've always hated being mad at people for more than a few minutes. His wanting gaze drew me in, and his eyes *sparkled*. That blue shirt of his must have had magical powers to magnify their iridescence. It's hard to stay angry at someone whose eyes penetrate your own—and sparkle while they're at it.

"Thanks." Kyle understood that my sigh and smirk meant his apology was accepted. With a genuine smile of his own, he lifted an open hand to his chest. "I hate it when people are mad at me."

"You're an enigma," I said while shaking my head.

"What does that mean?" he asked while watching the ground.

"It means I can't figure you out."

Making music

The music wasn't live this time. It was a record player. Large, dark, wooden, bass-rich stereo speakers sat on tables. In the protective shade of the lonesome bandstand were six empty stools and a couple of unopened black carrying cases, quietly waiting for the show to start.

We wandered through the thin, but growing, crowd and found Louie sitting at a picnic table behind the concession stands in an area marked off for staff.

"Papa!" Kyle yelled and waved.

Louie looked festive, once again in his lederhosen and felt hat. In his unique German-based accent, he shouted back, "Boys!"

Kyle nudged up to his papa while I plopped down across the table from them both. Louie one-armed-squeezed and kissed the top of Kyle's head again.

"Okay, now *this* is nice. You look like my Q-Tip today. Not so beat up."

"Careful, Louie; he doesn't take compliments so well."

Kyle sneered at me. I laughed once.

"Oh!" Louie brushed a teasing hand toward me, then refocused on Kyle. "You come to hear me play some more?"

"Ooh, coffee," I mumbled. "I'll be right back." I walked across the grassy patch to the gigantic chrome pot with Styrofoam cups stacked next to it; then I watched momentarily from a distance as Kyle and Louie discussed the bag. I paused there long enough to ponder what was in it. Finally, I poured and returned with two cups.

"You like sugar, right, Louie? I put two scoops in for you."

"You're a good boy, Tuckster. Did you put spirits in it too?"

I laughed.

"Well, next time remember a snort or two. I'll forgive this time."

"I hope I didn't cramp your plans by bringing shithead by," I said while blowing across the top of my hot cup.

I could tell that the nickname shook Kyle slightly, and that he'd pretended not to hear it. I felt like an ass for having said it.

"Not at all. You made my day." Louie ruffled a hand through Kyle's hair. "Wait 'til you get to know him. He's no shithead."

Wait 'til I get to know him? This wasn't temporary? I paused for a second to let their quiet admonishment sink in with me. Then I asked for direction.

"What time would you like me to come back and get him?"

"You're leaving?" Louie let go of Kyle. "Today's going to be nothing but fun."

"I promised Grandpa I'd clean his barn today."

"Hmm, I know how old man Tucker is about those ponies." They were two full-grown horses, but Louie always called them ponies. Then he leaned over the table. I moved in to meet him. "But can you stay for a little bit? I want you to see something."

"See something?"

"It's important. We start playing music at eleven. I want you to watch my first song. You can do that?"

"Louie, have I ever said no to you?"

The GOAT DRIVE

"That's my boy. If old Tucker doesn't like it, I'll send Q-Tip over to help you clean it up later."

"Oh, that won't be necessary," I declined.

"Don't be so hard on him, Mr. Taylor. He's a little squirt, but strong like two men." He wiggled Kyle back and forth hard enough to make his head bobble and smile. "And fast like lightning."

I left the towheaded duo for a walk of the grounds. The day was warming nicely and was still comfortable. At eleven o'clock, I made my way back to the gazebo with a freshly cooked brat dog lying over a mound of greasy fries in one hand and a paper-cup soft drink in the other. I heard Norwegian and German accents shouting inaudible words into the microphones and a few percussions of a drum warming up. I made my way to a picnic table and sat down with a local family of neighbors whom I knew by face but not by name.

The littlest musician

The remaining men emerged from the performer's tent, but with an extra band member—a half-sized man, dressed in the same brown shorts, white fluffy shirt, green suspenders, white socks, and green felt hat with a feather as the rest of them. His hair was white.

"Oh, my god!" I mumbled. *"That's* what was in the sack."

Louie had the accordion, so when they got ready to start, Kyle stood alone in front. One of the men counted, *"One, two, one-two-three…"* and the festive music crashed into the world. Kyle jumped up once, twice, then lifted one foot, crossed it behind himself, and slapped his heel. The music was lively, and so was his dance. Both hands slapped at his heels and knees in rhythm.

"No waaaay!" I put down my dog. "He's *good* at this."

Kyle knew his moves, at least enough of them to be entertaining. He was obviously partially-trained in at least some simple German or Norwegian folk dancing. By his smile beneath the feathered cap, I'd say that whether he was doing it right or not, he was loving it, and he was giving true entertainment pizzazz to his audience.

"Why's he such a little prick when he's with me?" I asked out loud. The couple I'd sat with looked over, then dismissed my comment and rejoined the show.

I ate my dog with a smile and a repeated giggle. I kept looking at Louie, whose eyes were on his little Q-Tip at least 50 percent of the time. Louie let out smiles at Kyle's moves, and so did the other band members. I saw the love. "Maybe he's not an eye-rolling, spoiled brat after all." I wished I'd had my camera gear with me, but it was all back at Grandpa's house.

I couldn't bring myself to leave, even for the twenty minutes it would take to retrieve my gear. I finished my dog and sat for three more songs. I heard comments from the crowd about the cute little dancer. People seemed to think he was ten or twelve, which made him appear even cuter. I overheard one woman ask her companion how old he thought the boy might be. Ten? Eleven?

"He's *fourteen*!" I righteously interrupted.

After the fourth energetic song, Louie introduced his grandson into the microphone. Kyle took a bow for the clapping audience.

"All right, you Swedes who are here today, here's a favorite I know you like: 'Johan Pa Snippen,' or sometimes I call it, 'The Johnny Oslo Schottische' played by my grandson, Q-Tip!"

People got up and clapped again. I had no idea what the hell was going on, but many of the people who were thirty or older wandered up to the dancing area and formed a big circle. Kyle, who had been handed Papa's accordion, sat on the stool and looked out over the crowd. He was almost too small for the instrument. One could see more of his hat than face. Kyle scanned the crowd until his eyes met mine. They lit up and twinkled. I saw it from all the way out on the lawn. Then he looked around at the band members and nodded. He started.

"One, two—a one, two, three—" His fingers flew up and down the keyboard like lightning. Not knowing the song, I couldn't tell if he was doing it right, but it sure sounded jovial. As the accordion bellowed its festive rhythm, watchers clapped, and the base-guitarist, trumpets, and drums joined in. The circle of men and women became a folk dance that looked like fun.

This song went on for a while with me laughing through the whole thing. I started to hear tones that sounded like they were probably mistakes, but the other instruments covered for him, and the tempo never slowed. Kyle mostly focused on his keys—I suspect he was making his share of mistakes, but no one cared. Every now and then, he'd look out into the crowd and connect with me. He'd smile. I'd wave and smile back each time, and then he'd smile even bigger and look back down at his keys.

Maybe he *did* want me to like him after all.

12

Morning Confessions

Spiritual connections between a mother and son can defy physical understanding, and to make this even more mysterious, the spirit isn't always connected to the physical relationship. In other words, a mother like mine, who doesn't seem to grasp her son's needs, can still feel his joys and pains in the spiritual realm, even from long distances. While her parenting skills weren't what I needed, and she didn't work hard to understand me, somehow Mom knew I was in serious trouble. She just didn't know what that trouble was, or what to do about it.

By Kyle Rickett

Monday morning, at about 7:30, I wandered into the kitchen where Papa, in his usual plaid shirt and suspenders, read the paper.

I was in my best mood in weeks because of the fun I'd had with him and Tuck the day before. You see, after playing music with him, I didn't take off my lederhosen and hat. I goofed off with Tuck at the fairgrounds until dinnertime. We rode the miniature steam train twice. It was like when I used to hang out with my cousin Scooter on the Fourth of July. I didn't change back into my street clothes because, unlike St. Tiberius's Catholic school, no one there was judging me as a freak and I liked the *positive* attention. I had become somewhat of a celebrity after performing. Some people asked if I'd ever danced on the monthly local TV show with Papa Louie's band.

> *Duluth had a local channel back then, and Papa's band had a show on it. All they did was play music for an hour. It was estimated to have had a hundred or so viewers. Papa always joked that his audience was more like a hundred TVs that were left on just for the noise in widows' empty living rooms. I disagreed. Papa was well-known in his small community, and I think people watched him play.*

I was too honest to take advantage of the easy attention. I admitted to the fact that Scooter and I had been seen with our grandfather on the show, but we'd never danced on it. I got a kick out of the smiles people gave me. One nice lady got me to sign the inside cover of her address book. I signed it *Q-Tip*. I hated the various hateful nicknames I was given at St. Tiberius's, but here, I was proud to have a nice one given to me by the man I respected so much.

But that was yesterday. This morning was going to be my first chance to be alone with Papa, and for that, I was happy. He rattled the paper when he saw me.

"I got gruel on the stove. You hungry?"

"Gruel?" I laughed, comforted to be in his presence. "Smells like oatmeal." Then I added, "I don't even know what gruel is."

"Whatever you call it, it's hot. Good morning, Q-Tip!"

"Morning, Papa." I couldn't contain my huge smile as I rounded the corner of the table and reached my arms around his thick German neck. Papa let go of his paper with one giant hand to stretch across my bare shoulder blades and squeeze once. I grunted comically, pretending I was being crushed.

Papa watched closely—real closely—as I wandered about the kitchen. He hadn't seen me in so long that maybe he was *soaking me in*. First, I grabbed a bowl from the cupboard, and then I went to the stove. After he'd seen as much as he could, front and back, he chuckled. I

The GOAT DRIVE

probably looked funny with my small bare back and large baggy Batman pajama bottoms, trailing behind each foot like dust mops from being two sizes too long. I'd probably chuckle too if I saw a kid dressed like that.

A mother's intuition

"You make good oatmeal," I complimented as I dished a scoop and turned to walk back to Papa. Then I asked, "How come you didn't teach my mom how to do this?"

"Pumpkin can't make oatmeal?" Papa had a nickname for all six of his girls, and all twelve of his grandkids. In fact, it was Papa who coined Scooter's nickname too.

"She boils water in a tea kettle and gives me packets of dry stuff."

"Hmm. She's too modern." He rattled his paper again and refocused on it. "The real stuff sticks to your ribs. She should know that."

I laughed and sat down. I wasn't a dumb kid to him; I was a real person. My chair clattered like a fart on the floor. I wiggled side to side to get comfortable. Papa had all the fixin's on the table already, so I began mixing in my milk, sugar, raisins, and cinnamon.

"I'm really happy I'm here. Thank you for letting me stay."

"Did you ask your mom if you could come?"

"No. She surprised me with it."

"She called last night when you was sleepin'." Papa folded his paper and put it on the table next to his coffee cup. "Third time now." He leaned forward. "She had a bad dream about you when you were on your trip. She's worried."

"She always has bad dreams. Did I turn into a donut or something?"

"Your momma's dreams can be funny. Not this one, though. She thought you died. She woke up yelling, 'Save him!'"

My eyes widened. "Save him?" I pictured the man on the train platform only two nights prior, holding his Twins hat after pulling me out of my suicide jump onto the tracks. I clearly recalled him telling me about the woman's voice he'd heard yelling '*Save him!*' Then he looked around and saw that he and I were totally alone. No one knew why he heard that woman's scream just in time to stop me.

"She was mighty worried. *Mighty* worried. She thought you were hit by a train."

Shivers permeated the whole upper half of my body. But with a tinge of vengeful anger in my gut, I puffed an arrogant laugh.

"A train," I muttered. "Sheesh." I shrugged my shoulders, stuck my spoon in the bowl, and drew out a serving.

"Q-Tip?"

"Yeah?"

"Your mama loves you. Don't think she don't…okay?"

I was pretty sure he didn't know the whole story of how I was sent away.

"Q-Tip, I see your face. You don't believe me. But I know my Pumpkin just like I know you."

"I'm sorry."

"I don't know what's going on out on that island right now, but Pumpkin was missing you pretty bad on the phone this morning. I heard it in her."

"Okay, Papa. I'll trust you…she loves me. I get it."

Papa's preliminary prodding

Papa repositioned himself. He rattled the paper again and grabbed his coffee cup. "You were much too sad on Saturday morning. Life's gotten hard for you, yeah?"

I chewed the first bite, and when I could speak, I said, "I'm happy now, Papa."

"But on your island…not so much?"

"No. Not so much." I looked down at my bowl and slowly scooped another spoonful.

"Did Connor leave for the summer? Left you all alone maybe?"

I smiled unexpectedly. My grandfather, who had never met my best friend from across the street, not only knew his name, but how important he was to me.

"No. Connor's still there, but my dad won't let me play with him."

"Is something wrong with the boy?"

"No." I took in a long, slow breath. "Something's wrong with me."

"Oh, that's silly talk! Nothing's wrong with my Q-Tip. You're as good as any of 'em." He poked his finger onto the table twice. "Something's wrong with your dad…that's what I think."

Papa was always extra tough on my dad, and he made no apologies for it, ever. For once, on that morning, I didn't take offense to it either. The story of how Connor and I had been torn apart that summer was so complicated that I had no way of even beginning to tell Papa how it had happened. The isolation that was forced onto me on Torano Island only made sense if you understood the complexity of the abuse I took at Catholic school, plus the velocity of my sister's sociopathic daily barrage of lies, and the unfathomable evil in my dad's best friend, Dr. Krieg. With God as my witness, *none* of those complicated stories were going to be disclosed to my simple, special, happy, loving grandfather. I jammed my spoon into the bowl, planting it like a flagpole.

"Can I live here with you?"

"Oh…" He paused and put his cup down, "Q-Tip…."

"Please, Papa?"

"No…no…. You got a family in Washington. They need you. I heard it in your mama's voice this morning."

"They don't need me. They don't even want me." My eyes turned hot.

He stared for a long time into my eyes and didn't push any further.

"Well, boy, if that's how you see it, then that's how I see it too." He nodded one time in agreement. "I can't move you in here. But tell me. What *can* I do?"

"I don't know. I don't even know why they sent me away. I got up one morning and there were my suitcases."

"Hmm. She didn't tell me that part." He drew his head back. His face turned a shade red. He suddenly looked angry. "So, you was sent away." He tapped the table once with a firm fingertip as if he were putting a period on the end of his new understanding. "And now you got no friends at home."

"No, sir." I was about to cry. "And they won't let me talk to Scott anymore, either."

"Ooooh, Q-Tip, don't tell me that. You and Scooter are Siamese Twins." Then he asked like he was truly confused by my report, "What the *hell* do you mean you two can't talk no more?"

"I don't know. They won't tell me. But he didn't come to the Fourth of July and no one will say why." I lied. I wanted to hear Papa's explanation to see if he'd heard it the same way I had. Fran had told me that the whole family needed to protect me from Scooter because he was gay and I was weak. Mom's version was different. She told me Scooter had changed and didn't want me hanging around anymore. I knew Papa wouldn't lie to me, so maybe—just maybe—he'd tell me a different version. A better one. I trusted Papa. He never lied to me, as far as I knew. I'd believe his version, no matter what it was.

"Maybe he was sick."

"That's what they said at first. Then they changed it. They told me to forget about him. That he's not my friend anymore." My words faded to a quiver. My hot eyes now welled up and I fought to keep from crying. I must have looked like a damned nine-year-old again. "Papa, what did I do? Scott and I will always be friends—won't we?" It took every muscle in my body to keep from crying now. "What did I do to make this happen?" My mouth contorted uncontrollably. "What did I do this time?"

"You didn't do nothin'." Papa shook his head slowly, with his eyes still locked into mine. He didn't have an explanation. His compassion on me was obvious just then, but he either knew nothing about this, or he wasn't willing to discuss it. I had no way of knowing which.

"Didn't you used to have a friend at school? Some piano player?"

My face turned red. How dare he call Andreo a friend?

"Oh." Papa saw the reaction, "Things aren't good with that boy either?"

"No." I shook my head and grabbed the spoon to resume eating. "Andreo and I don't get along anymore. Truth is you're my only friend."

"Don't say that. A boy your age needs friends who aren't crazy old men."

"I love your kind of crazy, Papa. I wanna be like you."

"In fifty years, you can be."

"And I'm not a kid anymore. And I'm not grown up either. I'm nothing. You're all I have—and I'm okay with that. I love you so much. And I want to stay here with you."

He shook his head, but with a compassionate smile, and changed the subject. "I'm going to play checkers a little later with the old coot next door. You wanna come along?"

"You mean Tuck's grandpa? Tucker Johnson?" I tipped my head while he nodded. "Is it far?"

"You know where it is. Next driveway over…so a few blocks. I can drive."

"Can I stay here, and if I change my mind, can I use the bike to come over?"

"Ya ya."

Time alone

The morning lingered. Soon enough, I had the house to myself—it was awesome. I'd never been alone there. I slid my pajama bottoms to the floor and stepped out of them to walk around stark naked for a while—just because I could. I slid the bathroom window up and left the door open so I could smell the warm summer breeze as I showered and blow-dried. Mom didn't have a blow dryer at home. This one was here because of the granddaughters and older grandsons whom Papa hosted. It was a treat to blow-dry my thick hair, especially since it was a bit longer than ever. I didn't exactly know how to do it, but since it wasn't *too* long yet, I really couldn't do any damage or make it look too wild.

I could breathe deeply here. I'd learned that being alone was the only time I felt safe. After my hair was dry, I flexed my then tiny muscles in the mirror and growled, then slipped on a pair of briefs, a tight-fitting pale yellow tank top, and my short blue running shorts. Nothing else.

I returned to the bedroom and drew in two lungs-full of summer air, letting it out with an "Ah" while pretending to live alone there in the summer sun. Then I folded yesterday's laundry neatly into a pile and pressed it firmly on the dresser to wash later. I hummed a German folk song under my breath while making the bunk bed and tucking my lederhosen back into their drawer. I zipped my duffel and suitcase and slid them neatly beneath the beds, then looked around the room. It was perfect. Like when I'd arrived.

It was still only ten o'clock. I put on my blue boat shoes, which were a pair of canvas slip-ons. The cream-colored soles made my feet look too big for my body—and they kind of were. My hands and feet seemed to be growing, but I wasn't, which made me feel more awkward and self-conscious. But no one was here to laugh at me, so I confidently went out into the yard to explore.

Papa lived on around fifteen acres of semi-wooded land, with a few gentle rolling hills and a creek about five minutes' walk back from the house. Being my first time alone there, it felt different than ever before. Peaceful. Heavenly. As a child I'd always seen all of it as a playground. Now, at fourteen, a newly matured appreciation emerged for the natural, serene beauty. It sort of took my breath away for a moment. But then, a peacefully deep rhythm of breathing made the entire experience even more blissful.

I walked, as if for the first time, the quiet, secluded grounds for a good hour. The air was still and quiet. No highway noise, but plenty of birds and chipmunks barking with a squeaky clicking sound. Every now and then, something would rustle in the bushes or tall grass. Probably a garter snake or a rabbit. Maybe a small bird. I'd look each time, but I never caught what it was. I'd talk to it, though: "Don't be scared. I won't hurt you." I listened to my feet pressing against the different soils, leaves, and rocks, pretending I had died on the train platform and was now walking with God in the Garden of Eden, in perfect peace and eternal safety.

I wondered if I could ever talk Papa into leaving the farm to me in his will so I could raise my kids there and then become the crazy old white-haired man who gave joy to all the grandchildren like he did. Each of the twelve of us grandchildren believed we were his favorite. Ever since Gramma died, he'd become that good at giving his attention to whomever he was with at the time. For us kids, this was always a happy place.

I reminisced about those past summer weeks I'd spent there with my favorite cousin, Scooter. We would make forts, hide from siblings, and make wooden boats to race in the creek. I always won, and I always knew it was because Scooter would let me. Even though he was almost three years older than me, we had always felt like we were twins. It was who we were together. Smelling the trees and the creek brought Scooter to life for me. I closed my eyes and could almost feel those big strong arms hugging me, and I could nearly smell the cologne he always wore. *Always*. It was even soaked into his pajamas. When my eyes opened and I saw how alone I was again, a hollow emptiness overcame me. I took a deep breath.

"Scooter," I sighed, "I wish you were here. I need you more than ever."

But he wasn't here. Today, the place was lonesome and quiet, but at least it was teaming with the ghosts of happy times.

After an hour or so, I emerged from the creek trail into the bright, hot sunlight and saw the GTO abandoned in the driveway.

"Oh," I said, smiling. "How long has he been here?" I wandered over to see if he'd left the keys in it again.

The GOAT DRIVE

13

Comparison

I've been talking all along about a friendship I was one day going to enjoy with Tuck Taylor. In looking back now, I think that the historic friendship took its roots while I played music in the gazebo on Sunday, July 28. But it wasn't until the next day, July 29, that the two of us began to recognize the possibilities we had before us. Me first.

By Tuck Taylor

It was almost 10:00 a.m., and I couldn't find the kid anywhere. I'd come looking because of Louie, who had dropped by to have coffee with Grandpa. When I walked into the kitchen, the two of them shushed—they'd obviously been talking about me. Louie then, for some reason, hired me to take out a bee's nest over at his place, and Grandpa told me I should "take the offer."

Something was up—that much I knew. So I played along.

After breakfast, I went to the garage and made a set of small torches, then drove to Louie's, humming that Johnny-something song Kyle'd played on the accordion the day before.

Nobody answered my knock, so I walked in. All I found was the wet tub curtain from a recent shower and the freshly stacked outfit Kyle had worn the day before. Even his suitcases were zipped and tucked neatly beneath the bottom bunk. For being such a mess when I'd met him, his tidiness seemed extra noteworthy. More evidence for me to assess that there was more to him than just angry eye-rolls.

Morning visitation

I held Kyle's folded blue shirt up to the mirror, but it didn't bring out the blue in my eyes that it did in *his* yesterday. I guess it wasn't so much the magic of the shirt as it was his outrageously blue pupils. I don't normally notice eye colors, but his were such an amazingly bright blue that no one *couldn't* notice them. They were literally the same color as the sky in that dream I'd had during my near-death experience.

"One like me...." I muttered the words from my dream a week back when I was trying to decide whether to leave or stay in Texas. A white dove against a blue sky had told me to show trust. When I asked to whom, it said to *one like me*. A shiver ran the length of my spine as I briefly wondered if Kyle was the *one like the bird*. I shook my head in disbelief. "No...that doesn't make any sense."

My search moved me from the house, past my parked Goat, and into the shop where I once again found no trace of life—even the bicycle was still leaning against its usual pole. I wandered back out into the dry sunlight and voilà—there he stood—admiring my beautiful car, probably looking to see if the keys were in it again. I couldn't blame him for his interest in the car; she was a great car. I even heard him whispering to himself, "Beautiful."

"That she is." I surprised him from behind.

"Tuck!" he whipped around, looking embarrassed.

"Did I surprise you?" I was taken in again by his eyes.

"Maybe a little. Why were you in *there*?"

"I was looking for you. You weren't in the house."

"Well—" His gaze darted toward the woods. "That's 'cause I was on a walk."

"Oh—all alone?"

"Well," he shrugged and looked down at his feet, "it's not like I have a lot of friends here. Pretty much just Papa, and he's at your house."

Youthful good looks

"Hmm." I nodded gently. "Good day for a walk, I guess." I looked up toward the sky.

He giggled.

"Did I say something funny?"

"No." He turned pink. "I'm sorry. It's just that...."

"What?"

"Well..." He nervously chewed his bottom lip for a second. "Why do you look so *young* today?"

"Young? I don't know." I laughed out loud. "Hardy breakfast maybe? You really think I look younger?"

Kyle wiggled his awkward adolescent head and shrugged.

"Maybe it's because I'm only twenty-one. *That's not really very old.*"

"But you look like you're sixteen. Or twelve..." Then he flashed a sinister grin, "or nine."

"Oh!" I laughed back, and shook a scolding finger.

He chuckled.

"Okay, maybe I deserved that one."

He stuck his tongue out at me, but obviously not to be malicious. He quickly followed it up with a polite laugh. I think he was trying very, very hard not to let yesterday's explosion happen again.

I laughed with him and shook my head.

"Maybe it's because you're dressed like a teenager today." He pointed at my designer jeans.

"A *teenager*?" I looked down at my own clothes. I was definitely a fashion-conscious young man, but a teen? Okay, I admit that at that moment, I *was* having a great hair-day. And my pre-faded jeans—like my car—*were* from high school. The butt was tight, the legs loose. The art of tightly wrapping the various fleshy bulges from neck to knee was part of the male dress-code in those days. Thick hair and the right accessories could make a plain-looking wallflower like myself into a take-a-second-looker. The long sleeves of my white linen shirt were hopefully rolled up high enough over my biceps to show the world I had a weight bench back home. Also, I had youthful skin. I only had to shave once a week back then, and my half-unbuttoned shirt exposed an obvious lack of chest hair—maybe that was part of it. I spent a lot of time in the mirror each morning making sure everything worked together. Perhaps, subconsciously, I *was* feeling kind of youthful that day. "Do I look bad?"

"No!" Kyle bolted back energetically. "I think you look *cool*!" He seemed to have surprised himself by admitting that. He blushed.

"Oh. But I look too young to buy beer."

"Yeah, you'd probably get carded today." He laughed and rested his gaze on my silver eagle pendant, exposed by the half-unbuttoned shirt. "Well, you're usually wearing taller shoes." His eyes pointed down at my open-toed, leather sandals. "Maybe that has something to do with it."

"I don't really think I look that different, Kyle. I might be a little shorter without my boots…it's your perception." I looked down at myself again, but this time, I raised both arms out to my sides. I really did dress like that almost all the time. I was barely twenty-one, and proud of my physique. That's a pretty normal attribute in young, athletic males. But after talking with Ronnie two nights before, I realized I wasn't quite as forlorn, or *depressed*, as I had been of late. I guess I did feel especially sprite that day, and I hadn't felt that way in a while. Kyle's comments told me that my energetic mood showed.

Self-reflection

Then I saw him break focus to look straight down to perform an obvious self-evaluation. My heart sank. I knew the look—or at least I believed I did. I'd seen it in my own reflection at seventeen when my hair had fallen out, my skin had turned gray, and I'd lost weight from the cancer medications. I was sure that with my athletic prowess gone, I had become a vulnerable and ugly outcast. I suppose that's why I'd become so conscious of how I looked now. Suddenly, it wasn't only his sparkling eyes that drew me in; empathy was prompting me to address his obvious self-esteem issues. And who knows? Maybe that's why Louie had sent me over. He knew from the Saturday morning meltdown that his grandson was suffering in ways a teen never should, but he didn't know why.

So, for now, here I was, standing in front of Kyle's awkward little self, wearing all the latest fashions, showing off my well cared-for swimmer's body, and feeling like a million bucks. While his overly fluffed hair looked like he'd tried to blow it dry without anyone first showing him how. His good looks were slightly tainted by his un-styled haircut, small stature, catalogue shorts, and boat shoes. I could see how hard he was trying to fit in—but I saw no evidence that anyone was showing him how to do that. Perhaps I could help the guy out.

Time to assess motives

This would be the historical moment in which I stopped using Louie as my excuse for hanging around with Kyle. As of that very moment, my heart had become engaged in this relationship. The kid admired me, and I liked it. He could be moody, but his upside was quite endearing. I was in this for me now. This kid needed a friend—badly. And, frankly, so did I.

He finally seemed to focus on our shoes. He first looked at his own, then at my cool leather sandals, then back at his department store boat shoes. His feet were huge, which would one day be an advantage, but for now, it made him look like a clumsy puppy. I felt that his self-evaluation had gone on long enough, so I reached into his moment and offered a rescue.

"Hey, I like those shoes. I have a pair too."

"You *do*?" It worked more quickly than I'd hoped. He snapped back and smiled.

"Same color too." I let myself smile, but I held back a laugh at his reaction.

"Really?" His inner world seemed to be gone now as fast as it had come.

"Heck, yeah. I love 'em, but I don't have them with me on this trip. They look *really* good on you."

"Cool." He smiled even bigger, then looked back down. "They're comfortable," he added with new energy in his voice. "I'm glad my mom packed them."

I hoped now that I could find a pair at Target or someplace to prove I had them like I'd said I did.

His eyes sparkled again as he looked at me, while his gentle fingers continued to enjoy the smoothly waxed finish of my car.

14

No Jealousy, Please!

As a lifelong student of human spirituality, I've come to understand jealousy as a wrong reaction to a natural trigger. Whenever I feel a tinge of jealousy, I have learned to recognize it as a warning to ask myself an important question. Why do I feel less than someone else right now?

Here's my late-life opinion on jealousy: If a person feels jealous, he feels inferior to someone. (No one is jealous of someone who has less than he does.) If the jealous person attempts to discredit the person he's jealous of, then he is practicing pure evil. If he believes in heaven and hell, then he's pointing his moral compass downward, not up. If, however, the jealous person uses his jealousy as a tool to work on himself and raise his own self-esteem without hurting anyone else, then he is properly leveraging the uncontrolled emotions of jealousy to bring good to himself without hurting anyone else.

JAMES F JOHNSON

By Kyle Rickett

"Surprised" is the best word I have for what I felt when I saw Tuck come out of Papa's garage. He looked so good. How come I had to be such a dork? Why couldn't I look as good as someone like him? He was so…so…*everything I wanted to be*.

As I leaned against his car, which was the car I wanted, and watched him saunter around like an athlete, streaming his fingers through the hair I wished was on my head, I couldn't help but be mesmerized by him.

It wasn't a sexual attraction. I didn't want to have him. I wanted to *be* him.

If he hadn't been so kind about how bad I looked that day, my admiration for him might have turned to ugly jealousy. I hated the kids at school who had better bodies than mine, better hair than mine, and parents who built them up instead of put them down. I hated them because they flaunted their good fortune and looked down at me for being less than them. Tuck was an actual nice guy who had all of that—a better body, better hair, and a GTO. The jealousy was knocking on my door, but thank God I didn't let it in that morning.

Tuck, being as cool a guy as he was, somehow helped me not to go down that awful road of jealousy. My sister, Fran, always took that road, and it always made her look as evil as anyone you can describe. If she had been there just then, she'd have laughed angrily, rolled her eyes, and accused Tuck of being too stupid to dress his age.

If jealousy were in my family tree, then my thankfulness for Tuck's gentle guidance is eternal. In more ways than I can even recall, Tuck has consistently shown me the way *out* of the family trend of attacking others because of jealousy.

15

A Job to Do

I began to like Tuck more and more with each conversation. But the real test now was going to be to see if Tuck and I were ready to team up. Or was this going to be like me and my dad, where I pursued his attention and he gave it to me when it suited him? Something within me wanted to turn my jealousy of his life into a positive thing. I wanted to rise above something that divided us and turn it into a bridge to connect us. I wanted Tuck to show me how to be like him. I wanted Tuck to like me, and I wanted to prove myself to him. I wanted to emulate him. All his moves were cool. I wanted to learn those moves.

By Tuck Taylor

"Well..." I got down to business. With a graceful jerk of the neck, I flipped the bangs from my eyes. To complete the cool move, I raked a hand through my hair, front to back. Abundant locks flowed through my fingers and draped theatrically back into my face, which is something I'd enjoyed doing ever since my hair grew back. "Louie hired me just now to take care of a bee's nest. I was hoping you'd want to help."

Kyle pushed out his lower lip, nodded, and flipped his head slightly, using his free hand to rake it through the side of his shorter hair, exactly as I had done.

I almost laughed, but I held back. At the same moment, I was caught off guard by an unexpected sense of pride. This smaller, younger man was trying to copy my cool moves. If someone had told me that being emulated by a younger man was a good feeling, I wouldn't have grasped it. The *experience* of him copying my hair-rake move right then and there was a deep compliment that warmed my chest in ways no one could have prepared me for.

"Sounds good. Sure." He continued to nod slowly. "But the truth is I don't know how to take care of a bee's nest." The fingers of his other hand continued to run smoothly across the top edge of a front fender. I was beginning to believe he liked my car more than I did.

"Oh, that's okay. I know how to do it." I didn't tell him that I only knew it in concept and that I'd never done it for real. "We're gonna smoke it, and then smash it up. The bees are all over in his shop, and he can't use it until they're gone."

"How do you smoke it?" Kyle casually stepped away from the car to move toward me.

"I made some small rags on sticks. I soaked them in liquid smoke from my old train set. Then I sprinkled kerosene over them. We'll put them in a metal garbage can lid right under the hive. It works."

"You sure?" He gingerly walked past me and looked carefully through the open shop door.

"How could it not? It's just smoke." I could smell the deodorant from his recent shower, which brought up fond memories of summers when I was his age and my friends and I would hang out after our post-baseball-game-showers. Reliving that memory with friends helped put me in an even better mood. Less lonely. More alive in the moment.

"Of course. I've done it lots of times," I lied.

"Aren't you afraid of getting stung?"

"Na. The smoke puts them all to sleep."

"Will it hurt the bees?"

"Who cares?"

"*I* care!" he charged back.

"Oh…well…*no*. I don't think so." Not used to people being protective of stinging bees, I kept up my role as an authority figure by speaking like I knew how things were done. "They go build a new nest somewhere else." Or so I hoped.

"Well…okay then; I'm ready." He turned to look at me. "Let's do it." His questioning turned into a sense of excitement.

"Excellent." I walked to the shop door and peered inside. A few seconds later, I smelled his deodorant again and felt ten gentle fingertips on my waist, five on each side. I peered carefully behind to see him crouching, but on tiptoes, craning his neck to try to see past me. I had to force myself to keep a straight face.

"What?" he asked shyly.

"Nervous?" I asked back.

"No," he lied.

"Do you know where it is?" I asked.

"The beehive? No." He let go of me and stood straight up. "*You're* the one they hired."

"Oh, yeah," I joked. "I guess I'm the one in charge, aren't I?"

He giggled and crouched back down to peer past me again.

"But…in all fairness, I didn't get much intel from my bosses. In fact, it's like Louie and Grandpa just magically came up with the idea to hire me this morning."

"They didn't give you any warning?"

"It was suspicious. Like they thought of it together…out of nowhere…this morning."

"That's weird."

"Makes me wonder if there even *is* a hive at all," I commented.

"They wouldn't make that up, *would they?*"

Grumpy old comedians

"Oh...it's possible." I unpropped the shop door to let it close, then stood and faced him. "They do goofy shit like that."

"They do?" He wandered a few steps back, out of the shade and toward the car again, but he shuffled rocks back and forth with his shoes while we talked.

"You should see them at night when they play checkers."

"How often do they do that?" The morning sun forced him to close one eye, squint with the other, and tip his head.

"They play once a week. They have for years now. They drink. They're funnier than hell. And don't let them kid you about the checkers—*they get together to drink.*"

"That'd be fun to watch." He smirked and put a hand up to his forehead to shade his eyes.

"It is." I laughed. "The booze turns them into smartass ten-year-olds. They make fun of people they know. It's hysterical."

"They make fun of people?"

"Yeah. Haven't you ever heard Louie do that?"

"Not really." He shrugged. "I mean...maybe a little, but...."

"He must behave differently when his grandkids are around. Parents and grandparents do that. I'm hanging out when he's drinking with his buddy. So...maybe I see a different side to him. His inner child." I chuckled.

"I thought old men were supposed to be wise."

"Oh, they're wise-guys all right. Your grandfather is a great man, don't get me wrong—but he doesn't pull his punches. Whatever he says, no matter how funny, is true by his estimate. Both grandpas are like that. They don't take crap from people."

"Are they *mean* wise guys?"

The GOAT DRIVE

"No, more like cynical wise guys."

"But only to people they don't like?"

"Yeah. But as it turns out, that's a lot of people." I tapped Kyle on the shoulder. "You should hear them go on and on about President Nixon. Louie wants him impeached, but Tucker says, 'All politicians are criminals; let him be. If you impeach one, you'll have to impeach them all!' Then Louie gets mad and says, 'Then let's impeach 'em all, you old coot.'"

Kyle laughed, obviously knowing it sounded exactly like something his grandpa would say.

"At least they're funny about it," I added. "They're like real-life comedians. I laugh so hard…I hope they never stop."

"It makes me like him even more." Kyle laughed too at the image. Then he said something that sort of embarrassed me. "I hope I have a friend like that when I'm old." With his hand still shading his eyes, he stared into my face for an extra-long second, which brought up a bigger rush of serious warmth from my chest.

"Yeah." I nervously smiled. I had made friends fast before, but if I was reading him right, never *this* fast. "I know what you mean." I awkwardly cleared my throat and felt more of that warm energy I seemed to get from him at times. "I hope I do too. I guess. They're pretty cool old guys." Nervously, I looked around at the house, the shop, and the white fence. I wandered closer to him and changed the subject. "They've built a good life here, huh?" I tapped his shoulder with a gentle fist to acknowledge and respect his obvious and touching reach for my friendship. "Anyway, they didn't give me much information." I looked back into the shop door and cleared my throat again. "So I guess we have to find it first then."

"'Kay." Kyle nodded once like we'd just made a deal. "Let's do it."

Going in

I took three cautious steps into the dark shop and gawkily waved a hand above my head until it met with a string to pull. A dusty bare light bulb came to life and swung from its cord.

Kyle followed uneasily, and he let the door swing closed behind him. We journeyed together into a dimly lit ancient world furnished with historic remnants, representing various phases of Papa Louie's long, energetic life. We explored through recycled lumber, antique tools in sturdy old toolboxes, retired saddles, leather straps, and six or seven big milling machines that looked like torture devices. The only spot not cluttered at the moment was the empty parking space not currently occupied by Louie's rusty, turquoise Ford Fairlane. In its place lay a sheet of galvanized tin managing a small puddle of oil.

I flicked the flashlight on.

"Looks like Louie's old Fairlane's a bleeder."

"Oh, I get it." Kyle seemed nervous now. He looked at me, then at the wet oil pan, and quietly repeated the punch-line "a bleeder."

I gently punched him again on the shoulder, and he laughed once. I pointed the beam into the spider-webbed crevices of the ceiling, rafters, and wall studs.

"Let's find this thing before it finds us," I said.

I thought it was funny how Kyle's alert eyes followed the beam. So I pointed it to the next rafter and he followed it. I pointed it at the oil pan, and he followed it. I pointed it at the door—.

"Hey!" He caught on.

I laughed.

He shyly smiled, then chewed his lip and pretended to laugh with me. He'd been hovering only inches from me since entering the shop, and by now I was able to feel his body heat. For a little guy, he radiated pretty hot. He didn't back away. My compassion for him exploded.

"You're trying hard, aren't you?" my smile faded.

"Huh?"

"I'm sorry, Kyle. We got off to a bad start the other day."

"Oh." He dropped his eyes like I had just accused him of something and he didn't know what to say about it.

"Don't take the blame for it, Kyle. Both of us were being jerks the last couple of days."

"I don't think you were being a jerk."

"Well, I do. And I'm sorry. And right now, I can tell you're trying extra hard to trust me, and I respect you for it."

He shrugged sheepishly.

"So I won't do shit like that again."

"It's okay. It was funny. It was just a joke," he said, but he probably didn't understand *himself* how hard he was trying to be what *he* thought *I* wanted *him* to be. "You were just playing around." Again, he forced out the most realistic smile he could muster.

It tore me up inside. I'd been there. Or at least I felt like I had. Maybe I knew what he was going through, maybe not—but I *believed* I did. And if so, then my assessment was that he internalized too much, and he needed someone to stop blaming him for everything, and to rebuild his self-image instead of tear it down. My friend, Trenton, had once been there to pull me out of my awkward adolescence and my self-esteem crisis during the cancer. He stepped up and showed me how to be proud of myself despite the opinions of the world around me. He'd been a formidable and dedicated mentor to me in the years before we'd become awkwardly uncomfortable with each other. The whole story was that Trenton, who was two years older than me, came out as gay when I was just fifteen. I didn't have a problem with his identity, but his family did. Especially his dad. I stood by his side for years as he rebuilt his self-image despite his father's disappointment. Then I got cancer, lost all my hair, weight and my self-image as an athlete, so he repaid the favor by not leaving *my* side throughout *my* entire ordeal. Then I spent the two years we were in Texas dedicated to him by always accepting, and protecting, him and his friends. But as time slid along, we grew apart. It seemed he needed to socialize with his friends more than he needed a leftover childhood buddy tagging along.

Regardless of how it ended up, Trenton's older-brotherly mentorship pulled me through the loneliness of cancer. He showed me ways to feel good about myself despite my sickly appearance. I suddenly wondered who was going to be there for Kyle while he looked for guidance on how to dress, blow-dry his hair, talk to girls…. I drew in a breath to say something; then I thought about whether I was seeing too much of myself in him.

I held that breath for a brief moment, changed my mind, and exhaled. We resumed our trek with backs arched, ready to turn and run if we heard a swarm. I politely swept the area with the flashlight beam, not knowing where to point next. Apparently, Kyle still trusted me. His eyes followed the beam until he spotted something I didn't.

"Oh!" whispered Kyle. "I see it!"

"Where?" I whispered back.

"Over there, behind the sucker." He whispered even quieter, and pointed to a large, wall-mounted vacuum device with black, six-inch diameter hoses jetting out of it like a giant squid reaching out to grab each of the machines.

"Why are we whispering?" I put the flashlight under my chin, and up-lit my face to look spooky and sound like a vampire. "I don't theenk they speak Eeeeng-lish," I kidded. "I doubt they know what we're planning to doooooo."

"Are you sure they don't understand us?"

"Huh?" Was he serious? "Kyle…" I was off-kilter. Was that a real question? "I don't know what kind of bees they are, but I'm…pretty sure they don't speak English."

"What if they're spelling bees?" He huffed quietly like he was chuckling under his breath.

"Oh…" I chortled out loud. "You got me!" He was kidding after all. "Let's hope they're not spelling bees."

He laughed politely.

"Knucklehead." I turned and pointed the beam toward the sucker. "Spelling bees," I whispered again and shook my head.

Here they come—there I go!

Five or six bees exited a melon-sized gray ball of fibers. Kyle screamed like a girl and ran for the door.

"Hey! Where'd you go?"

Kyle was simply *gone*. The heavy wooden door swung slowly to half shut and stopped. Beams of bright sunlight surrounded it. From outside, I heard a childlike voice.

"I don't want to get stung."

"Some help *you* are!" I teased. As I walked toward the door, my heart took on another warm sensation, reminding me of the dream four years ago when the white dove told me to *show them trust*. "This is my chance," I whispered. I searched the rafters, half-expecting to see that dove again, and committed to being honest from here on. *One like me.* I pushed open the door and peered out. Kyle was crouching *behind* the GTO, looking back at me through the windows. As funny as it was, this was likely a serious phobia around bees. I felt even more compassion.

"You were right earlier." I let him off the hook. "I'm the one Louie hired to do this. It's okay if you need to sit it out. I'll do this myself."

16

Pho-BEE-a! So-BEE-It

The desire for a mentor was strong in me, and I was willing to put everything on the line to get it. With my dad gone from the picture, my terror around bees was going to need to take a backseat to my need to secure a place at Tuck Taylor's side.

By Kyle Rickett

Man, once that huge swarm of bees came to life, my body ran on its own. My brain couldn't stop me, no matter what. I hadn't realized I had a bee phobia. But then, I'd never seen that many bees in one place at one time. Tuck had offered to let me off the hook. But I didn't want to be off the hook. I wanted to do this with him. I wanted him to see how strong I could be and how bravely I could stand up to the world. I wanted him to like me as much as I was starting to like him.

17

Bees!

Mentorship has a dual purpose, and I believe it is hardwired into us from ancient times. An experienced older man feels an internal tugging to teach a younger one what he knows, while at the same time, the younger man strives to impress the mentor. Neither wants to let the other down. Personal growth happens, but few people realize how important that growth is for both the mentee and his mentor.

By Tuck Taylor

"No! I'm not *that* scared. Only a little. I still want to help." Kyle stood tall and confirmed, "I'm not a baby. I'm fourteen. I can do this!"

"You sure?" Unexpected pride for him boiled up in me.

He nodded rapidly.

"Good." My smile brightened. "Okay then, tough guy—get the bag. It's in the backseat."

Kyle exuberantly ran around to the correct open rear window and carefully reached through. I was again impressed with his conscientious handling of my car—*as if it were his*. He snatched the paper sack and peeked inside as he brought it back. He presented it and I pulled out a plastic bag, sealed tight.

Kyle's eyes followed the bag so I lifted it to be directly between our faces. When I saw him change focus onto my eyes, I wiggled my eyebrows. He broke into laughter. I lowered and tore open the plastic. We both gagged.

"Stinks!" he shrieked, pinching his nose with two fingers.

I winked at him. He responded with another eye-twinkling smile. Inside were three thin wooden dowels, each with a shredded cloth, rolled and tied tightly, about the size of a golf ball on one end. They were greasy and smelled of kerosene. Kyle's anticipation grew when he saw the glimmer of pride in my eye. I used one finger and a thumb to slide a lighter out of my tight-fitting front pants pocket. "You ready?" I asked, still gleaming.

"Almost." Kyle's eyes pointed toward the shop door. "Let's go in there first. I wanna see it again."

"Okay." We walked in slowly, but together, forgetting how much we had once distrusted each other. Again, Kyle bolted back out the door when he saw bees shoot out.

"Oh, *c'mon*, Kyle! Do you want to help or not?"

"Yes!" the voice shouted in. "But I don't want to get stung."

"What's so scary about a few little bees?"

"It must be a new phobia. Maybe I got it from my mom. I didn't used to be so afraid of them, but…maybe…I'm just…getting her phobia."

"Your mom's afraid of bees?" I pushed open the door so I could see him, again cowering way over behind my car.

"Once she jumped out of the car because of a bee."

"Did she get hurt?"

"No. But dad was pissed when he had to replace the garage door."

"What?" I laughed.

The GOAT DRIVE

"We just got home from somewhere. We pulled into the driveway and a bee flew in her window. She stopped driving. She didn't stop the car...she just let go of the wheel and stopped *driving* it." He batted his hands around to impersonate her swatting crazily.

"And it ran into the house?" I laughed even harder.

"Phch!" He imitated a crashing sound. His hands recreated an explosion "The door came down in two pieces and landed on the hood of the car."

"No way!" I roared.

"Hey, it's a true story!" He laughed back. "He was *really* mad."

"Well, if that's how bad you and your mom are with bees, then...how are we gonna smoke 'em if we can't get close?"

There was a long pause.

"Kyle?"

"Do you have a beekeeper's suit anywhere?"

"A *what*...?" I shouted back, "Yeah. I think I—Oh, wait a minute. No! Gee. I just remembered. I think I'm fresh out of *beekeeper suits*...and space suits too." I thought for a second, then added, "I might have a pirate's costume in a closet somewhere."

A predictable pause followed as Kyle thought about his next comment. "That won't work!" he yelled back.

Where there's a will, there's always a way

Still standing in the doorway, I roared with laughter and slapped my knee. The door closed and hit me on the head. I couldn't tell how serious he was. "That won't work," I repeated under my breath and kept chuckling. I stood up, gathered my stance, pushed the door open, and stepped back out into the sun.

"You sure?" I kidded. "It's got an eye patch."

"Oooh," he growled at himself by the car. "I want to do this *so bad*!" He looked down at his own poorly armored body, then scanned the grounds for a quick second. "I have an idea!" He lifted a victorious finger. "Papa's overalls."

"Papa wears size *tiny* overalls?"

"Shut up! I'm not tiny!" he yelled firmly. "I'm just a little small for my age."

"Yeah, and a *lot* small for your papa's clothes. He's a big man."

"Doesn't matter. I can make it work. He keeps masking tape around. Lots of it."

This sounded ludicrous. But he was so pleased with his idea that I decided it would be fun to play along with whatever he had in mind. His energy levels soared now. He ran behind the house. Then after about twenty seconds, I heard his feet crunching in the gravel. Crunch, crunch, crunch, crunch.

Kyle emerged from behind the house with a large wad of dingy gray cloth cradled in his arms, and a full-up grin on his face. I suddenly realized I was enjoying his smaller stature because his cuteness itself was entertaining to me. His iridescent blue eyes sparkled once again. He had found the gray-and-white-striped overalls that Louie used to wear in the machine shop he'd retired from down on the docks of Lake Superior.

"Help me!" He grunted and bounced up and down on one leg, then the other while putting the overalls on. They were *huge* on him. His proud blue eyes once again looked like they had after I'd complimented his shoes. This boy was obviously starved for positive attention. And there, on that day, next to that garage, I was just the man to give it to him.

Passing youthfulness back and forth

"Yeah…yeah, I will," I answered through a big, genuine grin.

He winked at me as I had earlier done with him. His smile warmed my heart again. He held out a roll of tape, and I tore off a length. "Roar!" the roll hollered. My eyes remained glued on my youthful friend's glowing, proud face. It had been a long time since anyone had been able to make a morning feel so alive for me. I accidentally chuckled under my breath.

"What?" he asked through a smirk.

"I'm just having fun. That's all. I feel like a kid again."

"Yeah, well..." he jokingly repeated my line from earlier, "twenty-one's not *that old*, Tuck."

I laughed and tore the tape with fingers and teeth, and I then knelt to wrap it around his ankles, while he managed abundant reams of cloth with one hand and balanced himself against my shoulder with the other. Once again, his hand emanated an unusually warm sensation like he was transferring some kind of energy into me.

"See?" he remarked. "Now we *do* have a beekeeper's suit. It's fun inventing things, huh?"

"Well, it is with you," I confessed. And it was too. I was fourteen again while he drew my crazy imagination out from its grave.

Once the ankles were secure enough that even air couldn't get through, he held out his arms. I sealed them tightly around his wrists.

"Now my neck."

"How am I supposed to tape your neck?"

"C'mon; let's do it. I don't want bees in my shirt!"

"All right." We tried, but the seal wasn't good. Every time he turned his head, the tape let loose and opened.

"I have an idea." I went into the shop and found a roll of screen door mesh, grabbed some scissors, and cut off a generous length, then returned and wrapped it around Kyle's head like a dome. I taped its edges to his chest, shoulders, and back.

"Okay. That's the best I can do."

Kyle looked down again at his thin boat shoes. It seemed now that each crazy idea led us to the next crazier one. He looked at the shop and saw Papa's black boots and yellow hardhat inside the door. He grabbed them and waddled back over to me. I had to help him put them on. Both of us inventors were jovially giggling at ourselves, partly with pride, and also because this was some good fun. The boots were huge and went all the way up to Kyle's knees. We taped the tops shut. Kyle couldn't bend his knees now, so he had to walk stiff-legged like a mummy. We put thick mechanics' gloves on his hands and taped them to his scrawny wrists.

"Ready," I said.

"You *sure* a bee can't get in here?" he asked.

"Absolutely. And we'd better hurry before you have to pee. It's going to take a while to get you out of there."

"So I look good to go?"

"Actually, you look kind of ridiculous." I laughed.

"Shut up! We'll see who looks ridiculous when you're in the hospital," He pointed his full right arm toward town, "swollen up with bee stings," He pointed with his full left arm to Louie's house, "and I'm eating gruel with Papa."

"What's gruel?" I asked, laughing.

"I don't know for sure," he said, laughing back. "You'll have to ask Papa."

Going in hot; fire extinguishers and...Farmalls?

"Okay, okay. Put your arms down; you look like an overdressed scarecrow. I'll pull myself together."

We went inside. Now that it was nearly time to light them, my confidence in the untested, self-invented, fuel-soaked mini-torches fell short. I'd already lied to Kyle about knowing what I was doing, so I couldn't very well admit that I didn't know whether they would smoke or *explode*. I did the next best thing. I stopped and reached under a workbench to pull out a large red fire extinguisher.

"Here! If I start the building on fire, it's your job to put it out." I handed him the huge red canister with a short hose on it. "Do you know how to use this?"

"Yesssss! My dad has this same one, and he taught me how."

"Wow. Good boy."

"I'm not a 'good boy!' I know how to do *real* things!" He was slightly pissed. "I can rebuild a Farmall by myself."

"Wow." I lit a torch. *Whoosh*—we both flinched. At least it didn't fly into the rafters like a missile.

"Yeah, wow!" he said angrily. "Let's *do* this."

"Well, when my Farmall needs rebuilding, you're my guy, right?"

"Damn straight," he blurted arrogantly.

"One question."

"What's that?"

"What the hell's a Farmall?"

"It's a kind of tractor, stupid. Get it to Torano Island, and I'll fix it for you." Then he smiled fiendishly. "I'll only charge you double."

"Oh, ha, ha. Very funny."

The shop was almost 90° and my tightly wrapped little fellow hunter was sweating salty water into his eyes. I could see him blinking and instinctively trying to wipe them, but he couldn't because his hands were busy holding the canister and were taped into gloves, plus his face was inside screen-door mesh. He no longer smelled of shampoo and pit stick; he now permeated the odor of old, musty, oily coveralls.

Hunched, we snuck up on the hive. I looked back and whispered, "I'll bet you're hot in there."

He sighed heavily. "Thanks for reminding me, *asshole,*" he whispered back.

I giggled again and got back to work. The kid was asserting insults back at me now. I enjoyed him a lot more like this than when he was a small, helpless, touchy victim. I closed in on the menacing hive with all three of my flaming homemade smokers in hand, blew the flames out to a smolder, and they started smoking. I held them beneath the hive, like I knew what I was doing, then dropped them into the metal lid. Kyle couldn't see it too well because of the sweat in his eyes and the screen over his face. Also, Louie's hardhat was a bit too big and kept falling into his vision. I was starting to see bees exiting the hive, some onto the ground, sound asleep from the smoke.

"Hey! It's working!" I remarked excitedly.

"What do you mean, 'Hey, it's working?' I thought you'd done this before."

"I guess I may have made it sound that way."

FIRE!

"You *lied*?" That was the end of his confidence in me. "You've never *done this before*?" he sternly yelled. Then, as if on cue, my homemade smoker trio burst into flames again—must have been the kerosene. Then the beehive caught fire.

"Aaaah!" Kyle screamed. He pulled the pin from the fire extinguisher. It blasted toward the flaming hive, but he fell backward from the force.

"*Get up*!" I shouted. "We're burning the place *down*!"

Kyle sat up, but he couldn't see anything. He aimed the fire extinguisher as best he could toward his last-known direction of the burning hive. White powdery smoke clouded all around us.

"*Give it to me*!" I tugged the tube out of his hands, but I left him with the canister. "Now *shoot it*! *Shoot it*!"

He squeezed the trigger for me. Shoop! Shoop! Shoo-ooo-ooop! We shot directly into the base of the flames. The heat became intense, nearly scorching the skin off my face and knuckles, but it cooled quickly and things went dark…the fire was out.

"*Oh, noooo*!" Kyle squealed. He dropped the canister and got up, which was nearly impossible with the boots keeping his knees straight and his hands buried beneath humongous leather gloves. He clomped out the door with the grace of Frankenstein's monster on hot coals.

"Kyle, *stop*! I can help!"

Was he on fire? I urgently followed with the extinguisher.

He was screaming a single, long "Eeeeeeeeee!" sound.

I saw no smoke, so I laughed a bit at his clomping. I was easily able to run faster, and when I got in front, I saw why he was screaming. A swarm of bees was clinging to his facial screen.

"Holy *shit*!" I panicked and used the fire extinguisher to wash them away. I only shot short bursts so as not to suffocate the human within, but it was still enough to knock him over.

Everybody calm down!

Kyle stumbled backward, choking and coughing, and trying to wipe away the residual cloud. He fell and landed flat on his back, spread-eagle, arms out to his side, overalls rising and lowering from heavy breathing. I stared for a moment. The scene went quiet.

I looked up at the shop. Nothing moved. Then back at the boy. The overalls were breathing. The air was still. Then, from inside the pile of cloth, tape, and yellow hardware, a sheepish voice called out.

"Are they gone?"

A laugh grunted from my nose, finding an escape from my closed mouth. "Okay, now that's just funny." I looked at the extinguisher in my hand. "You weren't even on fire." The bees were gone. The flames were out, the rags were cooling, and Kyle was covered in white powder. Then I burst into the loudest laughter yet and reported, "Yup. They're all gone, Buddy."

I reached through the Goat's open window onto the dashboard, where I now kept an instamatic camera for emergencies and snapped five pictures as he tried getting up. I pulled him onto his feet. When he unwrapped the screen, his face was covered in white powder. He looked like he'd been in an explosion. I merrily snapped two more shots.

"*Hey*! I don't like people taking my *picture*."

"Another phobia?"

"Whatever."

"Calm down, 'Bee-boy.' You're not getting away with it. This could win me another contest. You look ridiculous."

Kyle looked down at himself. Only his face was uncovered now. He looked up at me, and to my relief, he didn't look angry. "You're sure the bees are gone though, right?"

I nodded. Kyle's bee-phobia dissipated and his face brightened. His mood turned silly. Pretending to pass out, he jokingly made a yodeling *uh-ah-uuh* sound as he fell backward onto his butt and then again onto his back, arms out to the sides.

I laughed and impersonated Jimmy Durante. "*Ev*-ry-body's a comedian." I kneeled in to peel off tape.

"Uuuuh," he moaned with a giggle.

"You're more fun to hang out with than I thought you'd be. I think I don't hate you quite as much as I did yesterday." I laughed once.

"I don't hate you too." He giggled some more as he spoke.

"We'd better clean this goop off your face. It's probably poison."

18

Cleanup

The easiest way to bond two people is to provide them with a common goal. In the case of the bee's nest, our grandfathers had given Tuck and me a job to do that would test our ability to work together as a team, both of us wanting to make the old guys proud of us. Tuck was right...they were a couple of wise guys. Very wise indeed.

By Kyle Rickett

We teamed up again, but this time to get me *out* of our super-duper-awesome homemade beekeeper suit. It had worked—not o*ne single bee-sting!* I was glad Tuck had helped me make it, but I was starting to panic from the heat. We stripped it off faster than I could believe, and then left it in a pile that looked like someone was still in it.

Drenched in sweat and foam, I was led quickly by the arm, stumbling to Papa's garden hose up by the house. I braced myself for a rough scrubbing when Tuck twisted the spigot and began to wash the white chemicals off my skin. Being that he was such a calm person, I was surprised by his urgency and by how he kept *apologizing*.

"I don't know what the hell I was thinking. Squirting you with a fire extinguisher was a *bad idea*."

"I don't care. It got rid of the bees, didn't it?" The washing felt unexpectedly calm. I relaxed quickly. Even through the emergency, he wasn't trying to rub off my skin.

"Man, you really hate bees, don't you?" He shook his head while gently waving the trickling hose to drench my sweat-soaked tank top in refreshingly cool water. "Still, if I had it to do over again...." He rubbed his hands firmly, but carefully, across the skin of my neck and shoulders above the tank top.

"Now you're the one who's blushing," I said through a teasing smile. I could see it so plainly. His cheeks were pink.

"That's because I feel like an *idiot*. I could have hurt you. That stuff's poison, I'm sure of it. I'm supposed to be the adult here." As he squeezed one of my obviously small shoulders, he accidentally huffed a single laugh. "You can *really* rebuild an entire tractor—by yourself?"

"Yeah." My heart swelled. He believed me. I was surprised by how proud I suddenly felt. "Just because I'm small doesn't mean I'm helpless."

"Yeah, well, *I* can't do that. Small or large...not many fourteen-year-olds can rebuild farm equipment."

"I can," I bragged. "I did one, start to finish, last summer when I was only thirteen." The cool water felt good in the heat, but more importantly, it felt nice to have another person show interest in my skills and experiences. Tuck's now fatherly eyes were focused on what he was doing. I found myself staring into them. How could I have ever thought anything bad about this man?

His eyes locked up with mine.

I smiled.

He smiled back.

"I don't want you to get sick, little buddy," he admitted.

"Little buddy?" I gave a laugh. The more concern Tuck showed, the more speechless I became. My head wiggled side to side from the gentle scrubbing. The moment began to feel surreal. Someone cared. And he had listened to what I'd told him. I hadn't realized, until now, how much I had missed the touch of another human being. Simple skin-on-skin contact felt comforting. I couldn't remember anyone ever handling me quite so carefully. Not a single stroke of the towel hurt. His grip on my shoulder was gentle, not a claw.

Tuck glanced into my eyes and smiled another time. When I smiled back again, he gently punched my shoulder.

"You should go take a shower, pal. And scrub hard. I've done all I can do without soap."

"'Kay." I slid my wet tank top off and rang it out while following Tuck up the stairs. "I'll shower up," I offered, "and then I'll make us a lunch. I make a mean tuna sandwich."

I showered quickly, all the while planning my menu. Then I scurried into the bedroom and fumbled around in my suitcase until I found a bright orange swimsuit. I also grabbed the deep blue shirt I'd worn yesterday—the one Mom said made my eyes sparkle. It looked like someone had moved it—it had to have been Tuck. No one else had been in the house. It briefly seemed intrusive that he'd been touching my clothes. But then I decided I kind of liked it. "This'll work!" I blurted out, and I carried them back into the bathroom, excited to get busy making a meal for my new friend. But then I heard a gentle tap on the door.

Up close and personal

"What?"

"Kyle?"

Pause. "Yeah?"

"Can I show you something?"

"What do you want to show me?" In the mirror, my face appeared a bit frightened.

"Would you like to see how I blow-dry my hair?"

I gasped. The face in the mirror changed. I saw a happiness I hadn't seen much of in weeks. Still naked, I thought about letting him walk in like I'd done with my older brother, Daniel, back in my room the night Krieg molested me. But that night had such an ugly ending when Daniel turned my report into an accusation that I'd *wanted* Krieg to do it. I didn't want to feel any of that energy again. I respectfully wrapped the towel around my waist.

"Come on in, Tuck."

He entered, rummaged through the cabinet drawers, and handed me a round hair brush and the blow dryer. His eyes drilled into me as he talked me through rolling the brush backward while blowing the heat forward. He explained that the direction of the heat would change the fluffiness.

When my hair was dry, I couldn't believe how good it looked. Like it was twice as thick as it had ever been.

"You're a good lookin' kid, Kyle."

"Thanks." I smiled shyly. Normally, I didn't believe people when they said things like that. But I kind of *did* believe Tuck.

He left me there and closed the door behind himself. I stared at my mirror image again. He was right; I didn't look like a freak after all. It struck me as important that *his* opinion of me improved *my* opinion of me. Feeling like a newly printed million bucks, I moved to the bedroom to put my clothes on so he could have the bathroom to clean up. Then I went into the kitchen to make lunch.

Tuck washed his hands and face, then went back out to the shop to be absolutely sure we hadn't left any smoldering embers. A short while later, fully satisfied the buildings were safe, Tuck joined me in the kitchen. I welcomed him with an energetic "Tada!" The table was set with plates, napkins, two glasses of milk, and two enormous, overstuffed sandwiches, each nestled between a sliced pickle and a small pile of potato chips. Tuck grinned at the excitement in my eyes.

The GOAT DRIVE

It's amazing what a little praise will do for a kid

We sat across from each other and ate.

"Wow!" he exclaimed after only his first bite. He held the rest of the sandwich out far enough to look at it. Then through his full mouth, he muffled, "How did you...? I mean...these really *are* good.... I thought tuna was tuna."

"It's no big deal. I toasted the bread and mixed some stuff together. I found onions and olives and horseradish in the fridge." I seldom bragged. Something about the way this guy showed interest drew the boasting right up out of me—the fire extinguisher, the Farmall, now my cooking—I couldn't stop.

"Well, whatever it is you put in here, it's terrific."

As I ate and watched Tuck devour his sandwich, I wondered if I should open a lunch counter back on the island. Food like this could make good money. Tuck only looked up at me a few times, wiggled his eyebrows, and hummed, "Mmm." His eyes locked onto mine a couple of times. He looked surprised every time I looked back at him. I assumed that he saw my eyes twinkle like my mom and Papa always said they did.

Something happened then in my head that I've never forgotten. I wasn't afraid that he wanted to touch me now. But I really liked thinking that maybe he found me good-looking. It was the first time I'd ever had that thought. Usually, I just "didn't want to be ugly." But starting with that moment, knowing how good my hair looked, and how my shirt brought out the blue in my eyes, I now wanted to be *attractive* to the people around me. Maybe...if I was good...he'd teach me how to pick out clothes so I could dress like him.

We cleaned the kitchen together and went back out and straightened the shop. We wiped everything and brought the fire extinguisher to the porch so Papa would know to recharge or replace it. I carefully perched the charred beehive remnant atop a fencepost as a trophy. We nodded at each other, then both looked back at the shop door, which was the center of the whole adventure.

"That was fun," I admitted.

"Damn fun!" he replied. "And nobody got stung."

Sharing my life

"C'mon. I wanna show you something." I waved toward the creek and took him on my tour of the grounds. I felt a brand-new compulsion—a strong one—to share the times Scott and I had spent there.

I climbed over the fence and jumped onto the pasture from the middle rail. Rather than open the gate like most adults would do, Tuck climbed and jumped like I did. It surprised me how good it felt that he would do that—follow me by my rules, like a friend would do. I led him across the small pasture to the trailhead that pierced into the woods toward the creek.

"Is this where you and Scooter spent your summers?" he asked. "Playing out here in these woods?"

"Yeah." I smiled ear to ear, and slowed down so he could catch up and walk next to me instead of following. "Papa has a nickname for each of us. He calls him Scooter…and so do I, I guess." My excitement was showing. "He lives in Portland, Oregon. We slept in the same room when we were little. We feel like we grew up here on our summers with Papa. We had some real fun. Do you know him?"

"I think I might have met him once about five years ago. He's older than you, right?"

"Two years and eleven months older. He held me on his lap when I was born."

"Oh, is that you two in the photo next to Louie's fridge?"

"Yeah, that's us. You'd like him. He's funny." I got ahead of him again but walked backward down the path while leading Tuck. "He's super big and strong. Whenever he sees me, he always says, 'Agent McBride at your service, sir.'"

"Sounds protective."

"He is. He's going to be a cop when he grows up. He told me once that when they put me in his lap, he thought they gave me to him. So he always says he *owns* me." I chuckled excitedly, and then showed Tuck the trees that once held our fortresses, and the creek areas we'd used as beaches for the Normandy Invasion, recreated with plastic soldiers in 1972.

As the warm afternoon lingered on, I noticed Tuck took an interest in *all* my stories, but more like he was a kid himself than an adult. He even climbed into the trees to check out the vantage points from where Scooter and I had spied on unsuspecting siblings.

"Those were great times." Not wanting to out my cousin—whom I had recently been told was gay—I still wanted to make my point that Scooter was still Scooter, "No matter whatever happens, Tuck, my memories will never change. He'll always be my favorite."

"He's lucky to have a cousin like you."

"I'd do anything for him."

We visited the graves of the four ponies that had once roamed the acreage. I put a flower from the field onto each.

"It hurt Papa when they died," I said. "Sylvester went last, and it hurt him the most. He couldn't even talk about it for a long time. It was the only thing I ever saw him cry about."

"I didn't know he'd cried over it—didn't even know he had *tear ducts*." Tuck laughed.

"He was standing right here, looking over Sylvester's fresh dirt. He cried pretty hard too. It made my heart hurt. But I never told anyone. And he didn't see me. I was up in a tree—crying quietly with him."

"Wow." He gently punched my shoulder. "I know how important they were to him, especially Sylvester." Tuck looked up into the trees as if he were putting pictures to my story. "I was little when he'd have all four pulling his homemade wagons in the parades in Duluth. The crowds always clapped when he came through. He'd have signs for the TV show hanging off each side like the wagon was an advertisement. One year I got to ride with him. The ponies looked proud."

"They probably were," I agreed.

"Hey, Kyle." It was Tuck who then addressed the elephant we had between us. "I'm sure sorry I didn't like you at first. I couldn't have been more wrong about you." He blushed again. "I see now why Louie brags so much. You've got a lot of heart."

I gently kicked at small rocks with the side of my foot. Being complimented felt good, but strange. I didn't know how to act.

Our conniving grandfathers

After a short while, we came out of the woods through the creek-side trail. It was about 2:00 p.m. by now. Papa's Fairlane was sitting behind Tuck's GTO. We went into the house and both chuckled to find our wise-guy grandfathers at the kitchen table, half-drunk and laughing. They were fumbling with a deck of cards and two glasses of golden liquid with ice cubes. Both of them wore plaid, long sleeve shirts like it was winter.

"Boys!" said old Tucker.

"Hi, Grandpa," replied young Tuck. "Kind of early to be hittin' the sauce, don't you think?"

Old Tucker waved a dismissing hand at his scolding grandson.

"Hi, Papa!" I said through the biggest smile I'd shown him yet that year.

Papa shot a glance at Tuck, then back at me, and responded to the new joy on my face with a raised glass and a big smile of his own.

"*There's* my boy!" He patted my shoulder. "And the bees. They're gone. Yeah?"

Tuck and I nodded together. The old men looked at each other and also nodded, as if they themselves had succeeded at something.

"Was my Q-Tip a good wingman?" Papa asked Tuck.

"The best, Louie. You should've seen him. Brave as a knight of the Round Table."

"I was not! I almost let the shop burn down," I admitted.

"Uh-Uh-Uh-Uh—" Tuck pretended to zip his lip, looked at both grandfathers, and said, "Shop's still standing. And I'd have him on my team any day."

"Good. Because I was thinking," said old Tucker.

"Uh, oh," replied Tuck.

Grandpa Tucker looked over at Papa. They nodded once at each other and looked back at us.

"I think you two are getting too old to be playing around like this."

"Playing *around*?" Tuck was laughingly indignant with his retort. "What the hell are you talking about? We just spent the morning in a death-defying act of saving Louie's shop from deadly swarms of dangerous bees!"

Tuck and I laughed, but the old men looked at each other like something important was happening.

"You are too old to be living off me for free every summer." Old Tucker pointed at his grandson like he was trying to look serious.

"You too, Q-Tip." Papa, in cahoots with his friend, pointed at me the same way. "Living for free's not a man's way."

"I...I was sent here, Papa. And...I don't have any money."

"You got two hands." Papa looked at Tucker. They nodded. Whatever they were planning had been set up in advance and they were ready to close the deal.

"You want me to work?" I was fine with the idea, but confused as to why it came up out of the clear blue like this. I was also quite curious what these two were planning to make me do.

"You two proved to us that yous are a good team," Louie started.

"Louie and I got a lot of work needs to be done between us," Tucker joined in.

"He says you're a good wingman, Q-Tip." Papa nodded toward me, then toward Tuck.

I kept quiet while Tuck looked at both old men who had obviously already discussed this. He inhaled a deep breath and looked over at me.

"They think we both need a friend," said Tuck, smirking at me.

I tried to laugh like it was a joke, but the old men were right—I *did* need a friend.

"And what's wrong with that?" Old Tucker jumped in. "You been alone too long, Tuck. You been sulking around since you got here. You ain't a bit happy unless you're with this little stinker." He reached with the hand not holding a glass and ruffled my hair. "And you're good for Louie's boy."

My heart skipped a beat and my face beamed. I couldn't believe what I'd heard. He wasn't happy unless he was with *me*?

"Damn right," Papa chimed in and also pointed at me. "And you too, boy. I never seen you so sad, Q-Tip. It breaks my heart." He pounded his own chest twice gently. "Tuck needs a wingman, and you need a friend. Look at that smile on your face now. You ain't smiled like that since you got here." Then he grabbed Tuck's shoulder. "You won't find a better friend than this one right here. I known him his whole life. He's good through and through."

"Good through and through" was my grandfather's highest praise for a man. That's what he'd said about both Eisenhower and Roosevelt. I pictured the scene from a couple of hours ago, when Tuck's smile was only inches from my face while he gently wiped off the fire extinguisher goop and apologized for spraying me in the first place.

"Besides, working with our old tools is dangerous. Who wants to be sawing out in the woods alone?" asked Tucker.

"Hey!" Tuck admonished. "You *were* just fine sending me out there alone with those old tools!"

Tucker dismissed him with that same hand gesture as before.

Tuck shook his head and rolled his eyes.

Strong backs for hire

"Sawing?" Did I hear him right?

"Both us old coots need firewood. There's trees what need cutting up on Norton Hill."

"Oh! Really?" Tuck seemed surprised for a second or two. With a half-smile, he then looked at me. "Grandpa's got some acreage about an hour's drive from here, up on a place north of Deer River, called Norton Hill. I was planning to spend a week up there, but…" He smiled as if he really liked his grandfather's idea, "if you go with me, we could get it done in three days." He looked at my arms and changed it. "Maybe two."

"You mean…like a *camping* trip?"

"I guess...yeah. We cut, split, and stack it to dry; then he hires a guy he knows to truck it down later in the year."

"Firewood?" I could barely contain my excitement.

"Then we've got a couple of weeks' worth of work to do down here. They both need a ton of fence-work here; the creek between these two lots needs cleaning. Between the two of them, we'd have all the tools, even a tractor," He teasingly tapped my shoulder, "and I can't keep that tractor running without an expert on the team."

"The team?" I almost burst into laughter. Cutting firewood was my greatest superpower, and I was *never* invited to be on teams.

"We might find bees out there, and like Grandpa said, I guess I could use a good wingman, especially up on Norton Hill."

I hesitated.

Papa saw the stall and pointed at me.

I stared back at him.

"Go with him," he said.

My eyes opened wide and aimed straight at Tuck—who was planning to *go up a hill*. A dream I'd had only weeks before flashed in my face. In it, a young man was walking up a hill with a growling cougar on a leash. A cougar that was the same color as Tuck's growling car. And those were the words from my dream—"*Go with him*." I never expected Papa to be the old man's voice that said them, but it all sounded exactly the same as in the dream. *This moment was predicted!*

I looked at Tuck differently, like he was appointed to me. First, I thought about staying home, but picturing a whole week *without* him felt dark and lonely. No way in hell was I going to pass this up, especially after what Papa had said.

"Yeah, I guess. Sure...why not?" Trying not to explode in excitement, I spoke slowly and held back a grin.

"Good." Tuck didn't hold back. His smile was genuine. "We leave Saturday. I'll take you shopping Wednesday for some gear...maybe even get you some new leather sandals."

While I finally unleashed a huge grin, Papa reached for his wallet like he'd done when he told Tuck to feed me at Center Park.

"Nope." Tuck put up his hand like a stop sign. "I've got it, Louie. He's *my* guest this time."

I smiled even bigger. Not taking Papa's money meant he wasn't babysitting me. This really was a work team. It was starting to sound fun already.

Of love and trust

Years ago, on a summer trip to Duluth, I mentioned to Papa that I liked writing but didn't do it much because I was too embarrassed when people read it. Papa didn't know how many serious secrets I had, but somehow he sensed that I needed some sort of an outlet, so on that same trip to Duluth, he surprised me with the gift of a brand new diary of my own. Then he promised he'd never read it unless I let him, and that he'd keep it hidden from my family and cousins. I often wondered if he and I were even more alike than I knew then. We both liked the accordion. We both liked to cook. Maybe he wanted to be a writer too. Then, as years passed, I never once found a reason to believe he'd broken his promise to keep my diary hidden from the other grandkids and from my mom.

That afternoon, after Tuck and Tucker left, I discovered it had been discretely placed on my bed. Late that night, while Papa snored, I let the bedroom light glare proudly, knowing that here in Minnesota I was allowed to stay up into the night and write on pages I wouldn't have to destroy. Nothing I did was acceptable or supported back at home. But here, Papa respected whatever was true about me—and he went a step further and always did something about it. I was bubbling up inside with the need to express, on the paper he'd given me, my thoughts. But I was finding them too confusing to communicate.

My entry this night would be more in my head than on paper. I *thought* a hundred words for each one I wrote. Through the window screen, I listened to the crickets. Scooter had once given me a private nickname that we kept between us. When he was in school and I wasn't yet, he noticed that my name, Kyle Rickett, could be written K. Rickett, so he started calling me Cricket. No one except he and I knew that. But on this night in exile with Papa and Tuck, I thought of Scooter because I could hear crickets, which were a soothing music rarely heard in Washington State. Here, in Papa's safe and peaceful world, I still had too

The GOAT DRIVE

much to think through, but at least the clarity of mind was better now than it had been.

I put pen to paper but didn't move. What would I write? A thousand thoughts wanted to be first. Only hours before, I'd been excited to go camping with my new friend, but now as I approached the witching hour, the moment of laying my head to pillow, my usual fears and worries emerged.

Did I trust Tuck? There was no doubt I wanted to. He gave me all his attention whenever we were together. He'd shown me how to blow-dry my hair. Maybe I could get some more lessons out of him. What if I could get him to teach me how to throw or catch a baseball without dropping it, or how to shoot hoops and actually get one in?

But why did he stare into my eyes so often? Lots of people did that, but Tuck was the only man who didn't quickly look away when I'd notice him. Mom had told me for years that my eye color was particularly interesting to people. Same with the hair. Krieg sure liked it. Andreo told everyone my eyes and hair made me look feminine. Why would Tuck like the things about me that made me look like a girl? I knew why Krieg liked it. And I'd seen how the men in St. Paul liked blond boys.

Since coming to Duluth, I hadn't vomited, but I did still wake up three or four times each night to feel dread and panic as all the confusion danced around and argued in my head. It seemed that the things I believed, and the things I *wanted* to believe, couldn't agree enough to shut up and let me sleep soundly. I meditated on the "T" word: Trust. Up until meeting Tuck, I hadn't really thought about who I did or didn't trust. I pretty much just trusted everyone, until the day came that I *dis*trusted everyone. Now I didn't know for sure who I loved. I mean, if I couldn't trust them, how could I love them?

Tuck and I had been through a lot together, but we really had only met a few days prior. So my ability to trust him was still forming. My pen still hadn't moved. It was nearly eleven by this point and I wasn't tired. But I wanted to write *something*. Then I could lay into the pillow and let the normal craziness begin. Through all the possible topics I could expand on tonight, I chose the newest idea of them all.

Monday, July 29, 1974

Dear Diary,

 It's official. I'm insane. First, I tried to kill myself, and then I got in a stranger's car. And now I'm best friends with him...the stranger! I'm totally crazy for sure. Pinch me. Maybe I'm dreaming.

 I stopped writing and stared at my pictures on the wall by the closet. My own family couldn't be trusted. What made me think this stranger could? A surge of emotion exploded in my chest. I wanted to trust him. So God damn it...I was going to. The pen began to move again, but this time more boldly.

 Fuck it, Diary. I'm going for it. Sure, maybe I just met him. Sure, maybe he stares at me. Sure, maybe he tells me how handsome I am...but fuck it, fuck it fuck it. I LIKE HIM! I've decided to make myself trust Tuck Taylor with my whole heart, even if it's the wrong thing to do. I can MAKE myself do it if I want to. It's my decision.

 There! Now it's in writing! I'll never go back on my decision. I'm going to trust him even if I shouldn't. I guess I'd rather have my arms cut off and be killed in the woods by someone like Tuck...than to live one more second completely alone.

 I looked toward the wall that had Papa's bedroom on the other side of it. I listened to his snoring for a moment. Somehow, I felt as if I'd just lived an entire lifetime in one day. I'd asked my grandpa to let me move in with him; I'd been alone for the first time in my favorite house; I'd walked the yard and reminisced so vividly about Scooter that I felt like I'd actually been with him; I'd faced one of my greatest phobias; risen victorious over it; impressed the coolest guy I'd ever met; pleased my grandpa by becoming happy finally; cooked what was received like it was a five-star lunch; gotten a job fixing fences; and accepted an offer to go camping alone with my new friend. My confusion started to lift. I knew what I wanted to say in my diary.

You know what? I'm fine. Papa says I can trust him. So I'm going to. No matter what. I'll never change that decision.

Shit. Summer's not going to last forever. How much damage can he do in just a few weeks?

Good night, Diary.

Cricket.

JAMES F JOHNSON

PART 2

A NEW ALLIANCE

Learning to Trust Myself

JAMES F JOHNSON

19

A New Alliance

    Behind my back, Tuck and Papa were about to form an alliance meant to help. It was good that, at fourteen, I didn't understand what they were doing because, at that point, I was too jittery to accept anyone getting into my personal world. Diary entries are mere words on a page. Though I'd promised in mine to let Tuck do anything he wanted in exchange for his friendship, my standard reaction to betrayal was changing. I was learning how to stop loving people whom I perceived had betrayed me. One day, I would learn to cut the person out of my life and never go back. My fragile trust issues were forming. I was becoming easily agitated when people got close to me. Those issues remain with me today, though I work at not letting them control me. This is the baggage I carry forward from a long history of being repeatedly ganged up on and attacked by my own close family and best friends. While some abused people become abusers themselves, I did the opposite. My motto: If you can't beat 'em...leave 'em."

By Tuck Taylor

"Louie!" I answered the door in gym shorts with a toothbrush jetting from my mouth. "It's only seven."

"That ain't early," he teased gruffly.

"It is for me. You're lucky I got up before nine this morning. Grandpa just went out with the horses." I removed the toothbrush and pointed toward the barn.

My eye caught a dove—a real one—fly up from the fence to the barn roof. "What the f—?" I mumbled.

"I come to see you." In one of his typical plaid shirts, a blue Ford cap, and denim bib overalls, Louie pushed his way in like he lived there. "Coffee's hot, yeah?"

"Drink a little too much yesterday?" I chuckled. As I turned to follow him in, I glanced back quickly to the bird and shook a disbelieving head. "Too weird," I whispered.

Louie ignored me.

"Yeah. Coffee's hot…but it's pretty disgusting—blah." I jokingly gagged while closing the front door. "I can make fresh."

"Just give me a fork—I'll chew it."

I laughed.

"This is business."

"Business?" I followed him in, rinsed my mouth at the kitchen sink, clinked the toothbrush into a water glass, and then, with a shiver of disgust, served an acidy-smelling, two-hour-old cup of percolated coffee while he bellied up to the table in his usual spot and took off his cap.

"I need your help." Big, sturdy Louie's face looked desperate. Vulnerable.

"You mean more than with fences and firewood?" I sat down with a tall orange juice.

"It's Q-Tip," he mumbled.

The GOAT DRIVE

"Well, that's no problem," I quietly responded. "I mean…I've been helping keep him busy since Saturday. It's been kind of fun." I listed a few activities, "I've been giving him rides, keeping him company, sharing chores…."

"He needs more than that." Thick fingernails rapped once on the table where his eyes focused.

"What's wrong?"

"I told you I seen his look before…" He raised eyes to me, "on a friend."

"Your war buddy?" I asked with obvious surprise.

"Maury." He looked back down at the table.

"The one whose gal had left him while he was fighting enemies?"

"That's right." He slowly rotated his coffee cup in circles. "Maury had a quiet way. Enemy fire was too much for him. His gal couldn't wait for him and moved on. He came back from the war, but the war never left him."

"And you're saying Kyle's like him?"

"That's right. He don't like enemy fire either."

"But I don't get the connection. We're not at war. Kyle's just a kid who lives on a quiet island. He couldn't have enemies…could he?"

"Why not?" His gaze—and his voice—rose boldly. "Something's makin' him look the same way."

"Life's naturally tough for teens," I said, minimizing Louie's concern. Comparing Kyle to a shell-shocked war vet seemed ridiculous. "When you saw him fall apart, it was after a rough three-day trip." I shrugged "That's not the same as coming back from a *war*. He seemed pretty happy yesterday."

"No."

"You don't think he had a good time yesterday?"

"I still see it. His face ain't sparkin' like it should."

"He's fourteen. Kids grow up. Sparks fade," I argued without giving much thought to Louie's concerns. "I think you can rest. Kyle doesn't appear suicidal to me, but—"

"No buts! You *listen to me!*" He angrily pointed directly between my eyes. "I'm *sure* of what I know. He's not right. Somethin's still wrong."

I paused while my face heated. I didn't agree with him, but I quickly felt the seriousness he wanted me to feel.

"I don't know how long I can keep him, and I don't want him going back until I know he's okay there."

"There? You mean his island? His *family?*"

Louie stared into my eyes, sending a clear message that I was to take him more seriously.

"Like there's actual *gunfire* there?" I asked. "Or…are you thinking 'his gal' left?"

"I never heard of no girl."

"So you're saying he has *enemies*, Louie?"

"Enemies could do this."

"But how could he have enemies? He's a nice kid."

"Sometimes bein' nice…" He tapped the table to make a point, "is what brings 'em on."

Target on the forehead

Louie's innate wisdom, masked beneath plaid shirts and broken English, was, once again, spot on. I'd foolishly fallen for the old paradigm that when people meet nice guys, they say, "He couldn't have an enemy in the world." I was suddenly embarrassed to have disagreed with the elder's assessment, especially after I had seen Kyle's vulnerability with my own two eyes. Kyle could easily be bully-bait. I had taken him into the shop just a day before and teased him with the flashlight. I now recalled the sad truth that he'd forgiven me without standing up for himself. I guess if I'd have been a lesser man—a bully, as it were—I'd have gotten a proverbial boner and kept mistreating him, counting on him just to keep forgiving, like so many douche-bags do to

The GOAT DRIVE

nicer people. The more I thought about Louie's comment, the more sense it made that a gentle person could easily have enemies. He was a target.

"And it ain't your runna' the mill bullyen', Taylor."

"How do you know that?"

"His face. I seen it." He lowered his voice. "*He's afraid for his life.*"

A chill ran down my spine. "And he won't talk?" My voice lost its edge. Less arrogance, more compassion. "He won't say what's wrong?"

"Not to me." He sipped the toxic goo I'd given him and grimaced, but he refused to ask for a fresh cup. Instead, he put it down and poured sugar into it.

"What makes you think he'll talk to *me*?"

"Because you're a college man and you know things."

"I'm a college dropout. I don't know—"

"You know *enough*!" He barked back with almost exactly the same fervency as the dove I'd challenged in my dream.

My heart jumped into my throat while a vision of the dove flashed across my memory. "What did you say?" More chills tickled my neck and spine. Those were the exact words given to me in the dream when I was struggling with my decision to leave school and come to Duluth.

"I seen you with him. He trusts you."

"But…I know *enough*?" Saying it again ran a third wave of shivers through me. "He *trusts* me?" Again, more words from my dream to teach trust to *one like me.*

"How old are you?" He leaned across the table and rested a heavy hand on my shoulder.

"Twenty-one. You know that. But I only went to two years of college. And not all of my classes were in psychology."

"And so, what did you do? *Sleep through the other nineteen years*? Why do you only talk about two years a' knowin' things?"

"Huh?"

"I seen you in that hospital years before you ever went to college."

"When I was *dying*?"

"I seen it in your eyes too…when you gave up."

"You think Kyle's given up?"

The weight of his hand increased. "Now, Mr. Taylor, you dig deep and remember back then what you thought."

"When I was *dying*…?"

"Then you look deep into my Q-Tip's eyes, and sure as can be…you'll see it there too."

"What are you saying?"

"I'm saying you been where he is."

"Death's door?" with slight cynicism, I tipped my head. "You seriously think he's at death's door?"

"You came out strong…a little quieter, but strong. You been living good for years since then." He let go and leaned back in his chair. "I'm sayin' you know enough."

"Jesus, Louie. If you're right…well…if he's afraid for his life…then…this is a big fucking job you're asking of me."

"No, it ain't. You already done the hard part."

"What hard part?" I wasn't trying to be sarcastic, but my head shook.

"He don't trust just anyone. Not like he used to. He takes the blame when things go bad with friends. He don't trust his mama no more. He won't even talk about his dad, not to me anyway. Scooter's nowhere to be found, and he tells me I'm his only friend. But then you come along…." Louie pointed into my eyes again and shook the finger to make a point. "You only known him a few days, but you got through already."

"Got through to where?"

"You're on his team."

"Like you and Scooter? You're saying I'm family?"

He affirmatively nodded once.

"After *three days*?"

"Has he been talkin' to you about his life?"

"Yeah. He's been pretty open with me."

"There ya go." He pointed back at me with his own sarcastic smirk. "He don't do that with me or his mama. He won't tell me *why* he's alone now."

I smiled from a sense of feeling honored.

"He looks at you the way he used to look at Scooter. That's a big deal you know. Scooter and him is like Siamese twins. Been closer than brothers since birth. But you…you're a stranger who's already showing him how to trust."

"Jesus Christ, Louie." These dream references were really starting to freak me out. "I'm showing him how to *trust*? Have you been talking to my sister?"

He looked at me like I was crazy, as well he should. My surprise at his use of the words from my dreams meant nothing to him. Louie and Ronnie didn't talk. Of course, it wasn't her who told him about the dove telling me to *teach them trust* and that *I know enough*. This had to have been a fluke.

"So…" I cleared my throat and tried to put the coincidental phrasing on the back burner, "all this talk about him and me needing to pay our way…."

"A ruse." He waved a dismissing hand. "His fences need mending a hell of a lot more than mine do."

"I don't get it."

"It's simple. I don't care if you fix my fences. I want you to fix *him*."

"Um." I was a bit dazed. What kind of superhero did Louie imagine I really needed to be? And why? Kyle was just a down-in-the-dumps teen who was reminding his grandfather of an unfortunate tragedy from years past.

"I didn't help Maury, and Maury jumped."

"Louie…honestly…Kyle isn't Maury. Don't worry so mu—"

"I ain't going to make that mistake again!"

"But I don't—"

"BUT YOU DON'T LET HIM JUMP!" He pounded his cup on the table, which made me leap three inches in my seat. "This ain't no JOKE! I *mean* it, Taylor!"

I was speechless. Obviously, he was intensely certain that Kyle was in grave danger.

"I don't care about no damn fences. *I want you at his side.* I known you your whole life. I trust you. You're a sad boy, but you got the heart of a brave man. One that came back from the dead! A hero. He sees it. I see it. Now you give me your word." He calmed down in volume but increased his intensity. "You *promise* me he won't jump."

"Louie...I...."

"Maury thought he was alone. That the whole world was enemies. I didn't know better to prove him wrong. I could'a stopped him if I hadn't been so full of myself—"

"Louie—" I interrupted.

"UH!" he counter-interrupted so he could finish what he was saying. "You be at Q-Tip's side. You fix this for me. You show him different. I'll keep him here as long as I can so you can prove he's got friends. That's all."

I glanced at the table. His quivering, muscular hand spoke louder to me than his words. The great Louie Dietz was truly frightened.

"God help me, Louie." With a heavy sigh, I stopped fighting him and clinked my orange juice glass to his coffee cup. "I promise. I'll do what I can."

"You promise me *what*?"

"I'll do what I—"

"You'll promise me WHAT?" He firmly interrupted a second time.

"I...He..." I suddenly knew what he wanted to hear. "He won't jump." My shoulders slumped. I'd now bought into Louie's assessment lock, stock and barrel. "With God as my witness..." I crossed my heart with a finger. "Kyle will never jump."

"So, good. You believe me now. That he's got trouble."

The GOAT DRIVE

I stared into his now-pleading eyes. He needed to be sure I wasn't just nodding to be polite. He needed me to prove he'd sold his argument. For the sake of his trust, I verbally summarized back what was going on in my head.

"Yes. You've made your point. I didn't see it until now. I don't know him like you do. But you've never steered me wrong. I believe you. He's gone dark." I sighed heavily. "I'll stick to him like glue. I'll do everything I can to bring his spark back."

Louie nodded and settled more comfortably into his chair.

I leaned back and continued to stare at his leathery, concerned face.

"I changed my mind."

"Huh?" I wrinkled my nose.

"We need new coffee." He slid the half-full cup to me and wiggled his brows. "This is shit."

JAMES F JOHNSON

20

Never-Ending Dreams

Sometimes I wonder if I'm awake or dreaming.

By Kyle

Dr. Krieg somehow became my teacher and taught math class while Andreo sat next to me. Andreo had finally apologized for slapping me, nicknaming me Homo, turning the entire school against me, and even for making the prank phone calls during my summer breaks. To my joy, we were friends again. In fact, the whole school liked me again.

I couldn't make sense of the numbers in the textbook because they kept changing while I tried to read them. Andreo leaned over to help me answer question number one, but that was when I realized I was naked. His hand went straight to my crotch and he cackled, "Homo!" Krieg grabbed both my wrists so I couldn't protect myself from Andreo. Classmates started laughing again. I couldn't run home because my parents had made it clear I was to deal with my own problems, and besides, Daniel and Fran were there. So I tried to run to my recently chosen hitchhiking spot on the freeway, but I couldn't escape Krieg's grip—and my feet weighed a ton each. My strong muscles could only move in super-slow motion while Andreo, Krieg, and the whole rest of the school laughed and pointed at me. A train horn blew. Was it coming after me?

Awake!

I woke up sweating and shaking. It was 8:00 a.m. My covers were on the floor. Not quite nauseous enough to dart to the bathroom, I lay still for about ten minutes, trying to be glad that it was just a dream and that in real life I was two-thousand miles away from all of them.

Moments later, a warm spray on my skin and the smell of soap and shampoo gave a physical distraction that allowed my tormented mind to shove those damned dreams back into the shadows where they wouldn't bother me in daytime. Singing a happy song in the shower magically lifted me even farther out of my dismal night into the brightness of the waking world. Blow-drying my hair using Tuck's technique put still a little more distance between me and the binding dreams, freeing me to feel even a bit more alive. The more I came into daytime, the further my vampire-ish dreams faded into the darkness of my mind's dark prisons where I could forget them and enjoy Papa and Tucker and Tuck.

I couldn't wait to see Tuck.

21

Covert Assignment

Back then, I saw Tuck as a wise older man. But the truth was that at barely twenty-one, he still had a lot of kid in him. The promise that Papa had pressured him into wasn't unfair, but it would definitely elevate his maturity levels to a new level. Tuck's superpower has always been his ability to assess the reality of the crazy world around him and find the most appropriate pathway through it. He is one of the lucky few enjoying a near perfect balance between a cautioned and an adventurous core personality. Papa had placed his trust well. I was being given over to good hands.

By Tuck Taylor

It was a tad past eight, and Louie was still in my kitchen. As we shared a fresh pot of coffee, he gripped my youthful attention by telling stories in the way of an elder. He spoke slowly in a cracked, but authoritative, low voice that filled the room like a baritone sax. He started a number of points with "The way I see it..." and ended them with a low-toned "so there ya have it."

As he spoke, the familiar wall-photo images of his family slid through my mind. But on this morning, his colorful words painted a *new* family portrait for me. One that exposed the back stories behind the familiar poses of the old ones. Anyone who knew Louie knew about his kids and grandkids' accomplishments. But that morning, after I'd promised to save his grandson's life, necessity forced him to peal the filter off the old familiar photos in m y mind and reveal a more complete version of the old truth. He dropped all formality and confessed to the murky things that few ever admit to about their offspring.

Marie

He described Kyle's mom, Marie, as "a jumpy car crash lookin' for a place to happen, ever since she married John Rickett." He said, "The way I see it, it knots her up when she thinks life should be simple," and "My Q-Tip's givin' her a real run for her money these days." He was worried because Kyle had become so complex that she was going to have a nervous breakdown if she couldn't somehow reclaim her easy-to-manage little boy soon. He warned me that Kyle didn't see her misery, but instead felt that his trip to Minnesota was due to her giving up on him and wanting him out of her hair.

Louie then made a comparison that Maury's final straw was his gal leaving him, so he hoped Kyle wasn't thinking his mom had done the same thing. Louie's biggest concern around Marie was that she was having dreams of Kyle being hit by a train. Louie, as sarcastic and realistic as he was, also had a propensity to believe in dreams and premonitions, especially when Marie was authoring them. "I don't know how to prove it," he said, "but somehow she *knows* things." He tapped at his temple.

Fran

Without realizing the implications, Louie was able to get a critical clue from Marie that I'm grateful he shared with me. Someone on Torano Island was advising her, or, in his words, "filling her head with crap."

The GOAT DRIVE

Kyle's sister, Fran, seemed to have the whole mess mapped out. That was a bad sign. All too often, the ones who verbally think they've got the tension figured out are somehow the ones pulling the strings in the first place.

In the phone calls to her dad, Marie repeatedly made comments like, "Fran says Kyle is trying to manipulate us all…" and "Fran says Kyle is acting out of anger at all of us…" and "Fran says Kyle wants something from us…." As Louie disclosed Fran's explanations for the family's confusion, I recalled some stories my sister had told me about a disastrous summer when, at thirteen, she'd tried to befriend Fran. Apparently, it ended in the backseat of a police car, with Fran rolling her eyes at the cop who was trying to scold her. Fran later laughed about it, labeled the cop an idiot, and bragged that she'd given Ronnie a wonderful experience to remember. The cop, on the other hand, told Ronnie to do a better job picking friends. Ronnie has since referred to Fran as "Louie's little narc." Narc being short for narcissist.

After prefacing that he was going to burn in hell for what he was about to say about his own granddaughter, Louie educated me on how different Fran and Kyle were. It seemed that he knew what Ronnie knew, but he didn't know the word narcissist. He said that Kyle was overly-emotional from a birth he and his mom only barely survived, while Fran was "cold and tricky." Having witnessed Kyle's emotional side over the weekend, I was able to track with Louie's words of worry. A tricky elder with an emotionally gullible child who wants to love his family is a bad combination. In an earlier comment, Louie flat-out told me that Kyle "trusts his family." Over the years, I've come to believe that trusting family is only a positive attribute for someone whose family can be trusted.

John

Despite Fran's explanations, Marie wasn't completely sure she'd done the right thing by sending Kyle to Minnesota. She'd twice mentioned not knowing what else to do except put some miles between him, Fran, and his dad, John. When I asked Louie if he had reason to suspect John was abusive, his response was eye-opening. He said John seemed peaceful enough, but then he instructed, "You look hard for bruises that might be hiding, okay?" That instruction made John look mighty suspicious. I'd cleaned fire extinguisher goop off Kyle's face, neck, chest, and shoulders, but I had yet to see under his socks, shorts, or armpits. The bruises and scars of family violence sometimes hide in those places. Up to now, nobody had talked much about John. I knew that an abusive husband can be skilled at getting his family to keep him out of the spotlight so as to protect the secrets.

On the topic of John and Fran, Louie told of a love/hate relationship that he called "like a married couple that fights all the time." Fran could both irritate more and get more favors out of John than everyone else combined. According to Louie, Fran's biggest problem was that John would never punish her for anything, so she grew up unhappy and selfish. That may or may not have been the best diagnosis, but it still shed a lot of light on family dynamics.

No allies

And finally, there was Kyle's friends. Louie informed me that he didn't know why, but some strange event, or possibly a series of unrelated events, had isolated Kyle from his cousin Scooter, best friend Connor, and some Texan boy from Catholic school. He reported the whole story of how Kyle had come apart in the kitchen Sunday morning with a claim that Louie was the only friend he had left in the world.

I had already promised Louie that I would do my best to be at his Q-Tip's side, but these stories, as he was telling them now, enlightened me that Kyle was definitely being tested by life's greatest fear—abandonment. Maybe Louie was absolutely right on the money with his assessment that Kyle was teetering on disaster. The most disturbing information of the morning was that Kyle's peers had faded away. Peers are the most important people in our lives. Being bullied by adults or authority figures is annoying or angering. Being bullied or abandoned by our peers is the loneliest curse there is. Believing you are utterly alone among your peers can *easily* bring on suicide, especially in someone who values friendship as much as Kyle seemed to.

The GOAT DRIVE (handwritten)

A walk in the trees

By 9:00 a.m., I had to take a walk. After Louie was finished assembling the details, I felt deeply compelled to try to sort through it all in my head. I snuck over to Louie's through the woods and retraced the steps Kyle and I had walked the day before. I used the familiar path to try to blend what I had learned about Kyle from his own words with what I had just learned from Louie's. I was confused about who Kyle really was—a sparking, humorous, excitable comedian, or a lonely, doomed orphan.

The physical walk through the area where Kyle had bragged about the fun he'd had was helpful. He was partially with me as I tried to understand his story. Why was he really here? What did he really leave behind on the island? What was really going to happen to him when he returned?

John might be abusive, but it seemed to me that an abusive father tends to turn a child bitter, not suicidal. Also, a family trying to keep a secret wouldn't have likely sent its victim out into the world unattended where it could not control whom he was talking to.

It's not bullying that turns you suicidal. Believing no one anywhere is on your side is what turns you suicidal. I couldn't help but lock in on Louie's haunting impersonations of Fran when he'd repeat what she'd told Marie. "Fran says Kyle is trying to manipulate *us all*..." and "Fran says Kyle is acting out of anger at *all of us*..." and "Fran says Kyle wants something from *us*...." It seemed to me that Fran had all the answers and Marie was as confused as Kyle.

By the time I'd gotten to the creek where Kyle and Scooter had once raced hydroplanes, I'd begun to put reason to my uneasy feelings around Fran. The way she kept saying "us all" and "we" was bugging me. Perhaps Ronnie was right about Fran being a narc. Narcissism is one of the attributes of a sociopath, and using "we" instead of "I" is a trick of sociopaths, whose goal is to make their prey accept they are grossly outnumbered, isolated, and helpless. First of all, sociopaths project. That means they tend to tip their own hands by accusing innocent people around them of the things they themselves are most often guilty of. By that reasoning, it was she, not Kyle, who was acting out of anger, and trying to manipulate. Secondly, repeatedly saying, "We all believe" is a dirty trick meant to make a point seem more valid than just "I believe."

While lumping "everyone" in to your story is a point-blank lie, the act of repeating a lie often makes it true in the listener's head. Maybe Kyle'd been hearing this "we all think you're…" his entire life.

This whole story was reminding me of the Cinderella tale. A gullible, good-hearted youngster is being surrounded and worked by his family, who bands together to let the child know he's not valued for anything other than doing chores and behaving quietly. The problem with Cinderella stories is that they are happening daily in towns all across the world, but despite the story, the strategy of waiting for a magic wand to bring a royal rescuer isn't the appropriate game plan. In real-life Cinderella stories, the victim normally has to stop waiting for a pumpkin carriage rescue and start looking at his family members for what they really are. From there, he needs to make some choices, none of which are to hope for a pumpkin to turn into a carriage. Somehow, the cop's advice to Ronnie was more realistic. Learn to pick better friends—and I'll add *family* to that advice.

Had Kyle been hearing this "we all" crap his entire life? Was this why in the long hours I'd spent with him so far, he had barely spoken of his family? Because he had come to believe that "they all" had lost connection with him?

I was suddenly beginning to hope John was a child-beater. If Kyle could expose actual bruising under his arms, socks, or shorts, we could call CPS and start the healing. But if the scars were invisible, then who was going to believe us enough to help? In fact, even Kyle himself would have to learn to trust, without any physical evidence, that the emotional scars were there so he'd begin to accept his own healing. Too many abused kids and adults are so convinced that they deserved what they got that they can't get it through their heads that it was abuse. No bruises? No scars? No problem! No one gets better when he thinks he's already okay. Without tangible clues, Kyle faced a long uphill battle just to believe in his own damage enough to accept his own healing.

The brother's role

I emerged from the woods overwhelmed. I was ill-qualified to make these assessments. I was also *not* a professional who had any business helping Kyle get his spark back. But just before releasing a scream of frustration, I calmed myself down because I remembered Louie's true request: "Be at his side." I didn't need to be the solver of the whole mystery. All I needed to be was his friend. I could do that.

Kyle had an older brother he hadn't talked about at all with me; instead, he had been admiring *me* as if *I* were the big brother. That was the leverage I needed to base the rest of the summer on. I'd never gotten to be a big brother, and Kyle seemed to need one. That win-win scenario helped me feel that the job I had committed to really wasn't going to be that difficult.

A string of unfortunate events

I had one final worry as I closed out that morning and prepared to meet my newly assigned little brother. Even if Kyle's entire summer was nothing more than a series of unfortunate events, or a "comedy of errors," he could still be in danger. I had once read that plane crashes are almost never due to one single cause; they are usually a deadly buildup of small coincidences that collapse when one final mistake brings the whole thing down to its fiery end.

This wasn't a plane crash, but in Kyle's life, it might as well have been. If Louie's hunch was right, and Kyle's life was maneuvering him toward death's door, then according to this theory, the series of unfortunate events had already pushed him to that dangerous altitude where one more problem could send him crashing. This was a prudent warning for me to tread carefully and keep a close watch on his activities.

Louie was able to bring me into his crisis because of a desire to strike before his boy "jumps." Having been a crisis line volunteer, I'd witnessed the fallout from people who'd waited until it was too late to help. One particularly heart-broken brother of a suicide victim called me during the darkest hours for several nights out of torment over having ignored his sister's signs before it was too late. I couldn't let Louie ever become that remorseful family member. I needed to help before it was too late.

People who are at the wrong end of a string of unfortunate events can live with "toes over the edge." They are sometimes highly vulnerable to acting on impulse at the wrong moments. We all walk over tall bridges, stand on busy street corners, know the location of a loaded pistol, or hold full bottles of pills in our hands on any normal day, but if a person is teetering at the edge of ending it all, those little opportunities can easily become high-risk moments. A single poor decision in a brief moment of agony brings them down to their fiery and final end because they happened to have a loaded gun nearby when they had the wrong fleeting thought.

Time to get started

At ten-thirty, I returned to Grandpa's house, where he and Louie were tinkering with an old green lawn mower that hadn't been started in years.

"What the hell are you two doing now?"

"About time you came back!" Louie chastised. "There's firewood what needs cuttin' down by the creek. I'll go home after you get him down there."

"Why can't you go home now?"

"Because we need to switch out."

"Switch what out?"

"I ain't his only friend no more. That's you now."

"You left him alone? After telling me how afraid you are for his safety?"

"He ain't alone no more, Tuckster. He went to bed last night knowin' you give a damn." Louie grabbed my shoulder. "Now you need to prove it's true. That you give a damn for real. I'm the crazy old grandfather. You're the friend now. You two's got firewood to cut, and he knows you need his help. So now he needs you, not me. Someone what thinks like him. Now git!"

22

When Not to Panic

Friendship is everything. I now believe that a person can survive a thousand enemies if he has but one trusted friend. If that summer had a specific purpose for everything it had brought me through, then that purpose was to show me how to untangle bullies from allies, or "separate the wheat from the chaff." A few good men were proving to me that they could be those few allies who would never change teams and who would give me the courage to stand united against an army of bullies.

By Kyle Rickett

On the fifth telephone ring outside the bathroom door, I figured out Papa wasn't home, so I ran to the kitchen.

"Hello?"

"Kyle!"

"Hi, Tuck." A smile beamed out of control.

"How'dya sleep?"

"Good," I cheerfully lied. "How about you?"

"Excellent. The fresh farm air is good for me."

"Me too. I can't believe it's ten-thirty already. I almost slept the day away. Did you just get up too?"

"Na. I've been up a while."

We small-talked a little, and then he asked if I was ready to go to work. Papa was there with him and we'd been hired for our first job. I started to get excited over being called into action like a real man. A couple of trees had fallen during the winter onto the creek, and both grandfathers wanted them cut, split, hauled, and stacked in their firewood sheds.

When I hung up, I scanned the peaceful, warm, quiet kitchen. I felt the urge to pack a special lunch—one that would wow Tuck and outdo anything I'd done yet. I glanced down at my white T-shirt, denim cutoffs, and cotton tube socks. I fingered my puka shell necklace. I was awake. The nightmares were behind me. I was wearing clothes. My legs were strong again. My friends were Papa, Connor, Scooter, and Tuck Taylor. Here and now, I had no need to run from anyone or to find a highway so I could hitchhike away.

I loved being awake and off that island.

Getting to know

Once we were in the woods, Tuck's staring was more noticeable than on Monday when we'd taken care of the bees' nest together. I was now in a more chipper mood and must have said, "Why don't you take a picture? It'll last longer" about four times. He laughed each time, but not energetically. On this day, while I felt happier, he seemed quieter, less amused by me, and more interested in whatever was inside my head. He did a lot of glaring like he was trying to peer through my eyeballs and read the writing on my brain. It's like he had something on his mind that had to do with me.

At first, I liked being interesting to someone cool like him. It made me less alone. I wanted to learn more from him, and it looked like he

The GOAT DRIVE

wanted to learn about me too. The arrangement with him made me feel like more of a man than a boy. Whenever I worked in the woods with Dad, I was the little helper. But here, I was an equal half of a competent two-man team on a real mission to clean up after an actual storm.

After a full hour with two roaring chainsaws, we'd cut the first entire tree into sixteen-inch lengths, or "rounds." Now it came time to split them. I shut off my chainsaw and caught him trying to rub woodchips off his tongue.

"Hey!" I teased. "Save room for lunch!"

"Very funny." He grimaced and spit. Then, in some automatic accidental move, he wiped his mouth with an arm, which only put more sawdust back in. "*God damn it!*"

I cackled and dropped my chainsaw.

We were both sweating and filthy. He slid his shirt off and sat down, spitting. "Gross."

"You're supposed to keep your mouth shut when you're sawing."

"Oh, *really?*" he answered sarcastically. "Thanks for the advice—*now that we're done.*"

"Better late than never, right?"

He shook his head. "Come on; sit down with me. We need a break."

"I don't take breaks," I joked. Then, when I was sure I had his full attention, I rolled my eyes up into my head and pretended to pass out like I'd done in the beekeeper's suit. When I fell backward into the soft leaves, I heard him laughing again. I sat up facing him. "Okay. Maybe I do need a break."

"Well, *I* sure as hell do." He jokingly flung his shirt onto my lap. "We have all summer to do this job."

"But we have a *lot* of work to do, Tuck." I tossed the shirt back, landing it at his feet. "After this, we have the trees up on Norton Hill. Then we have a bunch of fence work to do." The next words made me feel lonely again. "Summer'll be over before we know it."

"We'll get to the fences. Trust me."

"Trust you?" I giggled softly. "It's only been an hour and you're already sitting down."

"Jeez, Kyle, you're an evil taskmaster!" he griped. "I wish I'd have known about this side of you before I agreed to be your teammate."

"Sorry. My dad doesn't take breaks. He likes to keep moving."

"Your dad's not here now. You're in charge."

"Me?"

"But *I'm still taking my break*!" He shook a finger at me. "You know a hell of a lot more about woodcutting than I do. So as long as you let me take breaks, Kyle, you're in charge."

I was pretty sure I'd never heard "Kyle, you're in charge" uttered by anyone, anywhere, for any reason. My chest puffed up microscopically. I don't think Tuck saw it, but I felt it. I wanted to make my first command decision to see if he really meant it.

"You rest, old man. I want to move those five rounds up out of the water. Then I'll sit down with you."

"Whatever floats your boat." He nodded and let me do what I wanted.

I *was* in charge.

Sexualization—"the gift that keeps on giving"

I slid the T-shirt off over my head. When it cleared my eyes, I noticed he was intently staring at my chest and armpits. Heaviness came over me, like it did when he had followed me into my bedroom, or when he'd complimented my outfit that next morning. I wasn't turned on by him—*but*—maybe he was occasionally turned on by me? It's a little embarrassing to admit that after being ashamed of my looks for most of my life, being desired by anyone sort of felt…*good*.

> Here is where my story becomes difficult for me to tell, and you, reader, may find it difficult to follow. But that's okay. Consider it a peek into the disorder of the PTSD thought process. This confusion is part and parcel of what it feels like to

be me, fighting reality against rogue fears while dissociating under the stress of distrust.

He looked like the waterbed salesman ogling my legs in St. Paul, or like Dr. Krieg had when my arms were raised over my head. Why were visions of these two creeps flashing before my eyes now? Maybe because I was starting to see a pattern of lust whenever I was alone with men, and Tuck was a man.

My hypervigilance was also at play. I'd learned to watch every single microscopic expression in the faces of *everyone*, and to listen closely for any minuscule clue that might warn me when a person—any person—*was about to change into a monster.*

I tossed the shirt onto the ground next to his and turned my face away so I could expressively open my eyes wide and walk toward the creek. When I bent down to lift the round, I naturally assumed he was staring at my ass.

I didn't look toward him to check on my theory because if he was admiring me, I wanted to look cool. That's when I flexed every muscle I knew how to flex. *Good God, was I peacocking for him?*

No! I rationalized. *This can't be happening.* I admired him and wanted him to admire me back. That had to be all this was.

Thoughts were getting all tangled up in my head. I forced a memory of the diary entry and recommitted to trusting him. The confusion over wondering whether this was sexual or not was too much. No matter what he wanted, *I absolutely couldn't take any more loneliness.* I was willing to accept the bad with the good. Whatever the price, I'd pay it. With every fiber of my being, I wanted Tuck in my life every day, one way or another. He could be my very last chance at ever making a friend at all.

I lifted, carried, rolled, or slid all five rounds up from the creek bed to the clearing for splitting. That's when I noticed I was going into a time-warp again. The woods got quieter and smaller as I pondered why he was watching so closely.

A quick author's note:

Peacocking is the male act of showing off to potential mates. During my adolescent years, Krieg had stepped in and confused my natural order of physical reactions to people. Girls didn't like me because I was small and a bully-victim, but Tuck did. The peacocking was an involuntary reaction to the confusion. My brain's control over socialization was overriding my willpower to reserve peacocking for girls.

Don't let my admitting this to the readers color me in an inaccurate light. My goal for confessing these embarrassing and involuntary sexualized suspicions is to allow you to know how crazy and confused my PTSD and hypervigilance had gotten as I began a lifetime of wondering why some people want to be close to me and others don't. My relational brain senses the similarities when a current situation starts to look, sound, or smell like an old one and my brain uncontrollably expects that the same outcome is on its way to hurt me again.

Also, PTSD with hypervigilance has created in me a situation whereby at any given moment I am either totally safe or in total danger—never in-between. The slightest fear causes me to react with full-throttle fight-or-flight insanity. I respond to a hand-clap the way a balanced person responds to dynamite. Over-sexualization—for me—is the result of having been shown that some people can, and will, go to extremes to violate my boundaries without my permission, and it has left me unable to trust when and where…and who…will attack me next. Fight-or-flight, for me, has always been an on/off switch rather than a progressive and appropriate escalation.

Cutting into Sections

"Damn, kid." Tuck leaned back on his straightened arms. "Those are some real muscles you hide under that shirt."

"Oh." Panting, I didn't know what more to say. I smiled and wiped my chest with an open palm. "I've been doing this kind of work since I was nine."

"It shows. If you were nine, then you've been doing this for almost half your life. That must be why you're so strong."

"I guess, yeah."

"You must have to beat the girls off with a stick, huh?" he commented while still looking at my chest.

I faked a laugh that time. Beat the girls off with a stick? Hardly. No one would even look at me unless it was to laugh at my white hair or small size.

"What? A good-looking stud like you has no girlfriend?"

"I'm only fourteen." I blushed. "No. I've never had a girlfriend."

"I had a girlfriend when *I* was fourteen."

"Whoop-de-doo. Do you want an award?" I stuck out my tongue.

"It was just a comment." He laughed hard. "Jeez!"

"Well…I play the accordion. And almost all the girls in my class are taller than me. They don't—"

"Sounds like you have all the excuses memorized." He stopped me. "Are you excited to go back to school? See your friends?"

My look of surprise told him the answer was no.

"Sorry."

"For what?" I grabbed my shirt off the ground to use like a rag. I wiped my face and chest and sat down next to him.

"Louie mentioned you and some Texan friend had a falling out of some kind."

"Andreo. He's an asshole."

"I should have been more considerate." He kept staring at me. "You don't like school at all, do you?"

I shook my head without speaking the word no.

He reached behind himself for one of the ice-filled mason jars we'd brought with us.

"Here; you need to drink this."

"Why?"

"Just shut up and drink it," he teased.

"Thanks." I laughed. It was half-melted and refreshingly cool. But as I gulped, I could spy on him through it. He was staring at my armpit again. In fact, his eyes scanned the whole length of my arm's underside. I let it happen because I wanted him to like me and not leave me alone for so much as one day of my trip to Minnesota. So to keep him interested in me, I told myself I could do anything he wanted me to do. It didn't even matter if he hurt me. Because of Krieg, I had learned how to think about something else while unpleasant things happened to me. I purposely held the jar up high and enjoyed the final drips of melting ice. I purposely flexed too.

"Wow," he said.

"What?" I lowered the Mason jar and screwed the lid back on to keep bugs out while the rest of the ice melted for later.

"You were really thirsty! Do you want another one?"

"No, thanks."

He took the jar from me and returned it to the supply bag.

"I like summer." That was my indirect way of saying I didn't like the school year. I needed to focus my eyes on something. I looked at his face but only saw his scar. I distracted myself by wondering again how he'd gotten it.

"Who's Connor? Louie said you two are pretty close."

"What?"

Tuck's eyebrows dipped. "You okay?"

"Oh." I paused long enough to shake my head and get back to his question. "Yeah. Sorry. I drank too fast," I lied. "Got brain freeze."

"Brain freeze?" He tipped his head. "From *water*?"

"He's my best friend." I changed the subject. "I like him almost as much as Scooter."

"Yesterday, you told me Scooter was pretty important. That's great that you have a friend like Connor when Scooter's not around."

My face tipped downward in shame.

"It's not?"

"No—Yes—I mean...it is! Connor's awesome." I smiled as big as I could to fight back the confusion. Tuck was cutting my life into sections the way we'd just done with the fallen tree. This was starting to feel like man-to-teen questioning again. I was starting to shrink.

"You know what?" He stared into my face like he could see my confusion. "That wasn't brain freeze. It was me asking too many serious questions." He stopped looking at me and picked up the ax from at his feet. "I should be more like John Rickett—less talk, more work."

"*Don't be more like Dad*!" I accidentally blurted out. "I mean...I like you being...Tuck."

He stared again like I'd said something that shocked him, or like he had more to say, but like he chose to stick to his promise of less talk, more work.

"It's okay," I lied again. "You're just getting to know me. That's all."

"One last question then.... Are you glad your dad's not here?"

I paused for a long second. "I'm just having a good time..." I carefully chose my words, "the way things are right now."

He let it go. But the serious look on his face stayed.

Splitting

Splitting was my favorite part of this job. I could do it all day long. I liked axes better than chainsaws. The vibration from the gas motors could wear down my muscles, but swinging a wood-handled ax and breaking rounds into wedges stretched and invigorated those same muscles. I'd developed an eye for exactly where on the round to strike. My goal was always to split in one hit, three at the most. Four or more strikes made me feel stupid, like people were going to laugh at me for being weak, so any time I had to make a third one, anger swelled to force the ax through.

Time flew. His ax struck wood about twice for every three times mine did. It was always, always important to me to be the one working the hardest on any job. Sometimes, it was competitive pride, but mostly, it was because I was small and emotional, and if I didn't work harder than the people around me, it gave them something to humiliate me for. If I didn't overachieve, then I became disgraced—or worse, invisible...like I was at home.

"Time for lunch." Tuck panted as he pleaded, "Please can we stop?"

I laughed. "I'm not your boss. You can stop any time." I slammed my ax head deep into a round and left it.

"I know you're not my boss. But we're a team. I like keeping up with you."

I laughed at his pile of split firewood, which wasn't as big as mine. "But you're not keeping up."

"Hey!" He laughed back, leaned his ax against a stump, grabbed a pile of dry leaves, and tried throwing them at me, but they scattered and floated to the ground.

"Okay." I looked up through the trees at the sun directly overhead. "Lunch is a good idea."

Oh, shit

Then, as a symptom of hypervigilance, my nerves almost totally unraveled as he headed for the food I'd brought. Feeling like I was obligated to outdo yesterday's meal, I had decided that instead of making sandwiches, I'd take a risk by being, again, different than other guys my age. Suddenly, I wasn't happy with my decision to be different.

"Why the hell do I always have to be such a dork?" I whispered.

"Far out!" he shouted when he discovered two of his favorite root beers packed in ice.

I heard a "wow" when he unwrapped the foil off the top of our main course, but my chest was still thumping with fear that he was going to criticize the weird food.

The GOAT DRIVE

Our lunch was one of Grandma's old blue-and-white china plates heaped high with sliced cheese, sandwich meats, and some nuts I had found in Papa's cupboards. I'd pan-toasted half a loaf of sliced bread in garlic butter, hoping it would be crunchy when it cooled. All of this was on the plate with two spreading knives and a pile of fresh farm butter from a neighbor's cow. In the kitchen, I had been proud as hell over it, but now that Tuck was unwrapping it, I felt like he was unwrapping me. I was being exposed as a total freak of nature.

Big scare!

"My god, Kyle. Who the hell taught you to cook like this?"

"Don't you like it?" I panicked. My heart sank. I'd tried too hard. I should have just made sandwiches like a normal kid! *Oh shit, I was too weird for him!*

"No, no, no…. It's the other way around." Tuck's face shared my panic. "Kyle, I was complimenting you." He moved a hand toward me. "I promise. I was complimenting you."

I pulled back.

He froze, then nodded. "I like it." He grabbed a floppy slice of cheese and held it up to show me. "Mmmm."

I forced myself to smile so I wouldn't look so scared.

"Trust me, Kyle. I mean it. This is amazing." He nodded toward the plate in his hand. "I think you're a good cook."

I examined his eyes closely.

He grinned slightly and nodded again. He looked sadly compassionate. I felt like an idiot.

"A really good cook," he repeated calmly.

"It's not 'cooking,' Tuck." I shyly looked down at my bare knees. "It's all the same food that sandwiches are made of…I just put it on a plate instead…so you could make your own how you like it."

"I smell garlic." He was still smiling and looking into my eyes.

"I toasted the bread in it."

"Who taught you that trick?"

"No one. I made it up."

"Sounds like cooking to me."

I huffed a gentle laugh and finally started to smile.

"You're okay?"

I nodded through relief mixed with shame.

"Cool. I think this is a real man's lunch. I love meat. All men love meat." He looked at me and smiled like he was trying to cheer me up.

"Meat's good," I joined in, trying to pretend I'd never panicked.

"I'm sorry I scared you like that." He ruffled a hand through my hair.

"It's okay." I gently punched his arm.

"It is *not* okay, Kyle." He tapped my sweaty shoulder. "You can tell me to shut-the-hell-up once in a while. I'll still be your friend."

I looked at him, again not knowing what to say. Telling someone to shut up was a death sentence to any friendship I'd ever had.

"And you need to stop minimizing your skills." He locked eyes with me, smirked, and repeated a line he was starting to say a lot, "You rebuilt a *tractor*!"

"Ha!" Every time he said that, I laughed. His kindness was sincere enough to help me perk up. I leaned in and took some ingredients off the plate. I buttered a big slice of garlic toast and piled it with cheese, salami, and bacon. "This is a pretty fun day," I commented.

"I agree." He wiped a piece of toast over the top of the butter pile without using a knife, then made a meat and cheese sandwich for himself.

When he took his first bite, I tapped his shoulder. "I'm sorry I misunderstood you."

"I'm sorry too, buddy. I need to be clear when I get excited."

We both ate our first helpings quietly. Then when it was time for each of us to make another one, he slid down to the ground and lounged against the log. I grabbed the plate and slid down with him. Setting the food that I'd prepared and he was loving between us, I felt more relaxed with him than I ever had so far.

To relax even more, he kicked off his shoes and took off his socks. I copied him. He stared at my big feet a little longer than he probably should have, but he didn't make fun of me for them. I gently kicked at his leg and repeated, "Why don't you take a picture? It'll last longer."

He chuckled and started asking more questions.

Who gets me?

"Does your family…get you?"

"Huh?" I took a huge bite of my second sandwich. Crumbs rained onto my bare stomach. "Do they *get* me?" I muffled through a full mouth.

"Yeah. I'm amazed by you…and I'm wondering if they are too."

"Amazed?" I was lost. Such words had never been spoken to me. I didn't know how to answer him, so I kept attention on the food.

"You just don't seem like the kind of guy a family should send away for the summer." Then he held up the last few bites of his meal. "But their loss is my gain, right? I'm glad they did because I've never enjoyed working around here like I am this year, Kyle."

"Really?"

"You're fun to hang out with."

"So are you." It's tough to take kind words, so I turned them around to compliment him back.

"I just…." He nervously looked around the woods. "I just wanted to say that."

"Well, I thought this trip was going to be horrible." It seemed easy for me to say nice things now that he was saying them first. "Did I thank you for picking me up at the train station?"

He laughed.

I immediately felt self-conscious, but having just made an ass of myself at his last reaction, I wasn't about to let myself do it again. I had to trust that he wasn't laughing *at* me, but *with* me. "I don't remember if I thanked you. I was kind of a jerk that day."

"You thanked me…" He patted my knee and then looked around at the picnic spread, the two chainsaws, the cut wood, and then back at me, "in about a hundred different ways."

23

How To Teach Trust

God bless Tuck. I was trying so hard to trust him, and he was showing so much patience with me. I was sure he was laying the kind words on a little thick, but I still liked hearing them. He was becoming the big brother I'd never felt I'd had but had always needed, and unbeknown to me, I was the little brother who filled a deep void in his life also.

By Tuck Taylor

The Tuesday sunset lit the bathroom window to reddish-orange as I enjoyed a long, hot soak in Epsom salts. Afterwards, in sweatpants and with a towel across my shoulders, I shuffled, exhausted, into the kitchen to scoop up a bowl of Grandpa's nightly popcorn and then into living room to sit with him and watch the ten o'clock news while my hair air-dried.

"You look like you've been run through the mill."

"That little shit wore me out, Grandpa."

"Young'ns can do that to you."

"He's no young'n," I defended. "Just small for his age. But *man*, can that kid kick butt with tools." I tossed some popcorn into my mouth. "I'm humbled by him."

"Don't let 'that little shit' fool you." He smirked. "Louie called. Kyle's in a tub of salts too, now."

I laughed.

"He's a go-getter, that one. Louie's proud."

"As well he should be," I agreed.

"I'm proud of you too, boy."

"Thanks, Grandpa. That means a lot." I tossed in another kernel. "Coming here for the summer was a good decision…way better than staying alone in Texas."

"I'm getting my firewood cut, so it seems to be working out for all of us," he joked.

He stared for a long moment.

"What? Do I have butter on my chin?"

"You look tired…but you look good. That spark you used to have. It's coming back." He settled into his couch. "Now let's watch the news. See if that God-damned Nixon's been impeached yet."

New twist to an old visit

Grandpa went to bed at ten-thirty as always. I stayed up to watch Johnny Carson interview Orson Bean, but to this day, I don't remember a single moment of the show. I'd gone deep into thought before it started and had fallen asleep on the couch before it ended. I had always possessed a compassionate streak, but this promise I'd made to Louie was the first really heartfelt commitment I'd ever made that put someone else's needs as more important than mine. As I dozed off, Kyle's blank stares burned into my mind. It was as if he knew I had the power to save him—or *kill* him. While I was proud to have been trusted so much by my old friend, the emotional burden to succeed for Kyle's sake was heavier than any I'd ever felt.

Once asleep, I visited the dove, but differently this time. Instead of walking in the place I called heaven, I flew beside it through intensely blue skies.

"Do you trust me?" it asked.

I looked down and saw the earth. I looked up again and saw heaven. I was between the two worlds. I was safe. I'd visited here before and had returned home each time. I felt no fear.

"No matter what happens, you'll return to do your job."

The riddle made no sense, but somehow, I knew the bird was giving me good news.

"Do you trust me?" it repeated.

"I do now." I looked directly into the dove's eye. "You keep coming to me and everything keeps being okay. Of course I trust you. You make learning trust easy."

"But you're the teacher. Not me."

Something about those words shocked me. I felt myself instantly switch places with the dove. For years, I'd experienced the visitations...but...was I no longer the student?

I woke up when the National Anthem played. Back then, TV stations signed off with it every morning, not long after midnight. Still immersed in the heavy emotions of Kyle's conundrum, I stared into the ensuing static for almost an hour.

"You're the teacher, not me," I whispered. "What did that *mean*?"

What had I learned?

I couldn't get Kyle out of my mind. Was today a bust? I'd learned almost *nothing* about his mysterious situation. As I thought about him, I started chuckling. It was cute the way he kept flexing when he knew I was looking at him. I remembered being fourteen. I'd have done the same thing.

Louie wanted me to "fix" Kyle, but everything I tried to learn from him, Louie had already disclosed: Connor, Scooter, and Andreo were mysteriously out of his life; John was stern but Kyle was bruise-less; and we didn't even broach the topic of Friendly Fran.

I had literally taken advantage of every chance to examine Kyle's bare feet, ankles, and inner arms—hoping he wouldn't think I was some kind of a pervert—and to my surprise, I saw absolutely no sign of abuse. I was relieved and dumbfounded at the same time. But no visible bruises didn't prove anything. Something was telling me he had scars somewhere that weren't healing. Louie was right to be worried. The boy's cheerful demeanor and boundless energy had an inexplicable hollowness to them. At some moments, Kyle seemed free and easy, but then a panic would fly through him like a bullet—and at nothing! Then a gray hue would cover his face and he'd go slightly blank, like he was afraid of me, but only for moments here and there.

Empathy

Louie was my proof that you can't judge a book by its cover. Even a simple and silly old man who drinks too much and grabs attention wherever he can may harbor wisdom worth listening for. He acted a bit crazy, but he understood the world in ways a young man can't. His insightfulness was forged from his lifetime of experiences, both grand and small. His greatest gift was a naturally high emotional intelligence (EQ)—a term we hadn't coined yet at that time—which processed his past into useful wisdom for his, and my, futures. Whereas a lesser man would just bitch about how the world was going to hell in a hand-basket, Louie found ways to learn and grow—or to understand and harness whatever he experienced or witnessed.

He drew simplified conclusions that he didn't know others had already labeled with technical terms. For example, when he reported that I "knew enough" and "had been where Kyle is," he referred to a phenomenon taught in college called empathy. He also didn't know that my empathetic abilities weren't so unusual in the medical community. Empathy is a known force of power in the world of healing, and it is often the distinguishing difference between an adequate doctor and a gifted healer.

Louie also didn't know that I was good at empathizing, as I'd demonstrated the day before when I'd tapped into my own cancer

The GOAT DRIVE

struggles and then instinctively knew to compliment Kyle's shoes. I'd sensed Kyle's self-consciousness because it had reminded me of my own, and then I had responded with exactly what he needed to hear at the precise moment. My heart was talking to his heart. That's the power of empathy.

I intentionally recalled my own sorrow, as per Louie's wishes when he'd said, "Now, Mr. Taylor, you dig deep and remember back then what you thought.... Then, you look deep into my Q-Tip's eyes, and sure as can be, you'll see it there too." It was tough on me. For a couple of hours that day, I'd let myself live again in the sadness I had felt during the isolation of dying from a cancer none of my family or friends could save me from. I didn't know if Kyle could tell I was not my cheerful self that day, but the effort had paid off. Staring into my new friend's eyes while tuned in to my own grief created a remarkably insightful bridge between us. If a person can't judge another until he's walked a mile in his shoes, then I'd walked my mile and now could almost *feel* Kyle's energy rise and fall with our conversations.

I may not have learned much about his home life that day, but I did gain a better grasp of *who he was*. When he misunderstood my compliment at lunch, a window opened into his soul. That was hypervigilance if I've ever seen it. The moment he wasn't sure of what I meant, he defaulted to backing away and apologizing all over himself like he was sure I was about to turn into a monster and kill him. I knew right then and there that the boy lived on a daily bed of pins and needles. He likely had to say sorry to someone, somewhere a lot. Or maybe he had to try to please someone who could not be pleased by anything. It had to have been what caused all those stomach pains he seemed to nurse. Perhaps these internal aches and pains were the bruises and scars I was to be looking for.

I recalled him suddenly wanting to thank me for picking him up, as if he were soliciting my forgiveness again and again.

"Why does he keep making me forgive his one bad mood?"

The lesson plan revealed

That's when I got it. The bird made sense in a new way. For three-and-a-half years, that iconic vision had been visiting me during moments of intense grief or fear. Each visit ended peacefully. Because of the repeated positive outcomes, I was beginning to trust the visitations as positive experiences meant to guide me through difficult times. Whether it was a real spirit or a psychological trick, the dove was a trustworthy friend who was getting me through my fears.

"He needs to hear me forgive him the same way every time he brings it up. He needs me to be the same person every day." Then I whispered a little louder, "That's what the bird meant. *I'm*...the teacher. Consistent and predictable repetition is how to teach trust."

Energy began to percolate. I sat up spritely on the couch. I was on to something. If my theory about Fran being a narcissistic sociopath was even partially accurate, then, like all narcissists, she would likely say anything she wanted to say—honest or otherwise—even if it was a blatant contradiction to the *last thing she'd just said*. Narcissists don't so much love the people they're with as they compete with them. They typically only have one true goal: To triumph over the moment that's facing them that second, as if each and every conversation is an isolated war they feel they must win. Because of this shortsighted, competitive view on life, they contradict themselves and change their stories almost every time they open their mouths. How the hell is a kid supposed to trust an authority figure who does that?

Kyle's trust issues, therefore, made perfect sense. He probably tried to live as an honorable family member, believing everything he was told, even though he was intelligent enough to know it was crazy shit. After hearing him clearly tell me that he was glad his dad wasn't here while simultaneously refusing to say anything demeaning about him, I detected an inner battle—one he was losing. Within the few days I'd known him, I'd also heard Kyle say, "I love my sister, but..." a couple of times. I believed he was working to convince *himself* that his family members were on his side, even though they repeatedly proved they were not.

"I can't fix his family," I spoke aloud in order to help organize my thoughts, as if I were both the teacher and the student. "I can't even figure them out. But I can control *me*." I recalled Louie's advice simply to be at Q-Tip's side and concluded, "Trust is about *me* repeating *my* same messages so he knows what to expect from *me*. I teach *him* by example. By being the same *me* every day."

24

Credit for Trying So Hard

Tuck was a good guy but a bad actor. His overexaggerated compliments were obvious, but at the same time, they made him look like the nicest guy in the whole world. Because of his genuine efforts, his compliments were appreciated. Papa was right; Tuck was a good guy through and through.

By Kyle Rickett

On Thursday, August 1, I had slept well for the whole night. Thank God for small miracles. I'd set my alarm for 6:00 a.m. and Tuck called at exactly six-thirty, then showed up to the house at seven, exactly when he said he would. We used Grandpa Tucker's tractor and wagon to haul the split wood. We dumped half of it at his firewood shed, and then we delivered the rest to Papa's. Our plan was to come back on Friday to revisit both piles for stacking. It was strange for me not to finish the job while we were there, but our grandfathers had made it perfectly clear that we were only to work for *a few hours a day* so we wouldn't be so worn out every night.

Our grandfathers, who'd insisted we work for our room and board, seemed hell-bent also that we spend only half of our day working and the other half hanging out together. That didn't hurt my feelings. I liked both as long as I was with Tuck.

So, with Thursday's chores done early, Tuck and I both showered and then he took me out to lunch. We shopped for clothes, food, and equipment for our upcoming camping/firewood trip to Norton Hill on Saturday. Our first stop was a Target store.

"Shoes." Tuck pointed toward the back of the store.

"Why?"

"I promised you a pair of sandals."

"No, you didn't."

"Sure, I did. Monday night. I told you I might get you some like mine."

"I must have just figured you were saying it to be nice because I don't even remember you doing that."

Tuck stopped walking but kept looking toward the shoe department.

"What?"

"Do people really do that to you?"

"What?" I asked again.

"Do people really offer to do things for you and then never follow through?"

"Sure." I shrugged. "They get busy. Doesn't everyone do that?"

"Not me." He started walking again and purposely bumped my shoulder to make me chuckle. "Come on; I made a promise and I always—*always*—hold to my promises."

"Your record's clean, Honest Abe," I joked. "You haven't broken a single promise."

He smiled extra warmly at me.

The GOAT DRIVE (handwritten)

Out on the town

At Target, Tuck bought me sandals, two new tank tops, and a full package of purple licorice. He laughed while I sat on the sidewalk and swapped shoes for sandals as soon as we exited.

Next door was a magazine store, where I didn't have to beg because Tuck gladly wandered in with me. Then, without my asking him to, he purchased my August issue of *Disaster Island* as a gift. I had told him of my perfect collection of issues one through forty-one and how Connor and I had a ritual of buying them together on the first of every single month. He thought it was laughable that I lived on an island and read a comic book by that title. When we drove off, I wore the sandals and carried the little bag of treasures in my lap like it was too valuable to let go of.

Shopping with Tuck was more fun than with Mom and Fran. He didn't need to look at things. He'd find what we needed and get back in the car. No perusing or foraging for knickknacks. Men are hunters; women are gatherers. Men don't need to pick through the shelves like berry bushes. We find our prize, shoot it, and bring it home.

The first hardware store took care of most of our list. Then we headed for a safety supply store. After being pelted with flying chips the day before, Tuck had decided not to return to the deep woods without quality safety glasses.

Break from the break

"Hey! I have a Frisbee in the trunk." Tuck pulled the Goat into a gravel parking lot at the edge of a huge grassy field, tapping the throttle every few seconds to make my favorite sound.

"Now? We're not done shopping yet."

"I told you I like taking breaks," he said, expressionlessly.

"Um. Yeah. That's true." I thought back to Wednesday in the woods. "You definitely did tell me that."

"And well, nothing's changed. I'm the same person today as I was when I said that."

"Um. Okay." I laughed under my breath as he overexaggerated more promises.

After I'd thrown my first Frisbee off into the bushes, he asked if anyone had ever shown me how to throw one. When I confessed to being self-taught, he said he could tell; then he showed me the right way to fling a Frisbee. This was the second time he'd taught me something just because he thought I should know it. I hadn't noticed before how rare it was that anyone would do that for me—even once.

After a half hour of flinging it back and forth, running and laughing, he said he needed a break.

"You mean from our break? Cuz, we're *on* a break."

"Yeah." He laughed. "I need a break from our break. Now shut up and let's sit down."

"You shut up!" I laughed and charged him, arms open wide. As I reached his waist to try to tackle him, he spun me around, causing both of us to fall into the grass in hysterics. I started slapping the top of his head with my floppy Frisbee, and then he attacked me with the same move.

He got up first and started running. I chased after him until we found a shady spot in a picnic area near a drinking fountain. I slurped for a minute, then sat with him on the ground. I felt so comfortable with him that I actually opened up and asked him something personal.

"Tuck," I panted from the horseplay, "how come yesterday you were so interested in my life, but today you haven't asked me anymore about it?"

"I hadn't noticed."

"You haven't asked me about hardly anything."

"You want me to?"

"No!" I comically waved both hands. "It's more fun if you don't."

"Then what are you complaining about?"

"I'm not complaining." I plucked a handful of grass to fidget with. "I was just noticing. That's all." I dropped blades of grass one by one onto the ground. "Seemed like you wanted to know a lot yesterday."

"Yeah, well..." He smirked and tapped my shoulder once, "I guess today I know enough."

JAMES F JOHNSON

25

Finding a Single Spark

> *Tuck was working on his theory that being 100 percent consistent would make him 100 percent predictable, and that would help me learn to trust him. I can't say he was wrong. I also can't say it was all about teaching me. Tuck saw something in me that taught him about trust in himself as well.*

By Tuck Taylor

I couldn't believe no one had ever shown Kyle how to do something so simple as to toss a stupid Frisbee. Emotionally and physically, he appeared no older than eleven or twelve. I had to dig a bit to discover he was more than a kid, and that he had a vast array of adult skills. Nobody had taught him how to be a boy. But they had successfully given him a number of adult-level skills instead. The kid had rebuilt a tractor, for God's sake. I know I say that a lot, but in all fairness—at thirteen, *he rebuilt a freaking tractor*! He could cook, entertain an audience, and communicate far more clearly than an average fourteen-year-old. But he couldn't throw a Frisbee.

Why was he so goddamned unsure of himself? It seemed to go along with his nervous stomach. He was an overachiever, but only when doing things for other people. More proof that Cinder-fella's family members taught and rewarded things they needed him to do for them, but they didn't show him how to have fun for himself.

Chasing me down and slapping me with his Frisbee was one of the most endearing things anyone had done with me in years. While Kyle was enjoying childhood in a new way with me, I had all-but-forgotten the joy of childish horseplay myself. We were meeting in the middle and both becoming fourteen. Grandpa was right. My own spark was returning also.

I could tell Kyle was starting to see through my campy ways of overstating amazement at his accomplishments and skills, but at the risk of being seen as an overactor, I was more determined than ever to build him up with every word I spoke. He needed to see himself through eyes like the ones I saw him through. He needed to learn to accept his abilities. If I could at least *start* some sense of self-worth in him, the personal reward for me would be life-changing. The challenge of trying to right the wrongs of others by simply being the best person I could be was turning out to be deeply rewarding.

To give is to get

My family had been missing my spark since the cancer had mellowed me down, but now this kid was rekindling that spark by injecting a much-needed youthful vigor back into my body and soul.

Because of him that summer, my own mortality came into question. Why had I been suspecting my cancer was returning, and at the same time, choosing not to be tested? The intelligent part of my brain wanted a blood test at the very least. Perhaps I was afraid of the prognosis. If I had cancer again, I'd have to stop living my free life and immediately check into the prison of a hospital. I'd have to worry my family all over again.

Further thought then brought me to suspect a third reason. This is difficult to admit, but looking back, I'd say I just didn't want to enter back into a fight for a life I wasn't enjoying. Maybe it wasn't a full-on death wish, but putting up another life or death fight didn't seem to have a big reward at the end. To put it more simply, I didn't seem to realize I had something to live for.

Ronnie may have been right; I wasn't "forlorn." I'd been clinically depressed for years, but I didn't know it. When cancer struck, I became the recipient of sympathy, assistance, prayers, and love from all angles. Without realizing it, I had not only received love but hadn't been required to give it back. Kyle was turning out to be the first person actually to need *me* since cancer.

Ronnie wanted me to find someone who could help, and technically, I think I just did.

PART 3

TESTING PERIOD:

LEARNING TO TRUST WHERE TRUST HAS NEVER BEEN

26

Telephobia

    The problem facing our friendship now was going to be with my hypervigilance. I was learning to trust Tuck, but with my ticking-time-bomb-tendency to misinterpret and sporadically fly off the handle, could he trust me? As is common in people with PTSD, my fight-or-flight response was always set to "panic." Still is. Something like that never goes away. As an adult now, I've learned how to embrace and control it as a secret weapon, which gives boundless energy to complete any task faster and more thoroughly than anyone else can. But at fourteen, I didn't have any clue how to control it. This would tax Tuck's patience to its core.

By Kyle Rickett

    At six o'clock that evening, we were at Papa's house in the middle of a game of *Monopoly* when the phone rang.

"That's gotta be my Pumpkin. The five o'clock news hasn't started yet on that island of hers," Papa guessed on his way to answer it. "Hello?"

It wasn't Mom.

"Who?" Papa bellowed into the phone.

Tuck rolled the dice, intentionally tossing one of them into my lap. It seemed like he was becoming more and more playful as we got to know each other.

"Ha-Hooo!" I caught the die and threw it straight up, pretending it had bounced. "Still in play! You gotta take how it lands. And I hope for a one." I grinned and pointed at his next square—my hotel on Park Place.

"Q-Tip, it's for you." Papa held the receiver toward me.

I went cold. The die bounced against the tabletop. Papa might as well have been pointing a loaded pistol at my face. What the hell was happening to me? I was the victim of *another* bizarre reaction to an everyday event. A kindly old man held a commonplace phone receiver, and I felt like I had walked into an armed robbery. It's just that no one in my present world of Minnesota would call me. Only the past could be calling. Torano Island. Nothing good was happening there. And there was nothing in my past on that island that I wanted to hear about.

"Kyle?" Tuck calmly checked in. "What's wrong, Buddy?"

"Who is it, Papa?" My mouth dried. The room went two-dimensional. The moment wasn't real. I was in trouble. Someone might have been calling into my serenity to accuse me of something I didn't know how to defend.

"I don't know. Sounds like he's about your age." He shook the receiver one time. "C'mon, boy. He sounds friendly."

I got up, almost tripping on the table leg, and shot a look of concern toward Tuck. I honestly didn't know why this was so frightening. I was becoming the not-so-proud owner of yet another new phobia. First of bees and cameras, then of men like Tuck following me into my room or complimenting my cooking, and now I was afraid of *telephones*? What was next—light switches and ladybugs? If the list of my fears kept growing, I was going to be in a rubber room before turning fifteen.

The GOAT DRIVE

"Hello?" I whispered meekly into the scary device.

"Guess vat I huff in my hens rrrright now!" blared an impersonation of Inspector Carlen. "Issue forty-two. Two copies!" he proudly boasted. "No donuts today, though. And Mr. Hansen says hi."

"Connor!" I started laughing. My heart swelled in my chest. The room became real again. My fears vanished and I was myself in an instant. But Papa and Tuck's expressions were not so cheery. They stared until Papa tugged Tuck into the hallway.

"Kyle!" Connor shouted back.

"Thanks, man," I said into the phone, and then I breathed a long sigh of relief. "I should'a known my best friend would make sure I got my copy. I'll give you money when I come home." I didn't mention that my *new* friend had also bought me a copy, which made me feel like I was cheating on Connor and covering it up. It seemed like everything that happened around me made for another secret I believed I had to protect.

"Don't need to. Your mom paid for it. Her and my mom took me to the dime store today, and then they took me out to breakfast at the Dutch Cupboard in Stanwood. It was fun. Our moms are funny when they're together."

"You had fun...*with my mom?*"

"She's the one who gave me your grandpa's number! She knows I'm calling, but she told me to warn you never to let on to your dad."

"Mom said that?" My jaw slacked. A wave of warmth settled in my throat. I looked toward the hallway entrance where my two allies had ducked away. Maybe Papa was right about her loving me after all. Maybe those words she'd said as I was leaving were absolutely true—that she knew I needed a vacation from her and Dad and that this whole separation really was done for *my* good. I wished I could have figured out what was really going on in their heads, but my family members only told the truth *sometimes*. I had no way of predicting when and where their comments were genuine. "I'm sorry I didn't say goodbye...."

"It's cool. I was pretty bummed at how sad you looked in the taxi, so I begged my mom to call your mom that day. She said you were given this vacation as a surprise to make up for a bad birthday party."

"My birthday sucked."

"I know…I called you…I could hear them screaming at each other."

"Oh." I felt ashamed that he'd heard it. But now, at least, I could breathe easy knowing who was on the other end of the dangling wall phone that day.

"They've been talking a lot ever since." He politely raised the mood up out of my embarrassment. "I hope you're having fun…but when are you coming home?"

"Um. I—I'm not sure. I overheard Papa on the phone last night asking if he could keep me for the rest of the summer." The emotions were complicated. I was sorry Connor missed me and I couldn't wrap my brain around the fact that people really did like me this much.

"Oh," he mumbled. Then he perked up. "I got you a birthday present and I can't wait to give it to you. It's something you've been wanting. Mr. Hansen at the dime store even helped me get it for you."

I glanced through the wide open front door at the trunk lid of Tuck's signet gold GTO parked at the bottom of the stairs. "I can't even guess what it is," I said while rolling my eyes. The signet gold GTO Hot Wheels car was the one thing he and Mr. Hansen both knew I wanted. No doubt that's what he'd found.

"You'll be so surprised, Kyle!"

"I can't wait. And *your* birthday is next week. I'll bring you something from Minnesota. We'll have a private belated party…just you and me."

"That'll be cool," he mumbled again.

"You don't sound happy. Aren't you having any fun?"

"I'm doing okay. But it's the first time since I moved here that I didn't get to go to your party. Now you won't be at mine. It'd be a lot more fun if you were here."

"Sorry about that." Even though it was my family who'd banned Connor unfairly, I felt—as usual—fully responsible for his disappointment.

"It's not your fault…I guess. And I'm keeping busy. I'm reading a new series of books from the library and hanging out with Chad every couple of days."

History repeating itself?

"Ooh. Wrestling on the lawn?"

"Not any more. I'm avoiding doing that with him."

"Why? I thought you said it was fun."

"Let's just sayyyyy…" I could tell he was searching for a nice way of telling me something uncomfortable, "let's say he likes to wrestle in a little friendlier way than I do."

I half-heartedly chuckled.

"It's not that funny, Kyle. I really needed your support bad." He laughed half-heartedly. "He 'accidentally' stuck his hand in my pants the other day when I was pinned."

"Accidentally?"

"That's what he said. But I didn't believe him."

"So what do you do together now?" I felt sick. Blood started draining from my face into my gut.

"Ride bikes mostly. He keeps wanting me to go to the Torano Community Pool with him. He says now that he's sixteen, he can get us in with no lifeguard and we can have the whole pool to ourselves."

"No lifeguard?" Oh God. "*No, Connor!*" I shouted.

A gunshot rang through my head. My scream was accidental. I didn't know it was coming until it was out. My mind flashed back over four years to when Andreo was my official best friend and he was telling me he needed my support. The rest of the blood drained from my face. Andreo's story told of being alone with "an older boy" who grabbed him at that very pool. I'd never let him finish the tale. My own life went into the toilet right after that. I hadn't done anything to help. He had been a mess ever since. He'd hated me for over three years because of it. But Connor…he might have a chance if I could help him this time before it might happen.

"Whoa, Kyle. That hurt my ear."

Through the darkened doorway, Tuck backed in from the hallway, craning his neck my way. Then, as Papa stepped gingerly to join him, I turned and walked as far as the cord would let me in the other direction.

"Connor, listen to me. Don't *ever* go to the pool with him," I whispered so he could hear but they couldn't.

"Why? I've been swimming with him lots of times."

"Alone?"

"No, I don't think so."

"He's getting bolder," I whispered.

"What are you talking about?"

"Don't do it, Connor." My breath went sour. I tasted fear—or maybe it was anger.

"Why not?"

God, grant me the strength to fight back

"I...because I...I knew this kid once." Telling Connor about anything from Catholic school would be the most defeating set of words I'd ever spoken. I looked behind to see who was listening. I had to go on. Connor's safety was more important than my shame.

The men had gone back into the hall, leaving only us vulnerable boys to talk. I stayed conscious, but the room went flat. I was now a robot in a photograph, listening to myself speak as if the lines were written by an author above us. "I...I know him from...Catholic school."

"Whoa. Kyle, man, you *never* talk about school."

"I have to this time." I exhaled loudly. It was too late to hold back now. "He said an older kid did something terrible to him on a day when they had the whole pool to themselves. It was years ago."

"How many years ago?"

"Remember when they stopped letting kids under sixteen in the pool without supervision?"

"Yeah...oh, God. Are you telling me your friend was the reason they made that rule?"

"I'm pretty sure. It happened like the next day after he was attacked. He didn't know the boy who did it to him, but he said he was a couple of years older than us."

"You mean *Chad*?"

"Maybe."

"That's...kind of scary."

"I don't know for sure, but it happened on a spring break, and that's always when Chad's in town. I don't trust him all of a sudden. And if it's him, he's older now. More dangerous."

"What did he do that was so terrible?"

"He grabbed the kid I knew and stripped off his swimsuit. He almost drowned him and scratched his face all up. That's all I know. I never let him finish the story. But Connor—it turned my friend into a total shithead. He's been screwed up because of it ever since. Like maybe it traumatized him or something."

"What do you know about being traumatized?" He giggled lightly.

"I think," I ignored the rebuttal, "whoever it was hurt him bad. It changed his whole personality. I don't want that to happen to you."

Silence.

"Connor, I *mean* it! I don't want that to happen to you!" My eyes heated and welled. My breath began to quiver and my hands to tingle. Was he going to listen to me? I was sixteen-hundred miles away. The only power I had to save him was in getting him to promise he'd listen. Panic rose up again. "*Please*, Connor. I *can't lose another friend*!"

"Um. Are you *sure* it was Chad? We've known him for years."

"No one knows who the guy was," I said, pleading for him to listen to my words, "but promise me you'll *never* go in that pool unless there's a bunch of people in it. 'Kay?"

Silence.

"Even if it wasn't him, never go there with Chad—in case."

"Okay, Kyle."

"*Promise me*!" I stomped my foot on the floor, almost crying. The phone was shaking against my cheek. Papa and Tuck didn't hear the conversation, but they heard the stomp.

"Kyle, is everything all right?" Tuck stepped back in.

I nodded and looked away again.

"Okay," Connor conceded. "If it means that much to you. We were going to go tomorrow, but I'll fake a cold."

"To-*morrow*? No, no, no, no, Connor, please fake that cold!" I felt Tuck's gentle hand on my shoulder.

"I will. I told you!"

"PROMISE ME!" I screamed.

Tuck's hand squeezed.

"Okay, okay, okay…I *promise*. I cross my heart."

"Thanks, Connor," I said, calming down. "*Tomorrow*? Thank God you called tonight." I believed him, but the stakes were high and I needed one more ounce of confidence. "You believe me that it's important—right?" I turned to look into Tuck's worried eyes.

"You're freaking me out right now, so it must be. And after what his hand did the other day, I guess I should believe you."

"He didn't hurt you, did he?" I was ready to bawl. A tear streamed down my cheek. But I mouthed, "I'm okay," to Tuck and politely backed away again.

Tuck winced suspiciously, but he respected my pulling away. He turned back toward Papa but stayed close.

"No. But he creeped me out. He talked me into taking off my shirt, and then when we started playing, his hand 'accidentally' went up inside my shorts. Kyle, he grabbed my…thing. I needed to talk to you so bad that day."

"Oh, Connor." I held my breath to stop a wail from blasting out of my mouth. Just by hearing him say Chad's hand did that made my body hurt like Krieg was doing it to me right then and there.

The GOAT DRIVE

"It's okay now. I pretended I heard my mom calling and ran home."

"Oh, shit." I had to pause so I could breathe and hold back hysterics. When I'd calmed down enough to speak, I continued, "You're making me want to come home now."

"Why? To protect me?" He laughed for a few seconds. "You're the smallest kid on the block."

"Yeah, asshole! I may be small, but I'm the strongest hell-of-an-ant in the whole hell-of-a-hill." I nervously laughed back and wiped another stress-tear off my cheek with the back of a hand. "A million-billion times the strongest!"

Silence.

"Kyle, don't worry, okay? I know how you get."

"What the hell does *that* mean?"

"It means you're the most nervous kid I know, and you're probably shaking right now, and you're going to take extra antacids tonight from worry. So *don't*! Please, trust me. I'm your best friend. If it's that important to you, I'm going to hold to my promise and not go near him again. At least until we find out who hurt that kid you knew."

"Thank you, Connor." My nose started to run from the stress. Tuck handed me a paper towel. His head shook when he saw my hand quaking as I took it. "This is super-important." I wiped my face. "I'm your best friend too."

"I promise I'll be safe. And dooooon't worryyyy! You're going to get an ulcer. There's a ton of other kids I can play with a few houses up. If you're back in time, we'll go get issue forty-three together and Mr. Hansen'll be glad to see you too."

"One more year, Connor." I believed him now, and as my heart settled in my chest, my forehead started sweating.

"I know!" his voice raised excitedly. "I can't wait until high school! My school friends are going to like you."

"I can't wait to meet them." That was a nice compliment. I liked it better than what Mom had always told me—that whatever was happening in Catholic school would be worse in public school. Connor was easier to read than Mom. I trusted him more.

Papa Louie to the rescue

As I hung up, I heard the toilet flush and the faucet hiss. Seconds later, Papa came into the kitchen. He ruffled my hair.

"So you got Connor back, huh?"

"Yeah." I beamed. "Now I have more friends than only my favorite crazy old man." I chuckled.

"Someone snuck a phone number under old John's nose?"

"Did…you…?" I laughed like I'd caught him stealing cookies.

"I might have mentioned a little something to a certain pumpkin I know." His brows wiggled. "I told you there's nothin' wrong with you. I'm sure that boy was damn glad to talk to you."

"I was damn glad to talk to him too, Papa." I might have literally saved my best friend from being the victim of an ugly, ugly crime, one that my previous best friend had never recovered from. Now, more than ever, I wished I'd let Andreo finish his story. Whatever that older boy had done could never happen again.

I glanced at Tuck, who wasn't smiling. He looked angry.

"Q-Tip," Papa consoled. "Maybe life's not so bad, huh?"

"It's getting better fast." I grinned while Papa squeezed my neck. I shot a look to Tuck who didn't seem to buy my smile.

27

Reality Deepens

Tuck found it both easy and difficult to honor his promise to Papa Louie. No matter how much he wanted to help, at fourteen, I could be tough to deal with. I didn't mean to be, but now I was the one testing his ability to trust me.

By Tuck Taylor

Kyle's phone call seriously distressed me. It answered one question and raised a hundred more. His puzzling island drama was now more real to me than ever, but also more mysterious. If I could have heard both sides of the conversation, I might have been able to make more sense out of all that was going on. The weightiness in Kyle's voice and his shaking body proved that whatever it was, it was real and it was bad. It was *real bad*.

I now believed Louie's outrageous concerns to be more in-line than I'd originally thought. Kyle may indeed have had enemies who were causing him to be afraid for his life after all.

But damn it! How was I going to get him to talk without going into another one of his crazy spells like I'd seen him do at the gazebo?

28

My Crazy Place

PTSD wouldn't go away just because I'd made a new friend. In fact, becoming comfortable and letting someone get close may have actually tightened its grip. Tuck was about to witness for himself the increasingly uncontrollable and stark division between my clearly separated worlds. He was about to witness me go body, mind, and spirit headlong into my crazy place.

By Kyle Rickett

Tuck was quiet as we got back to our game. Was he mad? That's usually what the silent treatment means. I might have hurt his feelings by turning to talk to Connor. But I didn't have a choice. Still, I shouldn't have done it. I was rude.

As he sulked, I was becoming a nervous wreck. I needed to make it up somehow. He'd bought me sandals, licorice, and issue forty-two. What was the *matter* with me? I owed him now. Meanwhile, Papa had gone back to his *Gilligan's Island* reruns. Every now and then we'd hear him laugh softly.

"You trust me, right?" Tuck asked without looking at me.

"Yeah. A lot."

"Then talk to me."

I nervously bit my lower lip.

"Why did Louie have to sneak a phone number to Connor?" We faced each other, but his gaze was fixed toward his hand gently chopping at the table with a Get Out of Jail Free card. He'd rotate it and tap rhythmically. Click-clack-tap. Click-clack-tap.

I didn't speak. Muteness happens when I get scared. He looked angry and I couldn't deal with it. My family had always won almost every fight. If I ever got my way, they waited until my guard was down and punished me later. So I learned always to let them win the first time. I only suffered longer and harder if I kept fighting back, so when people were mad at me in those days, my mind would blank until the fight was over. The room would darken. My body would go numb like my brain had disconnected and floated off where it could feel safe.

"Yesterday you told me you liked Connor almost as much as Scooter. But that's all you said."

"It's true. I didn't lie."

"Louie's concerned. Says you told him Monday that you and Connor aren't allowed to be together anymore. You forgot to tell me that part."

"It's complicated."

"I'm smart. I can handle complication."

I bit my lip some more.

"Banning you from your best friend is a bit harsh, don't you think? He says you two were close. And so you know—I'm not above bragging; I'm the one who talked Louie into calling your mom about it." He smiled like I owed him a thank you.

"Thanks, Tuck." I half-smiled back. "But it's stupid." Fear gripped my heart and started squeezing. I could feel my entire life sneaking up from behind, ready to gush out onto the table if I answered any question too honestly. Silence was safety. I'd been a Rickett long enough to know that anytime my "allies" learned something new about me, I somehow found myself very sorry they had. If I didn't breach this dam carefully, the entire ocean of truth about the whole summer—about Krieg and me, and my memories of being with him other times—would crash in and destroy what little joy I'd been able to build here, sixteen-hundred miles from the real *Disaster Island*.

"Humor me. What's stupid about it?"

"Dad caught us talking about…sex." That was good. Honest, but not revealing. I slumped and secretly put a hand over my burning stomach beneath the table. I hated lying, but I was in no position to spill my humiliation.

"So?" Tuck's gentle laugh reassured that he might not be angry.

I let go of my aching gut and teasingly grabbed at his card between taps. It became an ax to chop at my thumb; his eyes locked into mine and winked. I smiled and blushed. He smiled and gently shook his head. I think we'd just had a full conversation with only our faces. I felt better already.

"You're fourteen," he lightheartedly announced, chopping at my thumb a second time. "I'd be worried about you if you and your buddies *weren't* talking about sex."

"The topic has never gone well for me." I leaned back. "It's a dangerous subject at my house."

"Catholics. Humph!" he grunted. "So you got sent to Minnesota because you were being a normal boy? You're here because of religious stupidity?"

"Nooo…my parents aren't stupid." I needed to change the subject from me and sex. "They've had a bad summer. Fran's been giving them trouble—Dad loaned Mom's car to her and Mom's so mad she sent me here so I don't have to put up with their fighting."

"So, if this is about Fran, why didn't they send *her* away? It sounds like *she's* the problem."

"She's an adult."

"Not from what I've been hearing."

I glanced up into his eyes. It seemed like he knew an awful lot about my visit. What all had Papa told him? This was starting to feel a lot like home where Mom, Fran, Dad, Daniel, and even Auntie Maureen seemed always to be discussing my life behind my back. Usually, it was so they could band together to talk me in or out of things. At home, I was always outnumbered and surrounded like I was one team and everyone else was the other team. I wished my life wasn't feeling the same way in Minnesota all of a sudden.

"I still think there's more to the story than that. First, you said this was because you were talking sex with a buddy, but now, you're saying it's about your dad giving in to Fran again. Neither of those things are enough to send a kid away."

Always the defensive stance

I swallowed hard. Why did I have to be on the defensive all the time? Why couldn't people accept my words as fact without challenging me? I was getting irritated as I thought of how close I was to telling too much. I knew how this worked. My face always gave me away. If I uttered so much as a single word that conflicted with what they'd been saying about me behind my back, I'd be labeled a liar, which would render every word I spoke after that useless. If I did try to lie, Tuck would know it because I hated lying so much that my face would turn pink if I so much as thought about fibbing. If I held back too much, he'd dig and make me say more. If I said one word too many, and if he were to start asking interrogating questions, I'd end up going into hyper-defensive jitters and my mouth would start confessing things my brain wouldn't be able to stop. This was almost a perfect checkmate. That's how it worked at Catholic school and at home with Mom and Fran. I learned that everything they knew about me gave them one more thing to criticize or even punish. I had to hold back. I couldn't let Tuck know who I was having sex with. He'd hate me for sure.

"When Dad threw him out, I knew he was gone for the whole summer. In fact, he told me on the phone tonight not to let Dad know he'd gotten this number."

"You're dad's abusive, isn't he? I can tell."

"No!" That brought a tinge of anger into my defenses, "I *love* my dad. He's quiet and hard-working. He gets..." I sighed, "stressed sometimes."

"Oh, I see. He only hits you when he's stressed." He frowned. "I hear that a lot."

"No!"

"Come on. He's *never* hit you?"

"No!" The questions were making me mad.

"Not even once?"

"No, Tuck. I promise! He's never hit me. He's never hit *anyone* as far as I know. He yells and makes us feel sorry for him so we'll stop doing whatever is stressing him out."

"Stressing him out? Two normal teen boys talking about sex *stressed him out*? Was he never fourteen?"

I shrugged.

"I don't see how your dad could be stressed over you talking about sex with a buddy."

I couldn't think of a single word that wouldn't leave me needing to explain that the sex was between Dad's adult best friend and his minor son. *That* would be "the stress he couldn't deal with." The ache in my stomach got way worse.

"Are you okay?" He stared at my hand on my stomach.

"I'll be okay in a minute."

His shoulders deflated as he exhaled. "You know what? Forget it. Let's look at the good things in your world." He let go of the card and let me snatch it. He then patted the back of my hand three times consolingly. "Connor's back in your life. At least someone's on your side."

"You and Papa *made* her give him the number." Angrily, I gave him back his card, rolled the dice, and counted out my move. "So yeah. At least *someone's* on my side." I pointed at him, then at Papa. "But no one on that stupid island."

"Louie says she loves you, Kyle. He's pretty sure of it. Moms can be fickle creatures." He purposely chuckled to help me lighten up. "Especially after a summer of arguing with a 'stressed' husband and a 'difficult' daughter. Louie says she's got her hands full there. And that your dad can be moody."

"Papa's always tough on my poor dad," I complained.

"Is he right? Is John Rickett moody?"

I wanted to say no, but the answer was yes. So I shrugged and nodded with a submissive half-smile.

"Maybe you could give her some bonus points for having to deal with your dad. Louie says she's miserable over how tough this summer's been on *you*."

"That's Papa wanting to believe nice things about his pumpkin."

"I wasn't supposed to tell you this, but she wants you back already, and Louie's refusing to send you."

"She wants me?" I laughed and looked down shyly at the game board. "Papa won't give me back?" My feet started kicking together and I slowly realigned the row of little green houses on my properties.

"But, Kyle, he's fighting her. He doesn't think you're safe there."

I flinched. He saw it. I closed my mouth tightly. There was no doubt in my mind that he had read my face and knew Papa was right—I wasn't safe there.

My crazy place

"Kyle, I'm getting seriously worried here." Tuck put his hands into his lap and engaged me eye to eye. "The conversation you had with your friend was serious. I think it had something to do with how miserable you were when I met you. And maybe even more the reason you're *really* here."

"What do you mean, 'the reason I'm *really* here'? Don't you believe me?" Uh, oh. Anger was bubbling. And not good anger, but righteous indignation. The *stupid* kind that doesn't think before it lashes out. I was about to lose control. Fourteen years of stuffing was about to gush.

"Oh, come on, Kyle. I've never seen anyone explode the way you did when you and Louie met up in the gazebo. I'm not an idiot! That's not how an almost grown adult behaves when his mom's car gets loaned out."

I couldn't speak. I couldn't think. Wait...what did he say? I couldn't remember the last words he'd spoken. How was I supposed to respond if I couldn't remember what we were talking about? The room was going two-dimensional again. Flat, like a meaningless photograph.

"Kyle...buddy...you're turning gray. Are you okay?"

"I'm sick." There. I had a response. It was a dumb lie, but it gave me enough power to control at least some of this conversation. "I think I need to go to bed."

"No, Kyle! Come *on*! You were just loosening up. It was getting good."

"I'm about to throw up." I got up. "I'll see you tomorrow, okay?"

"No! Where the hell are you going? *Don't you walk out on me!*"

I shuffled to my bedroom and closed the door. What was wrong with me? Tuck was the only friend I was allowed near, and I'd just walked out on him because he was trying to help. Anger felt fitting—but unwelcome. I was in a hurricane of emotions and thoughts. Heat boiled up out of my gut and the room was surreal. I was scared of the anger because I didn't seem to have control over it. But at the same time, it was delicious. I could taste my righteous reaction to the fact that the world sucked and, like a drug, I wanted more anger. I was a mess. I may have deserved to feel anger's sting, but I wasn't handling it right.

"Kyle?" Three taps on the door went unanswered. I stared, hoping he wouldn't come in—no—hoping he *would* come in. And that he'd grab me and make me explode and release all of it. Yeah. That was good. He'd let me rant and scream and pound on walls. He'd hold me back while I tore wildly at the wall photos. I wanted his help, but I couldn't ask him for it. I was desperate and needed him. I needed a grown man to show me how to get through this insane rage. I was so mad I was crazy with confusion. I couldn't talk. I couldn't think. My brain was out of my body.

He didn't open the door.

Why didn't he open the door?

Why didn't he charge at me, embrace me, and force me to scream into his shoulder, telling him the whole truth about everything?

When I heard the Goat fire up and gravel fly from beneath its angry wheels, all my rage left. Tears began falling down my face. I was suddenly hollow and lost just like at the train station.

"Oh, my God…." I stared intently at the silent doorknob. "What have I done?"

29

Total Frustration

Trust is at the core of everything for everyone—even Tuck, who was about to give up and stop trying to pry information from me. He faced a monumental task because if he was destined to teach someone how to trust, then he had two students: Me and himself.

By Tuck Taylor

I drove off angry—furious, even. Twisted like a pretzel. Kyle was pushing my buttons again like no one in the world could do. Couldn't he fucking see that I was trying to help?

I'd learned that my temper was manageable as long as I had some sense of control. Louie and Grandpa had fed my confidence into believing I could help Kyle. But God damn it, Kyle's walking off took away all the control and tore my confidence in half.

I'd dug and dug into his mind and could *not* figure out who was threatening him. I had no authority to force an answer. I wanted to help the little twerp, but he was pushing me away. He'd slammed a door in my face both physically and emotionally. It hurt. I was ready to leave, but at the same time, conflicted. I'd only known him five days, but that was already a lifetime. Could I leave and forget about him? Probably not. For me, those were five significant days. Considering where I was in my life at that time, somehow that kid had become my best friend—shit, he was my *only* friend. Why the fuck wouldn't he just open up and tell me what the hell was wrong? Was this to be the next in a long string of friendships I couldn't make last?

I turned right instead of left at the end of Louie's driveway. If ever there was a night for a long drive in solitary thought, this was it. I had no plan for where to go. Before me were unlimited choices of roads to drive on for as long and far as I wanted.

I didn't know where to go, but my right foot only wanted to stay on the throttle. There would be no turning around in the foreseeable hours. I glanced at the gas gauge. Full. I felt my back pocket for my wallet. It was there. I had all night if I needed it.

30

Papa's Scolding

Were my allies truly ready to stick by me no matter what? Papa, Scooter, Connor, and now Tuck? A growing sense of isolation is all too often the culprit that destroys depressed teens. All I had to do was stop blending them into the category with my bullies. They were the guys on my team. I needed to learn how to discern the difference between bullies and allies. It was up to me now to become their ally and then to accept that position no matter how tempting it would be to play their victim—as if they were the bullies.

By Kyle Rickett

"What the hell was that about?" Papa didn't knock—he barged in. "Why did he tromp out'a here?"

I teetered on the bed's edge, rocking to and fro, toes on the floor, clutching issue forty-two carefully but tightly. Sweat coated my face, neck, chest, and arms. My mind was still partly outside my body. The room was still more a photograph than reality. The skin on my face was numb, but my eye sockets were hot. The comic book was shaking in my grip, but I couldn't feel it. Had I blown my chance at the camping trip—with my only friend?

"Tuck didn't say anything wrong, Papa," I whispered loudly.

"That's what I figured."

"Why did I get so mad?" I wasn't fully inhabiting my physical body, and pushing out words was a chore for my lungs. I was struggling to breathe. My life with PTSD symptoms had begun. I didn't understand it at the time, but the numbness, dissociations, and depersonalization were locking in as a part and parcel of who I was becoming.

"That's what I want to know too. You was happier than ever. Now you're crazy sad. What's got you so twisted up?"

"He didn't do anything." I had a handkerchief to wipe tears and blow my nose. "I *hate* being mad. I can't control it. I'm scared." I was still struggling to speak, my words beginning to quiver. I had absolutely no control over my emotions.

"Why?" Softening his tone, he sat down beside me. "I known you your whole life. This ain't like you."

The bed sagged and I fell against his shoulder. The warmth of his body brought me back into mine. With eyes shut, I drew in the scent of his old flannel shirt, which made the room feel real again.

"I don't know. I just am. I try to be nice and everybody hates me." I heard my beating heart again. "If I get mad, they hate me even more. I want to see Connor and Scooter, but I'm not allowed. So I want to stay here with you. But now I don't have any friends here either." I was reentering my body quickly. Emotions began to overwhelm.

"You still got me." He pulled me in for a quick squeeze.

"I had another one, but he left…I made Tuck *le-he-heeeeeve*! I'm *so stupid*!" I started crying too hard to talk or think. It took a minute before I could add, "What's *wrong* with me? Why can't I have friends?" I sniffled. "And why is *everything* scaring me?" I threw an arm toward the door. "It's going to be *light switches* next. I'm scared of *phones* now! And I don't know why I get *so mad!*" I pounded my knee. My teeth clenched. I was definitely fully present in the room now—but not in control of myself.

The GOAT DRIVE

"You stay put. I'll be back with something nice." Papa gently pushed me aside to sit on my own. He left the room for about seven or eight minutes and came back with warm cocoa he'd made on the stove. I'd had those minutes to stop crying and think, but it did little good. I was as confused as when he'd left.

"Here, you drink this slow." He handed me the cup, took the comic book, and laid it on the dresser while I sipped. It's what Papa knew how to do; give me nice treats and take care of my possessions.

"Do you think he'll come back?" I sniffled.

"I called Tucker. He didn't go home."

"Where did he go?" My heart sank even lower and my chin wrinkled. Another tear fell.

"It don't matter where he went. He can't stay gone all night. Tucker will call me when he comes home."

"Oh. I'm so stupid."

"Now you stop that, boy. I'm tired of hearin' it. You ain't stupid. And I'm sick a' hearin' you got no friends, too. That whole thing don't make no sense to me. Something's wrong with all of it. But not because a you bein' stupid. None of my grandkids are stupid."

Papa was being nice. According to my poor grades, my need to play with toy cars, and my obvious lack of friends—I was definitely stupid. As far as I was concerned, he was lying to be nice. I was sure his kind words were not about me not being stupid, but about secretly reprimanding me to stop saying it out loud to him.

Reload

Papa eventually left me there to think, and to putter around the room trying to keep myself busy. I used the time to take the clothes out of my top drawer and obsessively refold everything, then compulsively stack it back in by color. The two shirts Tuck had bought were the last items in my hand. As I squeezed, I pictured the fun we'd had buying them. But then, in a fit of self-hatred, I threw them at the closet door.

"Damn it!" I shouted loud enough for Papa to hear from the kitchen. He ignored both my voice and the thud. I picked them up. They were a gift from my last friend on earth whom I had now offended. I held them to my nose and drew in the smell of the department store and the unworn cloth. Using my sense of smell seemed to be something that could help keep me from leaving my body at times—a trick that still works to this day. I folded them again, put them in the drawer, and looked around at the walls and furniture, assuming this room was going to become my new dungeon to lay around in the way my room at home had become. I rested against the dresser and stood facing the door to contemplate my future. With no ability to keep friends in my life, I was destined to live it alone. I needed to learn to get used to it.

31

Anger Drive

I can't say enough about Tuck's struggles. It's not like he woke up one morning and said, "I'd like to save someone today." Tuck was barely a man, yet he was being dutifully called into action by forces greater than himself. The fact that he'd willingly accepted the challenge didn't make it easier. His internal battles had to be dealt with alongside mine. The thing about young men is that they don't always recognize their own weaknesses until those weaknesses are exposed squarely in front of them. Tuck was about to remember that his own life needed stabilizing because it wasn't as well-controlled as he liked to think it was. Inexperienced or not, it seemed that his growth and mine had somehow both become his sole responsibility

By Tuck Taylor

"I know enough," I griped into the rearview mirror. "The hell I do! I obviously don't know shit from Shinola."

I'd been gone about an hour. My anger-drive took me right to the entrance of Grandpa's Norton Hill dirt road where I'd stopped to think. All I could hear was the low rumble of my idling engine. All I could see in my mind's eye was the white-painted bedroom door *not* opening when I knocked.

"I'm glad I saw his true colors before it was too late." All I could think of was how uncomfortable three days alone in the wilderness would be with unstable Kyle. "There's no way I'm bringing that ungrateful little nut-job up here."

Instead of heading up the gravel for the eight-minute dusty drive to the cabin, I gave into a wave of frustration that started in my chest and rushed like a hurricane to my throttle foot.

"No way, God damn it!" I turned the wheel and hit the gas, shattering the serenity of the peaceful evening with the hot rod roar of a ram-air 400 engine and the squealing of tires. I violently spun the car around in a hundred-eighty-degree half-circle and speed-shifted up to nearly ninety miles an hour, which is when my hot temper cooled and I hit the brakes down to fifty-five. I stayed the course, and the legal speed limit, back to the situation I couldn't run from. I could handle Kyle as long as our grandfathers were there to buffer our personalities, but there would be no way I could deal with that kid alone in the woods. I admit, the high-speed outburst was childish, but at least it broke through my internal tension and cleaned me out. It gave the long ride home a chance to clear my head.

All the windows were open. The sun dipped low enough to brighten my rearview mirrors. The air smelled peaceful and floral as the day began to wind down toward dusk. At fifty-five miles an hour, the Goat had a certain rhythmic hum that soothed the soul while bobbing me gently across the uneven roadway. I was mesmerized.

"How do people survive being actual psychiatrists? This is hard fucking work." I suppose what made it hardest on me was that I was personally invested, not only in Kyle, but in Louie and Grandpa, whose confidence in me added to the surreal pressure I felt at being expected—at only twenty-one—to single-handedly save a human life that I wasn't completely sure *wanted* to be saved.

"I'm not a goddamned superhero!" I shouted at my eyes in the rearview mirror. "This is so unfair to me."

The GOAT DRIVE

I turned the radio on, then switched it off immediately. Silence was better.

"The fucking kid has a split personality. That's what's going on here! God damn it! How am I supposed to cure that?"

Louie's words haunted me. *You don't let him jump.*

"Fuck," I blurted out while running aggravated fingers through my wind-blown hair. "I should have stayed in Texas."

With my outburst done, I drove in silence—for a while, anyway. Eventually, I glanced at the Frisbee on the passenger seat and immediately started to miss the kid's smile and sparkling eyes. I could almost hear his laughter in the buffeting wind. I grabbed my right forearm with my left hand and could nearly feel the warmth from his unusual touch. I pictured him ashamedly looking down at his ugly boat shoes and then bursting with joy the moment I told him I had a pair just like them. I saw his head wiggle side to side while I rubbed fire extinguisher goop off his chest—his sparkling blue eyes staring into mine. I pictured him proudly serving me food, and finally, I burst with an unexpected chuckle at recalling him flexing his small arms.

"God damn it!" I screamed out the window. "Aaaaaargh!"

I like the little fucker

"Shit." I gave in. "This isn't for Louie." With eyes closed, I shook my head. "God help me, I like the little fucker."

The drive back from Norton Hill was a particularly effortless one. There were fifteen minutes on Highway 6, which took me straight back to Deer River, then a left-hand turn followed by a full hour at fifty-five on Highway 2 back to Cloquet, and then just ten minutes or so into what we called *the Greater Duluth area*. Once eastbound on Highway 2, it was easy to get lost in thought for several minutes without having to focus any attention on driving.

Why wouldn't Kyle just open up and tell me why he was in Minnesota? He would come so close, but then he'd stop himself. Was he too confused to know why? Was he intentionally protecting a dark secret? None of my theories made sense. I doubted he was *on the lamb* from having robbed a bank or killed someone. I was still sure an abusive family wouldn't have let him go free where he could be interrogated without supervision by two crazy old men and a college dropout. I had already determined that his pot-smoking days were a fake when he showed no signs of knowing anything at all about drugs or alcohol, and he'd said there were no girls in the picture.

So what the hell was making him so miserable? According to his answers, Kyle's life was little more than a few friends lost, a stressed-out dad, a mom who missed him more than he knew, and an unlikeable sister who was giving his parents a rough summer.

"It doesn't make sense!" I blurted out. "He's not stupid; he's not crazy; he's not mean.... He's *got* to be keeping a secret."

Just then, as if on cue, a faded red Mustang flew past me in the opposite direction. "Trenton?" My heart jumped into my throat and I leaned toward my driver's door mirror to watch it vanish into the distance. It was painted black between the taillights. Trenton's was red front and rear—and he was in New York, last I'd heard. It wasn't him, but the moment of recognition showed me something I hadn't expected: Fear.

"Thank God that wasn't him." It was the first time I'd ever said that. As I thought deeply about what made me afraid of running into him again, I realized that in the months since he'd left me in Texas, I'd been lonely and abandoned, but at the same time relieved not to have his constant manipulative moodiness forcing me to live on eggshells around him.

Louie's words flew across my mind. "*Now, Mr. Taylor, you dig down deep and remember what you thought. Then, you look deep into my Q-Tip's eyes and you'll see it there too.*"

"Could Trenton be my Fran?" If Louie was right that Kyle's sister was a tricky manipulator, then he was also right that I could empathize with Kyle. Trenton was *my* tricky manipulator. Like Kyle with his sister, I loved Trenton. But after he took off, I realized a relief I hadn't expected. A drama queen like him could wear a guy down in ways he doesn't fully grasp until the relationship is over and the drama is forever gone. "Oh, my God! I've walked my mile in Kyle's shoes."

The GOAT DRIVE

There had to be a secret

I was sure of it now. Nothing else added up. The idea, however, of Kyle keeping a secret soured my gut. The only things worth keeping underground were abuse, drugs, robbery, money, murder…or sex…*with someone you aren't supposed to have sex with.*

"Well, I sure as hell understand secrets!" I screamed out the window to the trees whizzing by. "Stupid, fucking, God-damned secrets!"

I sighed heavily. If Kyle was protecting his secrets with the same fervency as I was keeping mine, then I had no right to question why I couldn't get him to open up. I still wasn't ready to talk about having been so irresponsible as to have gotten Shannon pregnant. I also didn't want to discuss having lost Micah, losing Shannon completely—the girl of my dreams—and then ending up in a bizarre, manipulative relationship…*with Trenton*—who after dragging me with him through *his* active sexual escapades, then accused me of having sex with his friend Mark, abandoned me, and left me so screwed up that I couldn't even finish school. Mark and I didn't actually have sex, but we came close, and in 1974, that was enough of a secret to die by. Louie may have said that I was living a good life ever since the cancer, but that's because I just never filled him in on the steady stream of life-altering mistakes I didn't want to admit I was capable of.

Kyle obviously admired me, but little did he or his grandfather know my private life was in chaos. For me, the secrets were as much about being too confused even to know how to talk about them to being quite sure at least one of them could get me killed. "No way would I *ever* tell him—or the grandpas—that I almost…not quite…but *almost* had an affair with a man. What…a…*mess.*

Circular thinking

One thought led to another. What if Kyle and I were walking in the same shoes even more than I had yet to realize? "Oh, God. What if he's gay and doesn't know how to live with it?" I deflated in the driver's seat. I'd just gotten out of that mess with Trenton and Mark. I wasn't ready to delve into it again with Kyle.

"I can't even figure out what the hell I'm all about. I'm not ready to deal with it for *him*."

Speaking my secrets aloud, in the privacy of my own speeding car, was a therapeutic way to verbalize things that had previously only been thoughts locked away in my head. There, in the safety and privacy of the car, I spoke aloud the things I'd pushed down deep enough so that I could never speak of them to anyone else. But as I broached my secrets, it seemed that they were all living together in a certain recess of my brain, and once I opened the door to look at one of them, the rest came to consciousness with it. Of all my secrets, Trenton's friend Mark was my most dangerous, but Micah was my most beloved. I was the only person alive who knew I believed I had been the cause of my son's death. That was a secret I wasn't ready to let out to anyone, anywhere, ever.

"I miss you so much, Micah."

Not long after Micah's death, Shannon's world darkened so badly that she journeyed away from me in search of a whole new life. After cancer, she, Trenton, and Ronnie became the only three people I felt truly connected with at the soul level. Her leaving devastated me. I had fully adopted the childhood assumptions that she and I would move into adulthood together. When it didn't happen, my brain couldn't make sense of it. I'd had no plan B. The loneliness and disbelief obsessed me for nearly an entire summer. That's when Trenton stepped up to somehow become my next drama. He was a tad older than me and probably took advantage of my emotional firestorm, but in the confusion I was in, he gave me something I needed. He surrounded and occupied my life, which—right or wrong—pulled me up from the worst of it. He was so different from Shannon that he kept my mind off of her. I couldn't hate him for that. The next problem in line was a return to the loneliness. Trenton's later abandonment dropped me back into the pity pot I'd been in when Shannon left. A very different partner, but the same hollow landing spot.

"I sure could use a strong shoulder to lean on now."

The misery was consuming me quickly.

"*God*!" I screamed. "I miss Trenton so *bad*!" I shouted it over and over into the solitude of the highway. I didn't mean it. I still never wanted to see him again, but the fact was that I missed some of what he gave me—companionship itself.

The GOAT DRIVE

Kyle had recently lost his favorite cousin and his best friend, apparently at the same time. Was I now feeling what he was going through?

"No wonder his stomach hurts all the time."

The magic car

"It sure is easy to be honest in a car." I smiled at myself in the mirror. "I can say *anything* here."

I drove in silence for only a few seconds while my mind wandered back to my mission.

"If only I could get Kyle to talk to me the way *I* can talk to me." I laughed as if I were talking to the Goat itself. "You're my best friend again!" I high-fived the steering wheel. "I can say things to you I can't say to anyone else. We can go places together."

I looked again at the Frisbee on Kyle's seat. Then again at my eyes in the rearview mirror. Then again at Kyle's empty seat.

"Holy shit. That's the answer!"

That's when the idea hit me.

"He loves this *car*!"

The GOAT DRIVE

32

Wisdom of an Old Man

Our mistakes don't define us. How we recover is how we show the world what we are made of. The measure of a true friend is not that he be slow to anger, but that he is quick to forgive. In the adversity of our mutual temper-flair, Tuck returned quickly and proved his spirit to be bigger than his human temper. He was a real superhero.

By Kyle Rickett

The phone rang. My heart skipped a beat. I tried to listen, but I could only hear Papa's dull low tones. Finally, he said, "Ya, ya, okay."

I stayed put. The creaky hallway floor gave him away. He was coming to talk to me. Within a few long seconds, he appeared in my open door.

"Okay, Q-Tip. He's coming back."

I thanked God through closed eyes and a silent prayer.

"Is he mad?" I mumbled.

"Ya."

"Oh."

"Are you?"

"No!" I blurted quickly, eyes wide open. I took two steps toward him. "I'll never get mad at him again—ever."

"Well," he smirked, "don't be too quick with a promise like that. Friends have scraps."

"Not us. I'm never going to fight with him again!"

"Q-Tip—" He stepped into my space and pulled my head to his chest with both arms, "you been here almost a week. You gotta start talkin'." He gently pushed me to arm's length away. "This is gettin' old."

"Papa, you don't know what it's like for me. What if I get mad again?" I sat back down on the bed. Papa sat with me. I didn't lean into him this time. Instead, I pulled a leg up and twisted to face him.

"What do you mean I 'don't know what it's like'? You think I never been mad? I was a boy once. I been mad plenty. You got a fire in your gut. You'll have it till you're old. All boys have it. I had it too. In the mountain shack in Austria, me and Teddy was startin' to grow strong and wasn't seein' eye to eye. My father had enough. He locked us in a room like this one because we couldn't stop yellin'."

"Did it calm you down?"

"We took to fists." Papa laughed. His older brother, Teddy, had been dead for decades, but we grandkids had heard enough lore to think we'd known him. "I tried gettin' out, but father held the door."

"That was mean."

"It worked."

"You talked?"

"We...took...to...*punches*." Words metered out slowly.

"How did *that* help?" I couldn't see the logic. "Who won?"

"We don't know. By the time both of us was bleedin' out the nose, we was laughin' too hard to keep fightin'." He chuckled again.

I gave up a gentle laugh with him. "I'm not going to punch him, Papa."

"I know that. You two's got a lot more in common than Teddy and me did…" He poked at his own forehead as he finished, "and I'm a lot smarter than my father. But you're even smarter than me. You gotta talk, boy."

"I can't. I don't know what to say."

"You listen to me." The room went silent. He didn't utter another word until I looked into his eyes. "I can see you two's good for each other. Neither a you is fightin' men, and I'm not usually a scolder, but I'm telling you now that *I want you to talk to him.*"

"But I told you; I don't know what to say."

"You do your best to figure it out." A finger tapped my chest firmly but caringly. "You hear me?"

I nodded.

"Don't make him go his way. He's not family—he can leave. And if you make him leave twice, I don't think I can get him back again."

I nodded in full agreement.

"He's almost a psychiatrist, you know."

I laughed, which pushed a few parked tears down my cheeks and forced me to need to blow my nose.

"See there? Me saying something about him makes you happy." He patted my bare knee. His big, leathery hand was warm. No one I knew had such a strong *and* comforting touch. "You only just met him. But I known him his whole life. He has a temper, but he gets over his mads quick—until he's had enough. He's like any man. Once he's had enough, then he walks away for good. Hear me?"

"I won't make him walk away, Papa. I promise."

A lesson on how to trust

"Good. Make yourself trust him, boy." He poked at my chest again. "You already trust me and I'm tellin' you to trust him, so take my word for what it's worth and make yourself do it. Once you do…once you trust him…your words will come. Somehow, you'll know what to say."

I smiled at his reassurance. He sounded like he knew what he was talking about. The room we sat in continued to become more real and three-dimensional as Papa put my fears to rest.

"Will you be holding the door closed?" I quietly teased.

"Won't need to." He stood up. "You're smarter than I was. And now you know you only got one more chance." As he turned to walk off, he added, "You'll be holdin' your own door."

Papa left me there to think. I sat on the floor and hugged my knees. I recalled my diary entry of promising myself to trust Tuck no matter what flashed to mind. Papa was right when he instructed me to trust his trust for Tuck. If I truly believed in Papa's ability to know people, then I could use that as more reason to put my faith in anyone he had faith in. He and Tuck together were teaching me some techniques to learn *how* to trust the right people. I sat perfectly still as the room began to darken and the crickets took to singing.

Off in the distant valley, I heard a rumbling train blow its horn. Tuck was only a few thousand feet to the west of us, but the room darkened more and more while I waited and waited and waited, not moving a muscle. Exactly when was he planning to come back?

The GOAT DRIVE

33

Return with Reservations

Tuck was mad, but our friendship was four men strong. He and I were both a part of an alliance now with two crazy old men who loved us too much to let either of us get away with acting like asses.

By Tuck Taylor

I was emotionally drained when I rolled quietly into Grandpa's driveway at 9:00 p.m. I'd been missing for nearly three hours. Dusk was coming down on us. Off in the distant valley, I heard a rumbling train blow its horn. Such a lonesome sound. Louie's words rang again: *"You don't let him jump."*

The Goat had burned three-fourths of its tank while giving me ample time to think. Definitely worth the eight dollars it cost in those days. I silenced the engine and enjoyed a few quiet moments of a gentle warm evening stillness.

At the moment I walked into the house, Grandpa called Louie. I wanted a break because I needed time to think about what to say to the kid, but Grandpa was too quick to offer a promise I'd return, so now I was committed.

What was I supposed to say when I got there? There was no way I could take Kyle up to the mountains now. No way I wanted anyone ever to have any ammunition to call me a pervert if they ever found out that I'd taken a minor "with secrets" into the mountains. Trenton had accused me of messing around with his friend, and I was never really able to convince him that I hadn't done it. I did not need that to happen again.

I needed to know more about Kyle. What if he were to proposition me while we were alone? I wouldn't begin to know how to respond—*he was a kid*. I think the greatest concern I had was that he was an emotional wreck who seemed to like my attention. While I'd been intentionally trying to get close to him, now I suddenly worried I'd done too good a job and had perhaps given him a wrong message. Was I prepared for that?

My final decision was that I wouldn't be alone with him again until I knew his secret was something I could deal with under scrutiny. I just needed to find a polite way to give him the bad news—that the trip was off. For the first time, I was going to break my promise to him, and I felt like shit over it.

For now, I'd go see him, as Grandpa had promised I would, but first I was going to eat. Slowly. The little shit walked out on me. He could wait a little longer as far as I was concerned.

34

My Personal Shrink

Tuck came back. He was different. He was far, far more of an elder than a friend this time. He was—once again—exactly what I needed.

By Kyle Rickett

"Knock, knock." Tuck's quiet voice cut open the silence.

I perked up as his shadow appeared within the open door.

"You gonna let me in this time?" The empty room filled with his soothing presence.

"I'm glad you came back.... I...I wish you would have come in earlier."

"You *wanted* me to come in?"

"Yes. No. I don't...uh!" I shrunk. "I don't know."

"Kyle..." His head shook angrily, "you didn't...." He sighed and aggressively finger-tip-combed his hair back once. "Never mind."

"I just know I'm sorry I didn't open the door."

"Yeah, well, so am I." He slid a hand up and down the wall until a light switch clicked and the room brightened fast. Apparently, the night had gotten darker than I'd realized while I'd been sitting there.

I almost smiled when I saw his face. Again, he looked like an older version of Connor, coming to visit me in my dungeon.

"So why didn't you?" he asked, still angry. "And why did you walk away in the first place? We were having a fun day and then, bam! You really hurt my feelings."

"Well, so did you!" I was the victim here—not *him*.

"Hey! I didn't say *anything* hurtful. I'm the one who should be mad. I was having the best day since high school, until you ruined it."

"Until I *ruined* it?"

"You walked off and wouldn't answer the door. That's got rude-jerk written all over it. I don't like rude people."

"Well, then...." Papa's words flashed back and so did the memory of the Goat throwing gravel. My face heated and turned red. "No! I'm wrong. I'm sorry. I was having a good day too. Best one of my whole life."

"Then what the hell...?"

"I was scared."

"Why?"

"It's complicated. My whole life is complicated."

"Complicated." He huffed a quiet laugh. "No shit, Sherlock. If you're anything, you're complicated."

"And I really did get sick for a minute."

"Because of some mysterious thing I said?" His voice was calm, but irritated. His eyes dropped to my feet where I was gently fingering my new sandals. "How am I supposed to trust you if I don't know what I say that makes you run off? That doesn't make me comfortable in conversations, you know."

"Trust *me*? How can you *not* trust me?" How could anybody not trust me? I'd never done anything to hurt anyone—had I?

"You walked off!" He sighed. "Maybe you thought I'd said something attacking—which I *hadn't*. I was asking questions to try to help somehow. How's that an attack? But when you abandoned me without saying why...well *that* was a bold move."

I stared into his eyes while trying to comprehend what he was telling me.

"How do I know you won't do it again?"

I pictured the moment I'd walked away and realized I'd looked just like Fran, who'd done that same move a thousand times. It always hurt Mom and me—which is exactly what it was meant to do. Tuck's point made ugly sense. Copying Fran's habits was automatic for me. It was my reaction to stress that I'd been taught through repeated witnessing. But at the same time, it was a *bad idea* that brought *bad* results. Fran didn't have any friends, and I was now headed in the same direction. I was quiet for a minute, now that I could see how offensive I'd been.

"Where's your quick comeback?" Tuck sarcastically asked. "I must have said something that got through. I'm right, aren't I? You thought I was bullying you. But maybe walking away was like a punishment or something. Am I right? Was I being *punished*?"

My mind started blanking again. How dare he accuse me of being the bully. I'm *always* the victim—but Papa was right. I couldn't let him walk away again.

"I'm sorry, Tuck."

"Oh, really? What specifically are you sorry for?"

"Uh...." Thinking had to happen quickly. What *was* I sorry for? "Uh...for not thinking about your feelings." That was good. Probably the truth too. "I've never thought of it like that. I was only thinking about myself. I guess I was kind of rude."

"Okay. Thank you. But now will you tell me what I said? So I know not to say it again?"

"I'm not sure. My mind goes blank."

"Blank?" His eyes examined my face for a few seconds. "I guess you did turn kind of gray."

"Am I still gray?" I asked only half-jokingly, from the floor, backed against the dresser with my knees in an elbow lock.

"A little bit. You sort of look like you did the day I met you."

"You mean pissed?"

"No." He chuckled quietly. "But definitely discombobulated."

"When I heard your car leave, I—" I didn't need to tell him I'd cried like a sad girlfriend. "I was stupid."

"You were what?"

"Stupid."

"Not stupid." He smiled politely. "You were being *complicated*."

"I…I don't know. I just…knew I'd screwed up." My guts turned to jelly. "I won't blame you if you cancel our trip to Norton Hill."

Just then, Papa called for Tuck. At first, the two men talked quietly near my door, but then they went all the way to the kitchen. I stared at my sandals and purposely breathed in the night air, hoping to slow the spinning down.

Friends again

"Hey." Tuck came back pretty quickly, and with a concerned smile. He took a heavy breath and asked, "Wanna hear something funny?"

"Yes, *please*!" I gave a dramatic sigh of comical begging.

"Louie wants me to be your shrink."

"I know." I laughed. "He told me."

"You know what else?"

"What?"

"I'm not a shrink."

"I know." I laughed nervously but genuinely.

"And I don't think we need to talk any more tonight."

"Really?" Even more relief.

"You're still a little gray."

"I don't know why I do that."

"I know you don't. And it really doesn't matter that you don't."

"Papa says I might be able to think straight…if I'll just…trust you."

"You don't trust me?" He jokingly teased.

"No. I mean yes. I mean…I don't…know…how to say it…."

"Kidding!" He immediately gestured me to stop talking. "I was kidding. I know you trust me. Don't fret over it. From what I've been learning about your family, you have the right to be confused about your own life."

"It's good that we're going camping on Saturday, right? We can spend time together and get more comfortable…right?"

"Oh. About that."

Instantly, I knew the trip was canceled. I looked up with a fake smile, preparing to say, "Oh, that's okay." That's how I was used to dealing with disappointment. By faking being okay. I knew the routine perfectly. Whenever I would screw up, my family would just cancel our plans and I'd go play with my cars and pretend the world was different.

"Kyle, I was thinking about our trip alone to the woods on Saturday."

"I know." The fake smile wanted to turn to crying, but I kept pretending.

He paused and stared into my eyes.

I stared back and bit my lower lip.

"I think we should leave tomorrow morning instead."

"What?" I coughed. Something lodged in my throat. I cleared it.

He laughed a little. "Did I surprise you?"

"Yeah. I thought maybe…."

"What? That I'd back out on one of my promises?"

Safe word

It was Tuck who suggested we pack the car, then go straight to bed, and get up early for an unscheduled gas and grocery run and an early departure.

I told him about the times when Connor's family had taken me camping with them and how Connor and I would spend the night sleeping in his bunk beds so we could get an early start the next morning.

Something about my excitement made Tuck suggest that since it was fun back then, and the house was set up with bunk beds for multiple grandkids, that maybe we should have a sleepover this night also.

First, we went together to Grandpa Tucker's to pack Tuck's duffel bag; then we drove back to Papa's and assigned bunks. Me on the upper and him in the lower bunk.

"We're doing pretty good, buddy." His voice carried softly up to my bunk through the night air. It's only ten-thirty and we're all packed. Tomorrow's trip is going to be fun, right?"

"It already is, Tuck."

"I been thinkin'. Don't put too much hope in me being your psychiatrist. This was Louie's idea, not mine."

"That's fine with me. I just hope I can stop turning gray."

"Don't worry too much about that. I'll bet that when we're in the car, and out by the campfire, maybe you'll feel more comfortable."

"I'll try harder."

"I'm not going to lie to you, buddy. I hope to find out what's got you so gnarled up." He paused for a minute, and when I didn't answer, he tagged on, "Is that scary for you?"

"Maybe a little."

"That's normal. I'm thinking I can help with that."

"How?"

"I learned a trick in school. If you start to feel like I'm getting too personal, you could say a safe-word and I'll stop—no questions asked."

"What's a safe-word?"

"Like a Get Out of Jail Free card. It's a word you and I agree on that makes me stop asking questions."

"Like what kind of word?" I asked.

"Hmm. Like a code. But not any old word, like Montana or baseball. It has to mean something."

"Trust!" I blurted out. It came to me the second he said the word had to mean something.

"Trust?" Tuck sounded surprised.

"Yeah. You're showing me how to trust."

"Well...." He seemed at a loss for words, but finally agreed, "Yeah. I guess I didn't realize it showed so much."

"It shows." I stared out the open window into the bluish moonlit sky. "Are you ever going to go back to college—you know—so you can fix people?"

"Well...um." He seemed off kilter. "We'll see how this trip turns out."

35

Scooter's Stand-in

Tuck's lesson on trust was about to go into the surreal. Any time a person learns true wisdom, he discovers that he is both the teacher and the student. Tuck was also learning his dual role as both the rescuer and the patient. After that highly emotional day, we'd both gone to sleep with minds and hearts softened like warm clay, wide open to learning about each other, about ourselves, and about the true depths of mutual respect, trust, and faith.

By Tuck Taylor

"Do you trust me?"

The dream had restarted from scratch. It was 1971 again. But as with any rerun, the story repeated the same while the experience of watching was different—this time I knew how it would end. This time in the dream, I felt secure with the dove, which was now perched on Ronnie's windowsill as it had been three-and-a-half years before. I looked down at my blue gown. I was seventeen, lying almost dead in a hospital bed in her living room. Off in the distance, I could see heaven, awaiting my now famous three-minute walking visit. A little to my left, a younger Ronnie hysterically begged me to stay, but beyond her, on the sill, that pure white dove, now a trusted friend, beckoned.

I stood. Draped in a hospital gown, I walked to Ronnie and gently grabbed both shoulders.

"I'm fine, sis."

"How do you know?" she sobbed. She was still in 1971, thinking I was dying.

"I've seen the future. I know how this works out. I have faith in the dove. You should too. I'm going to stay with you, Ronnie. I'm going to come back in three minutes. I'm going to teach someone how to trust."

"Who?" she asked.

"One like me," the dove interrupted.

I pointed toward the bird whose pure white feathers again contrasted the crystal blue skies behind it.

"You're the teacher, not me," it said.

"I figured that out already. I'm doing a good job of it. I use repetition and constant praise. I tell him over and over that he amazes me. I'm teaching Kyle how to trust me."

"Be honest instead."

"But it's working," I defended myself. "Praise is opening him up a little."

"It's you who needs to open up."

"I already am open!"

"You must tell me who you really are."

My secrets painfully flooded to mind. Trenton, Micah, Shannon, the car accident, the cancer. I'd become a master at pushing away their misery by not talking about them. Now, someone I'd placed my faith in was telling me I had to resurrect all of it? And why did the dove say *you must tell me*, rather than *you must tell Kyle*.... What did that mean?

"Oh, my God," I uttered. Faces flashed. I felt the mournful sadness from Grandma and Micah's funerals. I recalled the helpless agony of reading Shannon's goodbye note. Even Trenton's abandonment stabbed at my heart. I saw a wall between me and them. My anger at Kyle that night and my vow not to take him into the hills reflected my own fears of connecting to someone who'd leave me again. "It's…me…who can't trust."

"Yes."

"But I have a good reason."

"Yes."

"I lose everyone I love."

"And so do I."

Shocked by the comment, I focused on his face again. His eyes illuminated in accordance with the same sparkling blue as the sky behind him. Then they twinkled. Against the backdrop of his pure white feathers, the eyes looked just like Kyle's against his uber-blond hair.

"Oh, my *God*!" I scanned down to his feet. The dove was wearing ugly boat shoes. "Kyle!"

Panic

I woke up. The bed was shaking. Screams echoed from above me. Several thuds against the wall sparked panic in my chest. Someone was attacking the boy I was supposed to be saving.

"*Kyle!*" I jumped out of bed, ready to fight off his assailant. "*Kyle!*" I was disoriented but ready for a fight. The moon provided enough dim light to outline his thrashing movements.

I made it to him quickly and screamed his name again. "*Kyle!*" He surprised me with an elbow hit across the face. I instinctively grabbed and pinned his right arm with mine, and I blocked any more blows with my left.

He was alone. No one was attacking him, at least not for real. But as I held his pinned wrists, his anxiety went from bad to worse. He started thrashing to try to get away.

"*Kyle!*" I screamed again. "You're *dreaming!*"

He fought harder to escape my grip on his wrists, so I let go before he could kick me with one of those knobby knees of his.

"Huh!" He woke up—I think. At least he stopped fighting me.

"Kyle," I whispered. I could see through the dim moonlight just enough to know that his face was close to mine. His terrified breaths were hot and smelled of licorice. "There's no one here but me."

"Scooter?" he whimpered.

I gently reclaimed one of his wrists and felt it quaking.

"Scooter?" he repeated louder.

"Oh, my God, Kyle. No. Tuck. I'm Tuck. You're okay now. I'm here."

His inhale quivered with a sense of horror.

"You're okay. I'm here. It was only a dream."

"Oh. Shit." His feeble voice broke my heart. "I hate that dream. I hate it so bad." He started crying.

"Jesus, Kyle." Standing on tiptoes next to the bunk bed, I let go of his wrist and slid one hand beneath his face.

"Tuck, I'm so glad it's yooo-hoo-hoooo!" He wrestled himself up, threw both arms around my neck, and started bawling the way he had done on his papa in the gazebo that first morning.

My worrisome emotions of the past few days had finally reached their tipping point. I couldn't hold back this time. I started crying with him.

"What the fuck have they done to you?"

Why we're both here

Kyle's explosive moment of terror didn't last long like it had in Center Park that first day I'd met him. He calmed down relatively quickly and then let go of his death grip on my neck. I flicked the switch on a desk lamp, grabbed the box of tissue, and climbed onto the bunk with him. We sat together, feet dangling like dock fishermen, hands clasped in our laps, my left leg pressed tightly against his right.

"I still don't know why you're here, Kyle. But I think I've finally figured out why I am."

He shot a glance toward my face, but he didn't say any words. It was as if he knew my mission already.

I gently set the tissue box on his knees and slightly ruffled the cotton of his pajama bottoms with my fingers.

"I still don't get it," Kyle mumbled.

"You still don't know why you're here?"

"No." He shook his head.

"It's okay. You probably don't need to just yet."

"But I'm glad I am. In fact, I'm glad we both are." He smiled pathetically at me.

I smiled back.

"Tuck?" His demeanor seemed distant. "Why is life so complicated?"

"Oh, crap." I huffed a polite laugh. "I wish I knew."

He dropped his head onto my shoulders.

I glanced down at his hair.

"What?" He glanced up into my eyes.

"I was just thinking." I spoke quietly. "This must be what it feels like to be a dad."

"A dad? Where the heck did that come from?"

"Oh, I don't know." The dove's instructions were clear. I had to tell him who I was, and so I was delicately trying to broach the topic. But I'd kept myself shielded from dealing with the trauma of losing Micah for so long that I found it difficult just to blurt it out now. So I stayed a little mysterious. "I've only known you a few days, but I'm starting to connect with you. I just wonder if this is what it's like for someone like me who might…I don't know…have a son."

He smiled. "You'd be a good dad." He pushed his weight into me.

I almost started bawling. If his hair weren't so white, he might have looked exactly like what Micah would have looked like at fourteen. Suddenly, I realized a deep need to tell someone how badly it hurt to lose my own son. I held back any emotional outbursts, but a rogue tear fell from my eye.

"Tuck?" I know he saw it trickling down my face, but he acted as if he didn't. He said nothing about it.

I shook my head. I know I was supposed to tell him the rest of the story, but I couldn't.

"It's okay. Maybe when we're in the car, or by the campfire, you can open up to me." He laughed politely.

"Yeah." I grabbed one of his tissues and wiped the tear; then I did my best to cheer up. "We can both open up about our lives…tomorrow."

"Yeah. Tomorrow." He sighed. "We don't have to do it tonight."

"Are you scared?" I asked. "You act like you're scared."

"No. Maybe. Yes. I guess I'm just hoping it's easier than it was today." He sighed again. "Papa told me I *have* to talk…or I'm going to end up alone. I'm sick of being alone inside my head. I *want* to open up, Tuck. But I get scared. I still don't know what I'm supposed to say."

"You really don't know why you're here in Minnesota, do you?"

He slowly shook his head no. I believed him. He was as confused as anyone about his entire life.

"Okay, well…like you already noticed, life's complicated." I patted his knee. "Trust me on that one. I know, I know, I know how hard it can be to know what to say."

"Papa said all I have to do is trust you and the words will come automatically."

"He's pretty wise, huh?"

"I hope so. I think I trust you…but the words aren't there yet."

"But he says they'll come? The words?"

"Yeah."

"Well, he seems to know a thing or two about how you and I both think, so maybe he's right."

"I *hope* he's right."

"Well, if real life is too complicated to talk through right now, then let's focus on something simpler." I thought it was important that he have something to offer me. If I could open him up a little bit now, he might be comfortable to go the next step tomorrow. "Maybe you could tell me what the dream was about. It only happened a few minutes ago. Surely you can remember some of the dream. Why don't you just describe it to me?"

The Tree Dream

"Trees." He sighed and blew his nose.

"Trees?"

"And Dr. Krieg." He lifted to support his own head but continued to press our legs together.

Silence followed.

"You said you hate that dream…like it's bothered you before."

"About a hundred-million times."

"Who's Dr. Krieg? Are you like…chopping trees down for him or something?"

"Not chopping. Trying to escape. The trees tie me down and then go up my butt."

"Oh…shiiiiit." This time I felt my own face turn gray. In 1974, psychology was just beginning to focus on the existence of, reasons for, and problems with repressed memories and their connection to recurring dreams and irrational fears—of which Kyle apparently had both. Up to that moment, they were but a fascinating chapter in a textbook. But my blood started boiling with anger at the thought of him being a real-life victim of it. This moonlit bunk bed was not a classroom and Kyle was not a fictitious paragraph in a textbook. This dream was a true witness to something horrible. This room was in *my* neighborhood, and Kyle was *my* friend. He was my destiny. He was my sworn promise to teach trust to and to find the reason he might be suicidal. "Dr. Krieg…?" I paused.

"He's just my creepy doctor. I hate him. He's Dad's friend, but he's rude and tastes like cigarettes."

"Tastes like cigarettes?"

"I mean…*smells* like cigarettes." He shook his confused head. "I don't know why I said tastes. That's stupid."

"Why was he in your dream?" I knew why he'd said tastes, and I also knew to tread carefully now. School had taught to respect the fact that memories repress for a reason. Repressions are gifts from brains of trauma victims meant to hide things they can't safely deal with. Kyle may have had extremely good reasons for not remembering something very nasty, and I sure wasn't prepared to uncork that gasoline tank. Repressed memories needed to be dealt with by a fully colleged-up, experienced professional. Not a lonely, depressed dropout on summer break.

"I don't know. But…." He nervously tapped his own knee.

"But what? You look nervous."

"Can I…sleep with you tonight…? In your bed…?"

"Uhhhh." I didn't know how to answer. How much did I trust this kid? If this adult male Krieg guy was molesting him, how would my sharing my adult male bed with him end up? Would he expect something I wasn't prepared to do? Just then the dove, wearing Kyle's shoes, flashed across my conscious mind, reminding me that Kyle was important and that I had to move *my* trust of *him* to the next level if I was going to teach *him* how to trust *me*. "Sleep with me? Why?"

"It always works with Scooter."

"Scooter?"

"He lets me sleep in his sleeping bag whenever I have this dream. It makes the dream stop."

Trust goes both ways

Trenton's friend Mark was my story of a poor choice during a time of intimate sexual vulnerability. That choice had started with a simple backrub and ended up with me thinking I might have to defend myself for the rest of my life.

I had a lot to lose if rumors got out about a cute, confused blond boy sleeping in my bed. I was faced with a choice that needed to be made quickly. Was Kyle to be trusted or not?

"Scooter's helped you through this before?" I dug for clues to help me decide. "Just by letting you in his sleeping bag?"

"Yeah. He always says, 'Agent McBride at your service, sir' and then protects me the whole night."

"You have this dream whenever you're in the presence of someone you think can protect you?"

It seemed significant to me that Scooter was always there when this dream tried to get out of Kyle's subconscious. Perhaps his tormented brain was looking for someone who could help. Now he was having the dream while *I* was in the room. Was his subconscious reaching out to me?

"How does he protect you?" I questioned.

"He just...I don't know.... He just lays there, and somehow, I know I'm not alone."

"Alone?" My face warmed. The word dug into my already overly emotional state. "I guess I know how that feels."

"You know what? I'm sorry, Tuck." He pushed away a couple of inches. "It's not right for me to ask that."

"Wait." I put my hand on his knee again. "It's not that I don't trust you. It's just a surprise. It's not a normal favor that boys ask of me."

"I know. I shouldn't have asked. I'm really sorry."

"Stop. I haven't said no yet."

He looked at me with excitement.

"You really can't sleep after that dream?"

His face flushed, giving me the answer I needed.

I almost spoke, but I held my breath a second, then sighed, making it pretty obvious I was about to give in to him.

"I promise I won't hurt you." He giggled. "I'm totally harmless." Then he smiled at me with a cheesy, begging grin.

"Ha!" I shook my head. "I know you won't hurt me. If you think I'm safe enough for this, then dang it…come on." I jumped off the top bunk and motioned for him to share the bottom one with me. "Just make sure you keep your pants on."

He laughed. "Don't worry; I'm not that kind of girl." He jumped off and excitedly climbed in first, then held the blankets for me.

I switched off the light and got in to rest comfortably about six inches from him.

"How's this?" I asked.

"Scooter usually gets closer."

"Not gonna happen."

He giggled. "Okay."

We lay quietly for a while. I pretended his breathing, subtle movements and body heat were those of my own son, whom I imagined would have camped with me often in the hills.

"Good night, Tuck," he whispered.

"Good night, Micah."

"What?"

"I said, 'Goodnight.'"

A few moments later, I realized I'd called him Micah. But the kid, for whatever reason, never asked me why.

Sleep was going to take a little while that night, so I used a common relaxation technique of focusing on one muscle at a time, relaxing it, then moving to the next. I started with my feet and then moved inch by inch up my legs. Normally, I made it about to the belt line before losing consciousness.

Is there something wrong with me?

"Tuck, are you still awake?"

"No," I joked. "I'm sound asleep."

"I need to ask you something." He lifted up onto an elbow and looked down at me.

"Yeah?"

"Is this normal?"

"What? Us sharing a bunk?"

"Yeah. Does needing this mean I'm not normal?"

"No one's normal. There's no such thing."

"Fran called me gay because of it."

My eyes shot open wide.

"Do you think I'm gay?" he asked.

"No," I responded cautiously.

"Oh. Good."

"But I do think you're the frightened victim of a bad recurring dream." Then I asked, "Scooter sleeps with you. He's not gay, is he?"

"Fran says he is."

"Why would she say that?"

"She said his mom caught him behind a fence kissing a boy."

"Uh…" I perked up. "For real?"

"I don't know. I love my sister, but Fran's not always right."

"Do you believe her?" My mouth dried. I was in my underpants, in bed with a boy who was now talking about being gay. Hoping I hadn't made a grave mistake, I started planning my muscle movements for how I might slink from the bed to my left if he started advancing on me.

"I don't know."

"You've slept with him a hundred-million times, right?"

"He's never done anything like that to me, Tuck. He's never even said anything to make me think he wanted to. He's my cousin. He's like my twin."

I sighed heavily. This was a big, big topic for the middle of the night.

"Am I gay because I sleep with him in the sleeping bag?"

"Kyle…" I spoke with the seriousness of an adult teacher—not a peer. "You two were babies together, and up until now, you were just little boys. Considering how bad that dream is, I think it's normal that you need a little comfort at night."

"It really, really helps."

"Maybe you won't need to have his protection during the night for much longer now that you're almost an adult. I think it's normal for boys to be close, but as you get bigger, you'll lose interest." I then switched roles from adult teacher to curious friend. "What will you do if you find out Fran's right? What if he really is gay?"

"Don't care," he blurted out as if he'd thought this through already and was certain of his conclusion. "He's still Scooter. Nothing's changed."

"Wow." I was taken aback. It was 1974, and Kyle was Catholic. I'd never expected to hear someone like him say he didn't care about something so socially charged.

In honor of Scooter

"Scooter's the coolest guy in the whole world…. Oh! No offense. You're cool too."

"None taken." I chuckled. "I already know how you feel about him. But how can you say it won't make a difference? It kind of changes everything, doesn't it?"

"Not for me," he proudly boasted. Then he lay his head back down to stare at the bunk above us. "And I don't see how it changes him either."

"You mean, his liking boys isn't a huge change from liking girls?"

"Tuck, I've thought a lot about this. Scooter's still Scooter. If he likes boys now, that means he probably always did. Nothing's changed except that people know now."

"Wow. Insightful." I was amazed—and for real this time. No campy exclamations. Kyle was amazing. No other word fit. "If you find out he's been lying to you all along, don't you worry that'll hurt your feelings?"

"Nope." Again, he spoke with confidence. "I know all about why it's important to keep secrets. If it's true, that's a secret he has no choice but to keep. It's not his fault."

"Do you have secrets you feel forced to keep?"

After a short pause, he nervously whispered, "Yeah. I guess."

"Wow." Again, I had no other words.

"My first crush was on a girl named Ellen." He openly started rambling facts about himself, showing obvious comfort with me. "It was the fourth grade. I saw her face and just like…fell in love with her. Nothing could stop me from thinking about her. I couldn't control it. She never talked to me. I was invisible to her. In fact, she was kind of a mean person. But it didn't matter to my body. I couldn't stop thinking about her for like…a whole year."

"Why are you telling me this?"

"Because that's why I think Scooter is what he is. If I couldn't control whose face I had a crush on, maybe Scooter had the same problem but with a boy's face. What if he saw a face he couldn't get out of his mind, but he never told anyone? I've never told anyone about my crush—until right now. If I couldn't control my crush, maybe he can't control his. Why should I hate him for that?"

I lay motionless. Stunned.

"Tuck? Are you still awake?"

I laughed. "I'm still awake."

"Good." He started finger-tapping my elbow like it was a drum and he was keeping time with music I couldn't hear.

"Kyle?"

"Yeah?"

"You're amazing."

"You've said that before." He chuckled quietly.

"Not with this much truth. You never cease to amaze me."

"I just wish my family was like me. I don't think they're ever going to let me see him again."

"So...is all of this why you're not allowed to see him anymore?"

"I think so. I love Fran, but she called him a pervert and told me Mom is protecting me from him."

"Does Louie know about any of this?"

"If he does, he won't admit it to me."

"Kyle, I think you can trust him. He had a long talk with me last night. He says he doesn't know why Scooter's been taken out of your life." I reached up and grabbed the finger he was tapping me with. "People get really, really weird around this issue."

"They're idiots if they think he's dangerous."

We didn't speak again. My heart ached for him. Still not really understanding what may have driven his family to put him on the train, I was beginning to see a familiar story of people who may have thought they were doing the right thing, but who were isolating him—possibly by accident.

I eventually rolled away from him. Just before dozing off, I felt his hand come around my waist to rest on my stomach. His stomach pressed against my back and his knees against the backs of my thighs. After our talk, I believed I could trust his motives so I pretended to be asleep and faithfully allowed him to use me as Scooter's stand-in for the night's tree-dream relief.

All the while, I pictured him as Micah. This was no longer just about me teaching him. As his warm, motionless hand rested against the actual skin of my stomach, I lost all fears that he would try anything inappropriate with me. He was little more than a frightened child at that moment. I was his proud and trusted protector. He wanted to love me the way he wanted to love an older brother or father. What an honor for me to be that replacement. My heart and chest warmed comfortably with a sense that for the first time in many years, I was the one not alone that night.

JAMES F JOHNSON

36

The Manliest Goat Driver

> *Tuck was different from everyone I'd ever known in that he simply knew how to raise my poor self-image. He was technically an adult, but he bonded with me like a peer. He was the first person ever to call me a man, and even to get me to call myself one. For the first time ever, I began to believe in myself, all because of him.*

By Kyle Rickett

    The Goat hummed melodically through the hot summer breeze while I hummed to the radio, glad he'd come back the night before. Tuck and I both wore white tank tops and wire-framed aviator sunglasses. If my hair wasn't so white, I'd have looked like his little brother for sure. Whatever he wore, I wore—with the exception of jeans. I was in yellow gym shorts. It was summer—I couldn't wear *pants*. We both rested an elbow on doorsills. Tuck grabbed the rain gutter with a whole hand, but my shorter, fourteen-year-old arm used fingertips to reach the chrome roofline. I still looked cool—if my classmates on Torano Island could *see me now*.

Life here was good.

All windows were down for the hour-and-a-half drive to Norton Hill. The trunk was filled with chainsaws and camping gear. The AM radio played "Never Ending Song of Love." The aromatic breezes mixed with our deodorants and freshly shampooed hair. At the second chorus, Tuck spun the volume down and I stopped humming.

"So, Kyle. Thanks for sharing so honestly with me during the night. That's a big deal about Scooter. I hope things work out between you two."

"Me, too. It's so unfair. He's my favorite cousin and they all know it."

"I don't know your family personally, so I can't really guess why they're doing it to you. But, hopefully, things will get better with time."

"Problem is I don't know what they're telling him about me."

"What do you mean?" Tuck asked.

"Well…they keep saying he doesn't like me anymore."

"I hope you don't believe them."

"I don't *think* I believe them…I'm not sure. They're my family. I'm supposed to have faith in them, right?"

"Have they ever lied to you before?"

"Yes!" I blurted out without thinking. "Fran lies all the time. It seems like everyone always believes her, too. Mom lies when she thinks she's doing what's best for me. That's why I don't know what they're telling *him*. Our moms are twins. Auntie Maureen and Mom plot together a lot. What if his family is telling him that I'm the one who hates *him* now?"

"He would never believe that, would he?"

"Normally, no. But Tuck…he has a *really* big secret. He might be really embarrassed. He might think I am one of the millions of people who hate people…you know…like him."

Tuck shook his head. "I can't believe you're only fourteen," he said while watching the road. He seemed embarrassed to look at me.

"I can't believe you're twenty-one," I joked back, trying to keep the conversation light-hearted and safe. I also noticed that he looked young again. Like about sixteen. "I guess I don't really feel like I'm fourteen," I answered.

"Why not?" He remained serious.

"I always feel like I'm a little kid. Like I'm about seven."

"Well, you're not."

"Well, I feel like it."

"Well, you're not."

"How old do *you* feel?" I pestered.

"Twenty-one," he responded confidently.

"You look sixteen," I said, smirking.

He laughed without answering.

"You look sixteen, but you act—"

"Stop saying that." He slapped my shoulder kiddingly. "I'm twenty-one, and I feel forty-two."

"Oh, brother." I rolled my eyes.

"I think you've got screws loose feeling like a seven-year-old. You're ignoring what you're capable of." He half-smiled.

A manly man

"Oh, here we go," I teased.

"What?" Tuck asked.

"You look like you're going to say, '*You* rebuilt a tractor?' again." I laughed and casually turned away to watch the ditch slide past beneath my window.

"How did you know that's what I was thinking?" Tuck asked.

"Because you say it almost every day," I replied.

"Tractooooor." He hummed with a smirk.

"See?" I laughed loudly and slapped his elbow.

"Yeah, I guess I'm kind of predictable sometimes."

He checked his mirrors, then focused his gaze on me. "What did your dad say when you finished it?" he asked.

"He said I did a good job…."

"Good!" He slapped his steering wheel approvingly.

"But then later, he complained that it cost him more for me to rebuild than it was worth." I lifted myself up and repositioned, sliding my left foot under my butt and leaning back against the door, giving him all my focus. "He said he can't sell it because he can't recoup his money back out of it." I sighed deeply and looked down the hood with a final comment about myself. "I should have never rebuilt it. I caused him a lot of trouble because of it. He said he should never have let me do it."

"Of course he did." He deflated and sighed. "Even when he says yes to something, he comes back on you later. You can't win for losing."

"It's…." I looked down at my bare knee an inch from the gear shift. "It's just the way he is."

"No."

"No?"

"No. It's just *fucked up* is what it *is*! He has no right to treat you like that." As we came up behind a hay truck, Tuck tipped his head out the window, and with no hesitation, he sped up and moved into the oncoming lane.

"He's my dad. He kind of has the right—"

"He *should* have told you that it took a real man to accomplish what you did, and he *should* have been proud of you." He had to raise his voice to shout over the increased wind and the hay truck as we passed it. "He *should* have bought you a fucking beer and a god-damned cigar."

"A beer and a cigar?" I extended my right arm out the window and pretended to pull a chain. The trucker responded with two blasts of his air horn.

"I said, 'a *fucking* beer and a *god-damned* cigar'!" He pounded the wheel again.

The GOAT DRIVE

"Are you crazy? I really *am* just a kid."

"Na. Don't keep saying that. You'll start to believe it." He maneuvered us back into our lane and coasted back down to the speed limit.

"I *already* believe it." I laughed.

"How many guys in your class can rebuild a Farmall?"

"Probably none." With eyes lifted to the ceiling, I sarcastically answered his leading questions.

"How many guys your age can even make a *bad* tuna sandwich—let alone a gourmet meal like you did the other day?"

"Probably none." I dropped the sarcasm and joined into his line of thought to admit, "In fact, those sandwiches I made us were even better than my mom's."

"I'm sure they were."

"Trust me. They were a lot better than my mom's."

"Say it, then," he commanded.

"Say what?" I smiled apprehensively.

"Say, 'I'm a manly man.'"

"Oh, c'mon." I blushed.

"C'mon yourself!" He gave me a humorously scolding look. "It's only you and me. You're a man above men. You're 'an old soul.' We're in the car. No one else can hear you."

I stared.

"Traaaactorrrrrr," he sang.

"Okay." I laughed, then unconvincingly repeated, "I rebuilt a tractor. I'm a manly man."

"Oh, please. There's no one around but me, and I'm tellin' you, you *are* a manly man. Don't be embarrassed to say it."

"I'm a manly, *manly* man!" I cheered. Then I fell victim to a nervous giggle.

"Good. Now give me a tissue so I can spit on it and wipe your nose."

"Hey!"

Hope plus trust equals faith

"I have an idea," he proposed. "There's not a lot of traffic today."

"So?" The Goat began to slow quickly. Still sitting sideways facing Tuck, I grabbed the dash to avoid falling into it. The right tires dropped onto gravel. "Do you have to pee or something?"

"Nope." Tuck raised a brow when the left tires dropped. "Can you drive a clutch?"

"*What*?" I sat up straight and excitedly scanned the dazzling hotrod surrounding us. Had I just received an official offer...*to drive it*?

"What's the matter? Don't you think you can do it?"

"I don't know." I didn't know what to say. I wanted to drive it with every molecule of my body, but I didn't want to damage it.

"Don't you trust yourself?" He turned off the engine and set the brake.

"I...don't know. I think...so."

"Are you saying *I* trust you more than *you* trust you? Come on, Kyle. You rebuilt a tractor. You must have driven it."

"Yeah. I move trucks and equipment around the lot. I even tow with Dad's pickup. It's a three-speed. Daniel once let me move his Kenworth across the street." As the car slowed, reality clashed with fantasy deep in my head. Was this a joke? Was I *really* going to drive this gorgeous car? On the highway? "But what if we get caught?"

The hay truck steamed past us. I waved at the driver like we were friends. He tooted the horn one more time.

"So?" Tuck answered my question "You don't really think people go to jail for this, do you?"

"It's illegal."

"I've been driving this car on this road every summer for almost four years now. I've learned they only pull you over if you go ninety."

The GOAT DRIVE

"Ninety?" I blurted.

"But if you go ninety," he said, laughing, "they *will* pull you over. Somehow, they *aaaaaalways* know when someone's doing ninety."

"How many times did you get caught going ninety?"

"*Every* time." He laughed again. "I've never gotten away with it. But even then, I never went to jail. I just got a stern talkin' to. So…don't go ninety and no one will stop you."

"Okay." Things were happening fast. "Tuck, are you sure you trust me?"

"Absolutely!" His answer came quick.

"I just don't want to hurt it."

"You won't."

"How do you know?" I was a little nervous about what could go wrong.

"Because I have faith in you."

I laughed nervously.

"Why are you laughing?"

"You mean you *hope I won't crash it*."

"Nope!" he answered quickly. "I'm very sure of this. I have faith, not hope.

"Same thing."

"Nope!" He kept overexaggerating the word "nope" as if to make it funny. "Faith is an upgrade above hope."

"What does *that* mean?" I wrinkled my nose.

"Before you built that first tractor, you probably hoped you could do it, right? You didn't really know."

"I guess."

"But if someone asked you to rebuild another Farmall right now, you probably wouldn't say, 'I hope I can do it.' You'd probably say, 'I believe I can because I have done it already and so now I have faith in my abilities.'"

"O—*kay*...."

"So any customer who knows you've rebuilt tractors before can say, 'I trust your abilities, and therefore, I have faith you can do it again.'"

"Weird. I always thought hope and faith and trust were the same word."

"Lots of people do. They never think it through. But if you just use them in sentences, it's easy to see that evidence leads to trust, and *trust* plus *hope* equals *faith*."

"What sentences?"

"In Oklahoma, you can say, 'I hope that tornado will change direction and not hit my house.' You can't say you have faith because you really have no way of predicting. But you can say, 'I have faith that there will not be a tornado today' if you live in Seattle because you have evidence that tornadoes have never happened in Seattle.' You can change hope to faith when you have evidence to back up your sentence."

"So, Tuck, you don't have any evidence. If you've never seen me drive, why do you have *faith* in me now? You can only hope I can drive this thing. Right?"

"I've seen you prove yourself in other ways. How stupid would I be not to trust you with a car? I've *seen* evidence that you're good with equipment. A car is just another piece of equipment. I can't unsee it. I haven't caught you lying about anything yet, so I believe you when you tell me about having driven pickups, tractors, and a semi. You've shown me how good you are with your hands. Louie says you're competent and strong. That's evidence, evidence, and more evidence. That's why I trust you, and why I have faith—not hope—that you can drive this car."

"Okay." I wasn't sure what else to say. I got silly and gladly accepted his offer. "Wow...I guess, if you insist...I'll drive your super-awesome car."

"You're driving this god-damned car whether you want to or not," he teased back, "young man!"

"Okay, okay...I *want* to!"

"Good!"

"Good!" I responded mockingly.

"Good!" he bounced back with even more sarcasm.

We both started laughing.

Release the Goat driver

We flung our doors open. We passed at the back and slapped hands. We reached our new assigned seats and slammed both doors together. Before excitedly grabbing for controls, I forced a slow, deep, and calming breath, put my sunglasses back on, and then followed the proper steps to adjust the seat and mirrors. When I could successfully see over the steering wheel, I knew I was ready.

"I knew you'd do this right." Tuck's remark showed obvious confidence—faith—in me. "Look at you, getting everything right before takeoff."

"Fasten your seatbelt, co-pilot," I kidded.

"Do you know where first gear—"

"Eh!" I raised a blocking hand. "I've been driving this car in my dreams since Saturday." Then while he chuckled, I locked eyes with him and confidently slipped the car into first gear, wiggling my eyebrows the way he'd done when we smoked the bees.

"You're a nut," he mumbled.

"I'm a manly man. I know how to do real things." My heart sank only for a split second, and then it beamed with a refreshing jolt of pride. With my eyes, I focused only on the road, but with every nerve ending in fingers and toes, I meditated on the controls, hoping to move them smoothly and not piss him off or get him to correct me the way Daniel would have if this were his truck. I heard another low chuckle. Tuck was no Daniel. Grinning cheeks forced the sunglasses to rise up off my nose. I pushed them back down with one finger. "Here we go." The engine revved too high, then calmed. My head retreated like a turtle's. "Oops. Sorry."

"Easy there, Speed Racer; it's not a farm truck." Tuck wasn't scolding. He was laughing while speaking, like he was having as much fun as me.

A second rev hit the mark. The clutch smoothly released most of the way, then dropped, throwing rocks from the rear tires.

"Oops, sorry." But I kept going.

"No problemo; just keep driving."

The car floated onto the highway. I ran through the gears carefully, each shift smoother than the last. I leveled us off at fifty-five miles per hour, as was the posted limit.

"Thanks, Tuck."

"No need to thank me. I'm having a ball right now."

"It's just that…I never, *ever* dreamt I'd get to drive it while I was awake." I'd never driven anything this fast, and I'd only been on pavement once. I'd pretended to race around in sweet rides my whole life, and I had played many times behind the wheel of parked cars and trucks since I was a toddler. I now wanted this exhilarating movement of a real car at highway speeds to burn itself into my mind so boldly that the feeling of it would never end.

Hay!

But after several magical minutes, my dream was put to the test when we motored up behind that still slow-moving hay truck. I didn't want to do anything that could bring on criticism, so I focused on what the rules of the road probably were, and I tried to prove to Tuck that I knew them. I eased the driver's side of the car into the oncoming lane to peek around the truck. Nothing was coming. I looked back over at Tuck.

Tuck shrugged. "You're driving, not me." Then he casually added "Just be careful."

I smiled with confidence and made an obvious mirror check so he'd know I'd done it. No one was behind us. I used my blinkers, sped up to sixty-five, changed lanes, and overtook it. As the dual exhaust rose in tone, the exhilarating power of the amazing engine pulsated smoothly through my body.

"My God, this car is tight! Like brand new." My voice was two octaves higher than normal. I wasn't parked in a driveway making engine noises with my mouth—*I was in control of this mighty machine for real.* Awesome! Once again, *if my classmates could see me now.*

"This fucking car would burn rubber right now if you floored it...but *don't!*" he shouted. "I'm only bragging."

"I won't floor it." I laughed.

Tuck felt the exhilaration too; I could tell. While passing through the truck's shadow, he pretended to grab for hay. Escaped flecks and strands pelted his bare arm. When we made it to the cab, he pretended to pull the chain this time and the driver responded again with the air-horn. *Bahp-Baaaahp!* I pressed my thumb onto the Goat horn, *Breeeeep!*

"Yes!" I squealed.

"Woo-*hoo*! Kyle Rickett, you are the man!" Tuck cheered.

The shout was my reward for a job well-done, and so a wave of grateful peace flooded through my proud chest. I'd conquered my first obstacle, and I counted the hay truck as a point scored in my favor. Like I'd been doing it for years, I re-entered our lane and allowed the car to coast back down to the speed limit. I gently tapped the brakes to flash the brake lights and waved my small arm out the window. I heard a more distant *Bahp-Baaahp*.

"Not bad, Mr. Rickett. Not bad *at all*." Tuck nodded comically, drummed two fingers on his knees, and sang, "You're the king of the road."

"I watch how my dad does it." I couldn't contain a gloating laugh. I snorted and blushed. Tongue between teeth.

"Well, then you learn by watching. You've got passing down perfectly." He raised his hand and I high-fived him. This time, his eyes didn't wander down to my exposed armpit. Maybe Tuck wasn't like that after all.

Unable to lose the smile, I was tempted to thank him for having such confidence in me, but somehow, it felt more mature not to. So I nodded and accepted the praise—owning it for once.

Tuck stared at me for a few miles until the smile waned.

"You're the first person I've ever let drive this car, you know."

"What? You're kidding! Why are you letting me do it then?" I was smiling again. Maybe he was lying—but then maybe not. Either way, I was getting some mighty *positive* attention—and I liked it.

"Most guys I know aren't mature enough to handle this much car. You're the first man who's ever qualified for the honor."

I looked at him for only a second.

"You didn't punch it. Most of my idiot friends *would* have."

"Works for me." I couldn't think of anything else to say.

"So, as it turns out, Mr. Rickett," He was still drumming on his knee and bobbing his head as if to music, "my faith in you was well-placed, now wasn't it?"

Rollover

I guess I then lost focus on what I was doing and heard a loud thud.

"Oh, *no!*" Muscles tightened when the two right tires fell onto the soft gravel shoulder and the steering wheel pulled hard against me to the right. This was not a good situation at highway speeds in an overweight 1960s model muscle car designed for racing on *straight, smooth* pavement.

"Woah, *fuck*! Watch the road!" Tuck shouted over the squealing tires. His knees lifted to his chest, then slammed back down. "Oh, *shit*!"

The car fishtailed and my foot moved toward the brakes.

"*Nooooo!*" he screamed again. "*Don't touch the brakes!*"

"What do I *do*?" My heart raced. I set my foot on the floorboard, which was being pelted with gravel from below. The big wheel tried to fight its way out of my small hands, but I held on tight and steered against the fishtailing.

"Just hold it steady. And *don't go back on the pavement!*"

I couldn't look at him. I wanted to follow my instincts to hit the brakes and steer back onto the road, but my obedient nature to his authority was stronger. The car was slowing quickly because of the soft

The GOAT DRIVE

gravel. When we'd dropped to about thirty, Tuck coached from a shaking voice.

"Now, brake carefully...*carefully*...and just fucking stop this fucking car!"

With my bottom lip stretched tight from humiliation, I did as instructed. The shoulder widened, so I steered the left tires onto it to get us out of traffic. One little foot held the clutch, the other the brakes, and I felt like a total loser as the car stopped and filled with dust.

Gravel settled and the engine purred gently.

"I'm really sorry," I sheepishly whispered.

Tuck turned off the ignition for me and didn't speak. The keys dangled from the dash. His face was white as a sheet. His jaw trembled.

"I don't want to drive anymore." I could barely breathe because it felt like my lungs were so ashamed of me that they didn't want to work.

Clenching his seat on both sides, Tuck didn't move, but his eyes watered.

I lifted my door handle, but before I could push the door open, he raised a hand toward me.

"Wait, Kyle. I don't want to drive either. Let's just sit here."

I pushed open the door enough to slam it closed again.

He was staring, but I couldn't tell if he could see me. His blue eyes were blank against flushed pale skin.

"I'm really sorry, Tuck." The silence between us was deafening.

"Don't...." He exhaled and changed tone. "Let's just sit here for another minute." His bottom lip started covering the scar above it. I let him sit in silence messing with his lip until finally I needed to ask.

"How'd you get the scar?" I almost started crying because I suddenly thought maybe I now knew the answer.

"Rollover car accident," he droned almost too quietly to hear.

"Figures." I closed my eyes. I wanted to cry even more now. God, what a jerk I was.

"Stupid thing is…I don't remember it happening. And I was seven. I'm twenty-one now. I don't know why, after fourteen years, this shit still scares me so bad."

"How did it happen?" I shouldn't have asked, but I needed to say *something*.

"My friend Shannon's dad was taking us bowling. She said he did what you did, he fell half onto the shoulder, but he jerked the wheel back onto the pavement and hit the brakes. The car was older than this one. Kind of top heavy. Not like the Goat. I shouldn't have been so scared."

Again, I remained silent but my eyes must have given my curiosity away. The hay truck flew past us. The driver gave another friendly horn blast and his wind shook the car slightly.

"Shannon said we rolled three times. We had seatbelts on. Her dad didn't…. He died…right in front of us both. I guess I blacked it all out." His voice was low and void of energy. He swallowed hard and faked a smile toward me. "You did good." He unconvincingly praised, "Thank God you listened to me, huh? You controlled it like you knew what you were doing."

"Bullshit," I muttered slowly. "Stop being so fucking nice to me. It's creepy. I know you're faking it. I almost killed us."

He shook his head no.

I clicked open the door again.

"No, Kyle. You're going to get us back on the road and just…don't *fucking* do that again." He smiled, but it was phony. He looked more like he wanted to cry.

"Tuck, I don't want—"

"*Do as I say!*" His niceness turned to anger. "It could have happened to anybody. Suck it up." He released another breath. "You screwed up, but then you followed my instructions and didn't roll us over. That's called a learning experience. We all have them. You're doing fine."

"Suck it up?" I was *afraid* to drive another inch, but "suck it up" pissed me off. We sat for several minutes and didn't say much until Tuck finally reached for the key, started the engine, and told me to drive, but to keep my god-damned eyes on the road this time.

The GOAT DRIVE

I didn't throw gravel again. I drove silently and absolutely perfectly. Both hands on the wheel, both eyes on the road, and when we came up behind the hay truck again, he broke silence. His voice had calmed, but it wasn't joyful yet.

"I'm freaked out, Kyle...not mad."

The incredible shrinking me

I'd begun to shrink into the privacy of my head, like my body was still the same size, but my soul was turning tiny and hiding deep, deep inside. No matter what I tried to do, I seemed to screw it up. I wasn't a "manly man" at all. I was a—

"*Kyle!*" he yelled.

"What?" I stared straight ahead, too ashamed to look at him and way too afraid to take my eyes off the road even for a second.

"Kyle. I need you not to fade away on me right now."

"What do you mean?" It took all my strength to force words out. I just wanted to be completely alone and not speak.

"Don't pull this shit on me...*please?*"

I glanced over for a quick second and saw him staring.

"Don't make me live on eggshells around you."

"Huh?"

"I get mad sometimes. All guys do."

"I shouldn't have taken my eyes off the road, Tuck."

"I said *stop it!*"

I froze again and grabbed the steering wheel extra hard to try to keep feeling in my arms.

"Friends get mad at each other. Kyle, I need you to deal with that."

"I don't know how," I mumbled.

"I'll teach you how.... But for now, will you just look at my face? Please?"

I did, but I quickly looked back at the road.

"I'm freaked out. I yelled at you out of fear. Don't make me feel bad about that. I was scared to death, and I think I deserved an outburst. I need you to be my friend right now."

I couldn't believe what I was hearing. But I liked it, especially when he repeated it.

"I need you to be my friend, Kyle." He smiled. "I need you."

I smiled by accident. Life came back to my face quickly. I think I blushed from the release of nervous energy. I was able to glance at him comfortably several times. Again, I wanted to cry, but not from shame or pain. But because someone really, really wanted me—needed me—in his life.

"That's better."

"I'm really sorry, Tuck. I hope I didn't scratch the car with gravel."

"I have touch-up paint. You're new at this. I'm still happy with my decision to let you drive. Just…" He paused to wave his hand once, "shit happens, alright?" He sighed heavily and pointed at the truck we were following. "And don't pass him again. We're going to turn off in a little bit."

"Gotcha." I glanced quickly to see that he looked like he was recuperating okay. "I'm really sorry."

"Knock it off, Kyle. I said I'm not mad. You've already apologized. It gets kind of old when you keep doing it." He showed annoyance now.

"Sorry."

"Just…." He laughed at my apologizing for apologizing too much, shook his head, and continued. "All kinds of people make mistakes. It's how you recover that defines you as good or bad."

"Okay." I accepted his acceptance of me.

"You alright?"

"Better than alright." I nodded and smiled.

"Is that because you're proud of how you saved us?"

I quickly glanced at him again. "Because I'm with a *friend*."

37

Calm Acceptance

Tuck's plan to get me alone in the car was genius. Anyone who's ever had a long talk with a teen in the car will understand this: Tuck used the mystical power of the long ride to help open me up, and it worked. I felt comfortable and safe enough to begin sharing my inner world.

By Tuck Taylor

Except for the incident, Kyle drove like a pro. He was quite a kid. I, on the other hand, had just acted in a way unbecoming for a mentor—terrified of a little gravel. I looked like Kyle had the night before, shaking and screaming. Like with his tree dreams, something from my past sprang back to life in my head. Perhaps we weren't so different, he and I.

I respected Kyle's fears. I believed he had good reason for them, just like I did mine. He wasn't just a moody teen. But as an adolescent, he had a built-in challenge when talking to adults. Back then, too many adults talked *at* teens, not *with* them. Adults would coach and correct, minimizing or disregarding what the teens said. Why would anyone want to open up to people who didn't respect what they said?

Kyle thought of himself as a child. Most likely he was treated like a child at home. I certainly noticed that when I talked with him as a brother or a fellow kid, he connected quickly. But when I spoke as an adult, he struggled to stay with me. For this car ride, I needed to keep the balance between connecting as one of his peers and behaving as an adult.

"Are you sure you've never had a girlfriend?" This car ride had a purpose. I was still sure that he was holding onto a secret because of the phone call with Connor and the tree dream I suspected was sexual and also violent. Louie had originally put me up to this, but by now, it was personal. As I stared at Kyle's handsome high-cheek-boned profile, I got angrier and angrier at whoever was at the root cause of his moody explosions.

"*What?*" he looked over with furled brows. "Where did that come from?"

"Don't take this the wrong way, man…but…" I paused for a second to give myself the chance not to say it, "you're an exceptionally good-looking little dude."

He shook his head.

"What?" I asked. I blushed too. "Your dad's not here to catch us talking dirty. So spill it."

"I told you last night. I'm not that kind of girl."

"Ha!" I busted out laughing. "Doesn't mean you're not good-looking."

He didn't respond. In fact, he distracted himself by intentionally checking mirrors and squirming to get comfortable in his seat.

"C'mon, stud. Who else thinks you're good-looking?"

He ignored me. I knew he wanted me to stop, but I really wanted this car trick to work.

"I was sixteen the first time I ever had sex." I tried to bring myself to his level by talking about when I was closer to his age.

"Tuck." He looked at me even more nervously. "I told you talking about sex has never gone well for me."

"You've never had sex with anyone?" I ignored his excuse.

With that, I had pushed him too far. The car started wandering a bit more side to side in the lane. Kyle was biting his lip and starting to fade back out of his body again.

"Kyle!" I gently grabbed his forearm. "I was kidding. I swear. Just kidding. No more sex talk. I'm sorry."

He laughed unconvincingly.

I cleared my throat and worked to change the subject so I could get him back into his faculties again. "I know you aren't that kind of a guy, but I was sure impressed by how you see Scooter."

"Thanks." He wiggled his head and smiled slightly.

"But why are you like that?"

"Why am I *like* that?"

"It's not normal. Most people are afraid of guys like Scooter."

"Yeah, well, they're stupid. Scooter's awesome, and I know what it feels like to be treated like they're treating him."

"Empathy," I mumbled. "That's what it's called."

"What's empathy?"

"For some reason, you know what it feels like to be in his shoes, so you know how he feels and you feel it with him. Empathy."

"Oh." He blushed and responded quietly. "I'm not…in his shoes, you know."

"I believe you; don't worry. But why do you think like someone who is?"

He raised a shoulder as if to say, "I don't know," but at the same time, his face blanked ever so slightly.

"You're fading again," I openly reported.

He looked at me for longer than any moment since running us off the road; then he faced forward again to keep us between ditches.

"You told me last night that Fran accuses you of being gay." I was fishing for the answer I thought was out there. "Doesn't that piss you off?"

"I'm used to it. Fran accuses me of crazy things all the time."

"How do you get used to something like that?"

"She's my sister." He shrugged and then, in a rather non-animated, flat voice, he stated, "I love her."

"I don't believe you."

He gave a puzzled expression. "You don't believe I love my own sister?"

"I don't doubt that you love her. But that's not why you're used to being lied about. I know the *real* trick you use to get used to it."

"What trick?"

"You blank out." I was sure of it. Whether it was done to him by Fran, or by that kid he'd talked about on the phone to his friend, or by everyone on the island, Kyle had somehow mastered the ability to accept crap from people without fighting back. "Your problem is that because you can leave your body so easily, you have *too high a tolerance for pain*."

Too high a tolerance for pain

"I don't get it."

"Sure you do. How much time do you think you spend inside your imagination? Pretending to be somewhere else…some*one* else?"

He glanced at me again, but this time with a smile. "How do you know I do that?"

"I see it when you fade away. You do it all the time. I figure your imagination is safe. So that's where you go."

"Yeah," he sheepishly, but through a smile, agreed. "I have a whole world of people and stories in my head. I can do anything there. I'm always safe." He smiled even brighter.

I smiled back.

He laughed a little.

"Feels good, doesn't it?"

"What does?"

"Knowing I can see you."

The bully has a name: Frandreo

"The problem with going into your imagination is that I think it works too well. I think it helps you to take too much crap off of too many people." I paused for a moment. "Fran's not the only person who calls you names, is she, Kyle?"

He stared straight ahead as if he hadn't heard my comment. But he also started blinking more often, as if he were trying to wake up.

"Is she, Kyle?" I was getting into his head. I knew I needed to stride carefully at this point. If he was opening up, then I had a chance to harvest information. My task was to get what I could without shutting him down, or infuriating him as I'd done the day before.

He didn't respond. He was shutting down.

"Remember the safe-word, Kyle: Trust." I tapped his knee. "You say 'trust' and I stop asking. Okay?"

"Uh…" For a moment, it appeared he would use the word. Then he tightly clenched his mouth. Then he instructed me to ask the question again. "Keep going, Tuck. Papa told me I have to talk to you. So keep asking."

"Are you *sure*?"

He nodded, but slowly, like he was forcing himself.

"Fuck, Kyle. You've got balls. Most full-grown men wouldn't let me ask these kinds of questions. They'd just get mad and shut me down."

"I want to. But Papa warned me. So…*make me talk.*"

"Make you talk?"

He nodded.

"God damn. You are an amazing young man. I'm proud of you, buddy." I smiled slightly. "You're fucking amazing." He'd given me permission, but I knew he was close to shutting down if I wasn't careful. "Fran's not the only person who calls you names, is she?"

He shook *no* but continued to stare. Then he started chewing his lower lip.

"We're about to talk about the reason you're so understanding around Scooter's secret life, aren't we?"

He glanced at me with a questioning brow.

"For some reason, you know a lot about secrets that you are forced to keep. That's why you're able to forgive Scooter for keeping *his* secret."

"I..." He was almost starting to hyperventilate, "I hate lying, but...."

"But sometimes you have no choice, right? That's what you said about Scooter last night. So...it's true for you too, right?"

He nodded but still didn't use the safe word.

"You really, really hate school, don't you?"

He nodded, still expressionless.

"They do it there too, don't they?"

He drew in a deep breath, looked over at me, blew it out, and nodded.

"Will you share with me what they say?"

"*Trust!*" he blurted.

"Trust? Okay." I froze for a few seconds. Then I softly said, "I promised I would stop if you said that word...so...."

Without taking eyes off the road, he put his hand on my wrist. "Wait."

"Okay." I quietly enjoyed the warmth of his hand permeating my wrist.

The power of nicknames

"They call me Homo." He continued to push himself to be open with me.

My heart sank. "How often?"

"It's my name."

"Your *name*?"

"Might as well be. It's what they all call me...every day."

"Why?"

He glared angrily at me as if I should know the answer.

"What? You keep joking with me, telling me you're 'not that kind of girl.' So if you're not that kind of person, then I don't know why they would call you that."

"You saw me throw that Frisbee yesterday. I can't throw a ball either. I can't catch either. I can't do *anything* other boys can do."

"You're stronger than they are."

"Yeah, but it doesn't matter in sports. I'm not *coordinated*."

"Wait a minute...." I shook my head as if to wake up. "That's not the same thing as being a homo, you know."

"Well. It's why they call me one. They make me feel like I'm not one of the boys and I'm *not* one of the girls. I'm a freak—all by myself. No one likes me. I have to sit in class and be quiet. If I say anything at all, they giggle and roll their eyes. I'm not a human there."

"So being 'homo' means you're not like any of them. You're totally isolated—abandoned by your own herd." Then I added a tagline, "Just like Scooter, the guy you feel empathy for. Same thing."

"Not just Homo. Sometimes they call me a Fag and Fem too."

"This is...." I opened my eyes wide and in disbelief and looked at him again. "Feminine? No fucking way!" Kyle was all boy as far as I could see. "Exactly who started that ridiculous bullshit?"

"They all do it."

"That's not what I asked. I want you to tell me who the *first person* was who ever said that to you."

He drove tight-lipped for a moment.

"Don't you remember who started it?"

"Andreo," he mumbled.

"Who's Andreo?"

"The kid I told Connor about on the phone last night."

"The one who became a total shithead after someone attacked him?"

He nodded.

"Is he the Texan from Catholic school that Louie told me about?"

He just kept nodding.

"When did it start?"

"Fifth grade."

"Jesus Christ, Kyle. That's almost half of your entire education life." I shook my head in disbelief at what this poor kid had been taking. "I'm struggling to believe they all do it. There must be someone who does *not* call you that?"

"The teachers don't."

"That's it? No one else uses your real name?"

"Only sometimes."

"When?"

"Well...John Santana talked with me one day last year and said nice things about a painting I did in art class."

"One day last year?"

"Yeah, in the spring."

"*One* day?"

"Yeah...*in the spring*," he repeated. "I told you it's all of them, *all* the time." He mumbled, ashamed of himself.

"What was the painting of?"

The GOAT DRIVE

"A tree all alone in a desert."

"Okay, so John Santana doesn't call you homo."

"Oh, yes, he does. He did it a few days later when I dropped a fly ball in PE…and about a hundred times ever since in class and on the playground."

"No one else?"

"There was a new kid named Matt."

"He called you Kyle?"

"At first. We played alone on the swings a couple of times. But then…they trained him."

"What about your friends at home? In the neighborhood? Connor?"

Kyle looked at me with a firm expression. "My friends don't know about any of it."

"They've never heard the nickname?"

"Absolutely not. My life would end if they knew what the school kids know about me. I hated talking to Connor about Andreo yesterday on the phone. It's the first time I ever have. Up to then, Connor had never heard of Andreo."

"So, at home…."

"At home, I'm Kyle. All the kids like me there…but that's because they don't know the truth—and they never can!"

The despicable art of semi-organized mobbing

"The *truth*?" I stopped him. "How is calling you names that isolate you the *truth*?"

"They all do it, so it's the truth when I'm there."

"Wait just a cotton-pickin' minute."

"What?"

"You're telling me that once in a while, when you are *alone* with another kid, that kid treats you with respect, but when you are in class with all of them, they all treat you shitty?"

"I guess." He thought for a second. "I never really noticed that before. It's like they're only nice when no one is looking."

"Mob bullying."

Kyle tipped his head but kept his eyes on the road.

"You're Kyle at home and everyone calls you that. You're Homo at school and everyone calls you that."

"Pretty much."

"Well, there you have it."

"Have what?"

"School's the problem. Not you."

He looked at me as if waiting for more information.

Just stand up to them (Ha Ha)

"Your private school is like a researcher's Petri dish," I explained. "A closed test group. For whatever reason, Andreo's developed a boner for you and has manipulated a bunch of individual kids, who exist all day long in a closed community. He bonds them together by turning you into their common enemy and uses the power of mob-mentality to attack you from all sides. Each one of them is afraid to be the one who isn't on board with the insults. Each individual is as afraid as you are and wants to be on the winning team, and none of them are ready to be put on your losing team—which leaves you all alone there. He's created an anti-Kyle mob. You don't fight back, and so they keep doing it."

"Fight back?"

"Yeah. You're supposed to fight back."

"I *can't* fight back. You don't know what it's like, Tuck."

"I've been bullied. I've stood up to them. It's worked."

"But you're cool. You're Tuck Taylor. You're an athlete...with a GTO. I'm a small, white-haired freak who can't throw a ball past first base. I can't stand up to bullies the way you can."

"Why not? Haven't you ever heard that bullies are the scaredest kids on the playground, and when you stand up to them, they wet their pants and run off?"

"That's fucking *bullshit*," he firmly bellowed back.

"What do you mean, bullshit? It's true."

"*I can't stand up to them!*"

I stared.

"Don't *ever* tell me to do that again!" His face reddened. "It's not fair. I *can't* stand up to them."

"Sorry, Kyle. I..." I reached across the console and gently punched his bare arm. "Tell me why not."

He glared at me.

"Honest, Kyle. I really need to know what you're going through." I held my hands over my heart in a symbol of genuine humility.

He glanced at my gesture and smiled faintly.

I smiled compassionately back.

"It's *all* of them, Tuck. How the fuck am I supposed to stand up to *all of them*? They all call me a fag! And it's been years and years that they've done it. I can't stand up to them."

"You can't just tell them to fuck off?"

"No! I tried that to one kid last year, and he paid a bigger kid, Dennis, to try to make me cry. The whole class watched."

"Did you cry?"

"No. I was ten times stronger than him. But they all laughed when I got in trouble with the playground lady for fighting. All I was doing was trying to keep him off me. I'm the one who got punished and had to stand in front of them with my hands taped together for math class afterward."

"You're kidding."

He glared at me with the angriest look yet.

"Have you ever gone to a teacher and asked for help?"

The car started slowing, then speeding up again. He was losing focus.

"Sorry. I didn't mean to—"

"*Yes!*" he shouted and grabbed the wheel more tightly. "Yes, I've gone to the teachers. They punish *me*! One day in the bathroom, the boys all pulled my pants down and started dragging me into the hallway. I screamed so loud they stopped. I tried to tell a nun."

"What did she say?"

"I couldn't talk without crying." His breathing became shallow panting. "She told me to grow up and handle my problems like a man."

"You tried standing up to one and they joined forces and beat you down. Then you went to the authorities, who basically told you not to bring this to them again." I was getting angry now. "What about your parents? Have you told them?"

He huffed and sarcastically rolled his eyes.

"I guess that didn't work either."

"Mom told me never ever, ever, ever to make her or Dad come to the school because of me being bad."

"Being bad?"

"Fighting."

"Fighting is bad?"

"Yes! Even if I win, my parents or the other kids will retaliate later. If I lose, I lose now. If I win…*I lose later*."

"Checkmate," I mumbled.

He glanced at me and huffed in agreement.

"Why don't you ask to go to public school with your friends?"

"I've begged and begged my mom to let me out of Catholic school. I told her no one likes me there, that everyone hates me, and she said.…"

"Oh, God." I wiped my forehead with a disgusted hand. "What did she say?"

"She told me to ignore them because they were jealous."

I sighed. *They're jealous* is the parent's greatest copout. She should have given him permission to beat some of them to a pulp.

"Then she promised that no matter how bad it was, public school would be worse."

How bullying turns to mobbing turns to death

I turned beat red and began to see something the 1974 textbooks on bullying had never, ever, ever talked about. Some mob-bullied kids are simply too overwhelmed to "stand up" on their own. Mob-bullying isn't so much about name-calling as it is about an entire peer group rejecting someone. Kyle couldn't be expected to stand up to his *entire* peer group—especially while being ignored by the parents and teachers who had shirked their moral obligation to help. For starters, they'd convinced him that they were right to call him that name. Because he was so honest, he couldn't fight against what he had been told was the truth. By being a poor ball-player, they'd convinced him that homo was the correct term for his condition—then demonstrated to him that "homo" was a term that made him unlikable to them. Secondly, they'd proven both at home and at school that if he fought back, the abuse would increase. It had been proven to him that taking it was safer than fighting it. Finally, the abuse itself had gone on too long for a single, small, highly emotional boy to be able even to discuss it without completely falling apart. If he couldn't articulate his situation without becoming an emotional disaster, no one could take him seriously enough to listen to the truth.

Again, I focused all thought onto Fran, his accuser, calling him gay because she had him over a barrel with partially true information on Scooter. If Fran had had adult authority over him since birth and really had spent his entire life accusing him of one crazy thing after another, and if his parents and teachers had been telling him from birth to ignore it, then odds were good he was so used to living on the defensive that he couldn't even imagine what it would feel like to so much as find a *footing* in an offensive position. He was right: How the hell is someone who's been torn down since birth by a sociopathic older sibling and an entire school, and completely unsupported by his family, supposed to find the strength to stand alone against a punishing mob that encompassed his entire social environment?

I started to see why teen suicides happen so often. I had no reason to believe that Kyle's story wasn't happening to other kids in other schools also, especially those poor boys and girls who really were gay. They were all in exactly the same shoes he was in. No wonder their suicide rates were so much higher than those of straight kids. Poor Kyle still couldn't see through the entangled mess surrounding his life. He needed me to pick it apart slowly, piece by piece. I needed to find out about each piece individually.

Traumas replicate themselves

"Tell me why Andreo started all this." I was firm and angry. I couldn't figure Fran out at the moment, but this Andreo kid needed to be explored.

"I have noooooo idea."

"Well…how did it happen? Did you have a fight?"

"Nope. He turned mean without any warning. He was my best, best, best friend, and then bam, one day he slapped me across the face and I've been 'Homo' ever since."

"Why do kids believe him and not you?"

"No one ever believes me."

"Don't say that!" I didn't scold; I *reminded*. "I believe you. Louie believes you. Remember that, kid."

"Okay, okay. You're right." He smiled appreciatively. "I'll say it this way: They *like* him better than me. So they listen to him and not me. I guess they like his lies so they believe him. He's…." Pause.

"He's…what? Obsessed?" my sarcasm spewed back, "Because that's what I see—a very unnatural *obsession* by a stalker."

"He's…" Kyle gave up with a deflating sigh, "like Fran. They both lie. They know how to tell the perfect lies that everyone wants to hear. And so people believe them."

"Fran and Andreo? One at home and one at school?"

"Frandreo," he muttered.

I laughed. It didn't seem inappropriate. He was trying to be clever despite the ugliness of the topic.

He shyly laughed with me. "That's what I call them: Frandreo."

"Did anything happen the day before his mysterious turnabout?"

"He got beat up."

"By the boy at the pool?" The lights went on in my head. The fragments of the story were starting to connect for me. "This is what you meant when you told Connor that it turned him into a real shithead, isn't it?"

"Yes."

"So that's how this happened? He got beaten up and then he hated you?"

"There was a little more."

"I'm listening."

"He tried to tell me what happened at the pool, but when he said the kid pulled his swimsuit off, I wouldn't let him finish."

"Why not?"

"I don't know. I just couldn't handle it. I think he hates me because I didn't support him."

"Whoa, whoa, whoa!" I angrily waved both hands. "Didn't *support* him? You were *ten*!"

"I was his friend."

"You were *ten*!"

"Still—"

"Have you *seen* what a ten-year-old boy looks like?"

He thought for a second. "Pretty small."

"Yeah. *Very* small." I was getting mad. "He had no fucking business trying to get a ten-year-old to help him work through being raped at the pool."

"*Raped?*" Kyle almost panicked at that word.

"That's…what…happened…you know. You told Connor that he'd been stripped and beaten."

"Yeah, but…"

"Kyle…" I suddenly realized naïve Kyle didn't realize it was a rape, "if you think that older boy just wanted to strip him for no reason…or to look—"

"Andreo's a boy."

I stopped breathing. How far did I need to take this? "Trust me on this one, Kyle. Boys can be raped too. And you couldn't listen to his story because…."

Kyle's face flushed like he'd seen a ghost. He started to fade and turn gray. I needed to rescue this moment and change direction before he ran us off the road again.

If it looks like crap, don't call it pudding

"I'm sorry your former friend was attacked, Kyle, but…that is a steaming pile of gooey dog shit."

"What is?" He weakly cleared his throat.

"This whole entire story! Him! His almost four years of psychotic *obsession* with you! Taking his misfortune out on *you!*"

Kyle's grayness started to pink up a little.

"How many boys have you kissed?"

"None!" He was coming back into his body.

Reactions were difficult for me to discern. When he shouted "none," he *sounded* convincing but *appeared* unsure. This entire Minnesota visit could still be a sexual secret that he himself was too emotionally overwhelmed by to confess. Hell, no one in the 1970s ever considered boys to be targets for rape, but I assure you, they often were targets.

The GOAT DRIVE

At this point I needed to stop pulling information out of his poor aching mind and celebrate what he'd willingly given me. It was time to summarize our talk by explaining some dictionary definitions.

"Then you're not a homo."

"But I can't throw a ball."

"Doesn't mean the same thing."

"But—"

"Homo means you kiss boys. You don't kiss boys. So they're wrong."

"But—"

"They're *wrong*!"

"But—"

"And even if they were right, one day you're going to find out that some of the kids who are calling you homo right now…are *actual* homos themselves. They're just keeping it secret."

"But why would someone who really is one treat me like shit for it?"

"Because they don't want to be on the losing team."

"But—"

"But nothing. You don't hate Scooter for being like that. So even if you were like that, it still isn't reason to slice you out of your peer group and isolate you by shaming you for being who you are."

"But—"

"So say it."

"Say *what*?"

"Say, 'Andreo is a steaming pile of dog shit.'"

He nervously giggled.

"Come on; this isn't about you being unlikable. This is about Andreo being obsessed and dishonest. In fact he's really creepy if you ask me. His obsession with you is super, *duper* creepy. He's made up a lie and he's the one with the problem, not you. So say it; I *mean* it."

"Andreo is a steaming pile of dog shit," he mumbled.

"Now shout it."

"Andreo is dog shit!" he shouted but not convincingly.

"Kyle, this isn't a parlor trick. I'm telling you the truth…Andreo's just like Fran. This has nothing to do with you. He's fucking you over for his own sick, twisted enjoyment because he thinks he has the *power to do it*. He's a worthless sociopath. A fucking bully, and you have the right to shout that truth out to the whole wide world. He truly *is* a steaming pi—"

"*Pile of dog shit!*" he released with a vengeance. His body shook. He leaned into the steering wheel like he was going to wrap it around himself.

"That's my boy!" I impersonated Louie.

"FUCKING ASSHOLE!" Kyle's rant came to life on its own. "He was my *best friend*! I fucking *trusted him*!" He leaned his head out the driver's window and fist-slammed at the steering wheel while he screamed at the top of his lungs "*Andreo Castro is a steaming, sucking, pile of smelly, icky, sticky dog shit!*"

After he came back into the car, he looked over at me, panting like he'd just run a mile. I started laughing and so did he. We high-fived. His face took on more pink and more spark than it had all morning.

"Now pull off and let me drive. The dirt road to the cabin is coming up right here at the end of this fence."

"You don't think I can handle a dirt road?"

"It's not that." I smirked. "I just want my car back. I miss driving it."

38

Photogenic Musician

The power of trust is almost too big to understand. As I finally began to believe that another person truly had my interests at heart, my view of the world began to evolve into a more reasonable, less fearful place. Feeling alone and constantly criticized changes you. Being bonded with a friend, who is okay with you just how you are, changes you back.

By Kyle Rickett

Tuck drove the bumpy driveway, steering around deep grooves. I memorized where they were in case I could talk him into letting me drive us out on our last day.

But then road dust filled the car. We both coughed and frantically rolled up the front windows.

"I'll get the back!" I squealed. I threaded my little body between the bucket seats to roll up the back two. Then, while still lying on my back, I waved dust and laughed. My heart felt huge like it was a basketball.

Admitting Andreo was an asshole, without making myself feel sorry for his situation, sort of cleaned my gooey insides and filled my body with new, clear energy and peace. I'd been letting out old, trapped, moldy secrets, and it felt awesome!

I took in a deep breath. A really deep one. One that seemed deeper and easier than any I'd drawn in in years. I sat up, one leg still draped on the console between the seats. The other up over the headrest of the passenger's front bucket. With a smile I couldn't contain, I stared at the side of Tuck's head, wishing I could stay in Minnesota and never go home. I loved Tuck Taylor! I knew it with every fiber of my being. I loved him. I could tell Tuck anything and he wouldn't call me a liar for it. Tuck—not Daniel—was the best big brother I'd ever known, and I wanted to stay there and let him adopt me—*as if you could adopt a person as a brother*. I surprised myself by whispering out loud, but too quietly for him to hear over the rumbling tires and the engine noise. "I love you, Tuck." I meant it with every molecule of my body, but saying it out loud was an accident. Normally, I was good at keeping my thoughts hidden inside. I was changing. I was opening up.

He didn't notice how intensely I was staring at the back of his head until my bare knee started bumping his elbow. He glanced into the rearview, and I laughed as we locked eyes through it.

Music by the campfire

"Hey, you," he playfully reacted. "Camping trips are fun, huh?"

I nodded, still chuckling.

"Too bad you didn't bring your accordion."

"My *accordion*?" I laughed louder.

"What?"

"Ha!" I rolled my head back. "You're joking, right?"

"No! Music by the campfire is nice."

"*Guitars* by the campfire are nice!" I waved both hands. "Unless you want to polka with a bear, I don't think the accordion fits in."

The GOAT DRIVE (handwritten)

"Why not? Music is music. You're good at it. Maybe you don't think *you* fit in."

"Oh, blah-blah. You're just being nice."

"Oh, ho ho, no!" He comically rose a finger straight into the air. "I would never—*ever*—let a poor musician think well of himself." He laughed. "Music is a sacred art."

"Yeah, well I really only know a few songs." I lurched forward and grabbed his shoulder. "And *don't ever tell anyone* I play it at all." I let go and flopped back into the seat. "I have a hard enough time making friends."

"Kyle...."

"Girls like guitarists and drummers...not accordion dorks."

"Boy, I don't know for sure about that. Looked like the whole crowd was enjoying you at the Railroad Riding Days thing."

I shrugged.

"In fact, Mr. Rickett, it appeared that *you* were enjoying it too."

"Yeah, well...that's between you and me. It's another secret identity."

Secret "dork" identity

"I think you have too many secret identities."

A vision flashed of the three-sided paper I'd drawn up in my bedroom the night I'd broken through the memories of Dr. Krieg molesting me for years. I'd folded the paper in half so it looked like a greeting card. On the front side, I'd written *Home* and my name, *Kyle*. On the back side, *School* and my name, *Homo*. And then inside the fold, like inside a card, I had written *Krieg's favorite boy*. Then I taped it shut so no one could see that side. I saw how the three different identities could exist at once, but never on the same page because they couldn't see each other. Like my three lives, no human could see all three sides of the page at once. But no matter which side was facing one's eyes, the other two sides were just as real, but unseen.

"Kyle?"

I glanced back into the rearview to see his eyes trained on mine again.

"You still with me?"

"Yeah," I chuckled. "I just got lost in thought for a second."

"Well, welcome back to reality." He shook his head once with a smirk. "I was just going to say that if you like something, you should do it."

"You mean, play the accordion?"

"Yeah. The accordion fits anywhere you want it to fit. I've seen drummers wow the crowd on plastic buckets. It's not the instrument that you think doesn't fit in, is it?"

"It's the one instrument everyone laughs at."

"Fuck them. It links you to Louie. You enjoy it. Why not do it if you like it?"

"People will call me a dork."

"I thought they already did."

I went into an expression of shock.

"Well? At St. Tiberius's, they've already given you the most isolating nickname they could think of! So what more have you got to lose? Your reputation? Already lost. Right? Connor, Scooter, and me...we wouldn't call you a dork. So go for it."

As I pondered Tuck's interesting new take on dorkism and accordions, I jumped on an urge to blurt out, "I like classical music too!"

"What?"

"Mozart. He's my favorite! And Schubert too. And...Vivaldi."

"Wow. You know their names?"

"Antonio Vivaldi. He died 233 years ago last Sunday...July 28, 1741."

"Uh...*why* do you know that?"

"It's on the record label. I check out records from the library. My parents don't know. I listen with headphones."

"Another secret?"

"Only you know…and Mrs. Noell…the librarian. She won't laugh at me. I…I only check them out when *she's* there."

"That's quite an interesting secret, Kyle. You sure put a lot of thought into how to get away with something most people *don't care about*."

"Vivaldi calms me down when I'm alone. I wanted to know what he was like, so when I was at the library, I read his biography. I did the same with Beethoven and Schubert. Schubert wrote 'Ave Maria.' I guess I wanted to read about them…because…I wondered if these guys were…you know…anything like me." My voice trailed off. "See? I'm a dork. What other kid even knows who those guys are?"

"You wondered if they were anything like you?"

"Is that stupid?"

"You're looking for people to connect with. An identity you don't have to keep secret. I think the way you seek them is inspiring. Yeah. Inspiring, I guess, is the word."

"Inspiring?" I wrinkled my nose.

"You are…so…complicated."

"I know," I said sadly. "I shouldn't be so nervous all the time."

"No!" He batted at my knee. "You have your reasons. How you fight to try to find your way out of the pain, well…that's what makes you awesome! It's a good kind of complicated. Inspiring. More people should look for mentors like you do."

"Really?" I was honestly surprised at his reaction. "But I also like John Denver. And the Rolling Stones. I'm normal *sometimes*."

"Becoming normal shouldn't be your goal, Kyle. Normal people don't change the world. You appreciate *all* kinds of music. That's a sign of intelligence, Kyle. Not dorkism."

I shrugged. "Yeah. I guess I do…kind of…. I even listen to country."

"That was some real joy in your face at the gazebo that day with Louie. Kyle, I really think you should let yourself do that more often."

"Really?" A smile forced itself across my face. Tuck was right; the joy of music was bubbling up on its own out of my body and into my smile. He made a lot of sense when he reminded me that my reputation at school couldn't go any lower.

"I just wish I'd have gotten some pictures."

Pictures...uh oh.

"Why?" I grimaced.

Papa was right; the more I trusted Tuck, the more I could open up. Not only to Tuck, but to myself. The truth was setting my brain free. When Tuck mentioned taking pictures of me doing things I normally was embarrassed about, something in my memory trail broke free right then and there. For the first time in my life, I remembered Krieg telling me, *"I've got pictures. You keep the secret to yourself, and I'll keep the pictures to myself."*

"Because you and Louie have a cool bond. I think I could have captured a once-in-a-lifetime moment on film if I'd had my camera."

"But I—"

"I know, I know. You hate cameras." He stared intently into my eyes through the mirror.

I intentionally made myself look like I hadn't just faded away while I mentally processed his desire to take pictures of me in short pants. I was still tracking with Tuck, but barely. The memory was a pretty big shock. Had Krieg really said that to me? Was it a dream I'd had? I wanted to disappear into my own obsessed brain and live with the horror for a minute, but at the same time, I wanted to stay conscious, in that hot, dusty, bumpy car ride with Tuck. So I forced myself not to obsess over the new memory.

He was *not* Dr. Krieg. Tuck had integrity. He hadn't broken a single promise since the minute I had met him. He wasn't trying to get anything from me, and so I had no reason to distrust him. Again, I remembered my diary promise to trust him no matter what. He was turning out to be a good person—the best I'd ever met. I *forced* myself to rely on my thoughts and not my feelings. "*No!*" I screamed.

"No?" he asked.

"Oh...." I realized I'd shouted that out loud. "I wasn't talking to you."

He laughed and elbowed my knee. "I'm the only one here. Who were you talking to?"

"If I didn't hate cameras..." I ignored his question, "what kind of pictures would you take of me?"

He looked at me again, shocked.

I shook my head and shrugged. "Well?"

"I'd ask Louie to set up another gazebo event. I'd literally recreate last Sunday and take action shots of you, him, and the crowd. I'd look for chances to capture the trust you have for him and the way he cares about you."

"You can do all that with a *camera*?" I imagined the pictures of my relatives in Papa's house. All of us smiling like mannequins, year after year with the same half-assed grins on our faces, but with different haircuts and different Sunday church clothes. There was absolutely no personality in those pictures. In fact, the only photo on Papa's wall that hinted of a personality was the one with young Tuck and Papa proudly holding up a fish. "You can make a camera see what people *care about*?"

"Absolutely. I am an arteest!" He pretended to have a French accent.

"That's cool, I guess." I was on a mission to push myself into getting past this stupid phobia. I wanted his assurance that the photos wouldn't end up somewhere that would humiliate me. "Then what would you do with the pictures after they're developed?"

"Uh, I don't know." He appeared genuinely confused. "Why does *that* matter?"

"I...I just don't know what you'd do with pictures of me in an embarrassing costume."

"Okay, well..." He cleared his throat, and glared into my eyes more intently. "I guess if they're good enough, I might ask your permission to enter them into contests or something."

"With my permission?" Another sentence no one had ever really said to me before.

"Yeah. You should know me well enough by now to know I wouldn't do things with your image unless you told me I could."

"But I look stupid in that costume."

"I don't agree. You said the accordion didn't fit in, and now you say the clothes don't fit in…. Kyle, I really think you feel like it's you who doesn't fit in."

"No, Tuck. I do look stupid in that costume."

"Oh, you do *not*! Louie and Scooter wear them too, and you don't say they look stupid in the same costume! And it's not a costume. People around the world really dress like that when they're celebrating. It's appropriate attire for a German-themed festival. If everyone else looks fine in lederhosen, why don't you?"

"It makes me look stupid."

"Why is it everything you value is something you're ashamed of?" He didn't sound scolding. His tone was compassionate. "Other people wear lederhosen and are fine with it. Other people play accordion and are fine with it. Other people are blond…small…wear boat shoes…. Kyle, you're too hard on yourself."

I sighed. I hated looking at myself in mirrors and photographs. All I could see in them were my stupid white hair and my small body. But Tuck was a nice, nice guy. He really seemed to like me, and I sure as hell liked him. I needed to trust his camera—that it would somehow show me a different kind of picture. One that exposed me the way *he* saw me.

Maybe I could try it

"Welllll…." I shyly asked a special favor, "do you think you could guarantee that no one in Washington will ever see the pictures?"

"No one? Not even your family?"

"Especially them." I knew that if Fran were to see a picture of me having fun doing what I really cared about, she could fill my head with her critical bullshit and ruin it all for me for the rest of my life. There could be some real hell for me to pay after that.

"Kyle, I'll do what I can. I'll keep them out of Washington State."

The GOAT DRIVE

"Wow." I absolutely didn't need Andreo or anyone at school getting a shot of me in shorts and a feather hat playing for old people. But I wanted to be what Tuck wanted me to be. I needed to endure a little more of that pain he said I had too high a tolerance for.

"What say you?" he asked.

I wiggled into a sitting position, still in the backseat, leaned forward, put a hand back onto his right shoulder, and answered loudly, boldly, over the rumble of the tires, "Yes."

"Yes what?"

"Yes, you can take pictures of me and Papa when we get back."

"Oh, good. What changed your mind? So I can use that trick again."

"I just bet you're a good photographer, and I...trust...you."

"Why do you say that? Are you just being nice now?"

"No," I said, laughing. "I would never let a bad photographer think well of himself."

"Ha!" He laughed with me. "That's another sacred art. But what makes you think I'm a good photographer?"

"You see things that I can't. I want to see me the way you see me."

He paused for a second and looked over at me with the kindest smile I'd ever seen.

I smiled back. I truly soulfully felt bonded with him.

"You've never viewed my work. Why do you think I can '*see*' things?"

"I haven't viewed your photos, but I've seen your work."

"That was poetic," he replied.

"I guess I have faith in your camera because I've seen evidence that you see things in a better way than I do."

"Hmm." He coasted us into a parking area near a small cabin. The rumble stopped. The engine fell silent. The place was stone-silent except for some bird noises, and he was able to lower his voice. "I am pretty good with a camera, Kyle. And you're right. My teachers told me I had a knack for putting feeling into my shots." He set the brake. "I've been dying to start working with people instead of birds."

"I hope you brought a camera along today too."

"I did." He twisted in the seat to stare face-to-face at me. He looked excited. "I was going to take pictures of the terrain. I'd sure like to take a few shots of you chopping wood, but only if you're *really* okay with it."

"I am, Tuck." I patted my chest a few times to indicate that I was nervous, but willing. "As long it's *you* taking the pictures."

39

Tuck! No!

When it's time to die, do we know it? Do we go peacefully or do we fight to the end? Some say that the brain shuts off pain sensors so that, no matter how bad the damage, the dying person just doesn't feel it.

By Tuck Taylor

Kyle gave permission to photograph him and I was excited. I had a lot more experience with animals, birds, and scenery than with people. I wasn't thinking of Kyle as any kind of a model, but he had so much character to his face and head that I couldn't wait to see if the artistic glory would manifest onto film as dramatically as it did in my head. Trenton was my former subject because he had talked me into taking several shots of him for soliciting modeling jobs, but—and I say this with the utmost of love—Trenton was far more delusional than he was photogenic. Kyle seemed more the other way around.

Kyle's face was one of those that expressed both joy and pain more poetically than most. His eyebrows were flat, not arched, and so close to his eyes that they seemed to touch them. That's an almost must-have characteristic to this photographer. Eyebrows close to the eyes signifies a person with a close comfort zone, which translates to a face that draws viewers into it. His eyes themselves, as they faded in and out of focus, told stories words could not. My greatest curiosity was around the camera's ability to capture the intensity of his charisma—his endearing spark. Face to face, the kid was mesmerizing. I had no doubt that bullies weren't the only people drawn to him. He most likely didn't realize how many truly good people were attracted to him also.

Could I adequately exhibit the elegant combination of his deeply troubled heart with his brightly attractive spark on film? I was finally going to get the chance.

Friendship solidified

We unloaded the camping gear into the musty smelling cabin. We took the saws and axes down a hill into the woods about fifty yards to where limbs and trees had fallen beneath the weight of last winter's snow.

All the while, Kyle was more talkative than he'd ever been with me. He began sharing stories about his family that were more telling than before. I think his trust in me was loosening not only his voice, but his inner dialogue. I was sure that his reasons for not opening up before were as much about his inability to know what to say as his shyness around the newness of our friendship.

His stories had a pathetic sense that he had accepted too many abnormal things as normal. He wanted to be a pianist, but his family—who appeared to have a lot of money—refused to buy a piano or pay for lessons because they said he'd quit and they'd be stuck with a piano they didn't have a need for. So Louie was teaching him accordion instead. His love for the classic greats may have been a sign that if he'd been given his chance at his true passion…the piano…well. I guess we'll never know.

Fran, as I had suspected, was a real problem, but Kyle constantly tried to soften his own opinions of life on the island with opening lines such as "*I love her, but*…she calls me awkward and clumsy," or "*My family loves me, but*…they don't trust me to know what I want." Those

The GOAT DRIVE

introductory lines are usually not meant for the listener, but for the sender to reinforce his own delusion and remind himself to keep a lid on his true feelings.

Kyle was a good soul. He wanted to love his family members, and he didn't want to be responsible for me thinking poorly of them, so he started every sentence with "*I love them, but….*" I, on the other hand, would rather have simply heard the second half of each sentence, allowing me to form my own opinions based on pure fact.

I began to hope that our friendship would last for as many years as it would take to stumble onto chances to help him see through his delusions and admit the truth. That his family was holding him back.

This kid had more potential than any teen I'd met yet, but his family was draining him of it. My guess was that Fran, Andreo, and perhaps even others, were jealous fiends who intentionally knocked him down because they hated what *his* successful talents said about *them*. He wasn't responsible for his family's idiosyncrasies, but every time he processed their behaviors through his *Mr. Nice Guy* filter, he would take full responsibility for their image. The clear truth was that his parents were selfish and his sister was a jealous psycho. It wasn't his task to make the world think she wasn't by starting every sentence with "*I love her, but….*"

I'd brought my camera to the worksite and let it sit ready for photo-ops, but we needed to get started working first. As the chainsaws roared to life, the clock went into fast motion. A good hour flew past, and before I knew it, my back hurt from bending over the logs. Kyle shouted for me to take a break.

"Ha!" I shouted back. The heat from the chainsaw's exhaust made the day seem even hotter than it was. I wiped my brow with a forearm, being careful not to let the chainsaw get too close to my sweaty face, and shouted back, "I don't take breaks!"

"You're a good man, Tuck!" He laughed at me and shut down his saw.

I wanted to keep the banter going, so I purposely walked over to one more tree, winked at him, revved up my saw, and laid it across a tree that was leaning against another one.

"Tuck, NOOOOOO!"

I heard a crash, saw a flash of green fly toward my face.

Then silence.

The kingdom of heaven is at hand

Nothing hurt. No more work needed to be done. The temperature wasn't hot anymore. Or cold. The smell of the chainsaw exhaust wasn't even in my memory. The dove appeared. He hovered quietly. The silence and peacefulness were as beautiful as always.

We stood face to face, the dove and I, with only crystal blue skies as his backdrop. His white feathers and blue eyes made me feel welcome and important, again matching my new friend's interest in me.

The oddest part of all these visits with the dove was that each time I was in his presence, I felt as if I'd never left. This visit seemed to be on the same day as the very first one, making the three-and-a-half years in between only a flicker.

"I'm glad you made me stay close to him," I admitted with a huge grin. "I haven't felt so alive in years."

"He loves you too."

My heart warmed. I hadn't thought of it as love, but the word fit perfectly.

"You've accomplished what you set out to do. He trusts you."

"I can't believe I've only known him a week."

"His prayers go back years, and now you've answered them."

"What do you mean 'now I've answered them'?"

He moved to the left, and before me appeared heaven once again. The grass was perfect, the sky pristine. The slow-moving river glimmered like gemstones. There were no shadows. It would be a glorious place to spend eternity.

"Are you ready for this?"

"What? Ready for...*No!*" I panicked quickly. I had many times wanted to stay there, but not this time.

"*The tide is turning.*"

"*No*! That's *bullshit!* He needs me...or he'll die."

"*You've always wanted to stay.*"

"Not anymore! *No!*" I'd been in this place several times, face-to-face with this dove, and I had even walked in heaven, but this was the first visit to drive me to panic. My heart throbbed. I couldn't leave the boy when he needed me this badly. "He needs me!"

Right now, it's you who needs him.

"What? I'm...I'm confused."

"*Hold on and fight, Tuck Taylor. Hold...on...and...fight...*"

The vision started to fade. Excruciating pain overpowered all my thoughts.

"*...or it's you who will die.*"

He vanished.

Everything went dark.

JAMES F JOHNSON

40

Turnabout

In the woods, around tools, things can change quickly. When they do, shock must be dealt with rapidly. Somehow, the crack of a tree forced Tuck and me to switch roles. I was now the person in charge of a life-or-death rescue. And I didn't have time to think, so I acted.

By Kyle Rickett

"Tuck! *Tuck*!" I'd never panicked this much before. "I can't lift it! I can't lift it! Oh-ho-my God!"

The log had fallen across his stomach. The chainsaw looked to have torn into his right leg…badly. My instinct to lift the log off him drove more panic when I discovered it was so heavy that it seemed glued to him.

His eyes opened, but it didn't look like he could see me. I fought to lift or roll that god-damned tree off his possibly crushed stomach and legs, but I was too small.

"*Ow!*" he shouted in pain. He was waking up.

"*You're alive!*" I shouted back. "Oooh, God...thank you!" I looked up to the sky. "*Please* help me get this tree off him!"

What in the world was happening? He and I had just been laughing about...something...so how the hell did we end up like this? The moment was in slow motion. Thoughts raced, but I didn't go into a crazy dissociation like I had done when I was being attacked by Krieg. I was actually thinking *more clearly* than usual.

He seemed more coherent as he came to. I hoped that was a good sign. But I still couldn't free him.

"*Tuck!*" I looked into his face. My hands gently covered his cheeks. "Fight, Tuck. Please fight. Tuck, don't die. *Please*! *Hold on and fight, Tuck Taylor. Hold...on...and...fight....*"

41

Ninety Miles an Hour

True friendship either transcends selfishness or blends with it. Tuck and I had each become more concerned with the other's wellbeing than with our own. Was it because we had become unselfish? Or was it because selfishly, we both valued the friendship, and so we did what we could to protect the other?

What difference does it make? The warmth of friendship is rewarding either way.

By Tuck Taylor

"Kyle!" Pain shot through my torso. What was happening? Thoughts raced at lightning speeds. I was confused about myself, but I was worried about Kyle. He needed me, and I had made a promise to save him. All his friends had left him. I couldn't leave him too, could I? The dove instructed me to fight for this, so God damn it, I was going to give it all I had.

I called out to the dove in my internal voice. *"You will not take me! Please don't take me. I can't die now. I won't! Not now!"* It wasn't the first time I'd been at the edge like this, but I'd never before wanted so badly to turn around and go back to my pain-ridden body. How cruel could fate be to put me in Kyle's life only long enough for him to bond with me and then force him to watch me die?

Another burst of pain finally panicked me when I tried to take a deep breath, but it only sent what felt like a knife through my right lung and spine. The weight of the tree on my chest wouldn't allow me to draw much air in anyway. My face didn't hide the panic.

"Oh, *shit*!" Kyle's fear transformed to pure, red-faced anger before my very eyes. "Tuck! Noooooo!"

I tried to shake my head *no*, to show I agreed with him that this was *not* going to beat me, but I hurt so badly I couldn't tell whether I'd shaken my head or not. I just knew I had tried.

He pushed away and threw his shoulder into the tree trunk just over my torso. With a raging, *raging* roar, he heaved. I actually heard the dirt push away beneath his feet, and I felt the ground move below my back.

Hold on and fight! The words from the dove rang through my head like a song I couldn't get rid of. So, as the log lifted only a smidgen, but not off me, I pushed upward with my left arm. The pain was the worst I'd ever felt before or since—from the hip, through the back of my neck, and to the top of my head—but I think I had pushed just the right amount to help Kyle move the log enough to free my lungs at least enough to breathe. I tried to roll out from under it, but I'd given all I had, and now I was paralyzed.

"I can breathe now. Go get help!" I tried to yell, but my lungs barely pressed out words.

"No way!" He looked around to assess the scene. "There's animals out here, Tuck. I'm not leaving you alone with them."

"I can't move."

With sweat dripping into them, his eyes darted from the log to my face, then to the branches still on trees above, then up toward the Goat, and back to the log and to my face. "I can block-and-tackle it!" An idea was alive in him. He yelled, "I brought rope!"

While I lay still trying to figure out which muscles I could manipulate, Kyle ran to the car. In a minute, he came back and planted himself on his knees at my side. He held one end of a long rope in one hand and a shovel in the other.

Tow the line

I wasn't able to see what the other end of the rope was tied to because I was stuck under a big log, but within the window of visibility I had, I watched in amazement as the boy who claimed he couldn't catch or throw a ball mightily tossed the free end of the rope over another tree in only one try. As the tail of it landed on the ground next to him, he grabbed it so fast that I couldn't follow his movements. He tied it to the tree that was pinning me and then ran out of my vision toward that other end. The pain was worsening fast. I wanted to vomit.

"Hold on, Tuck," I whispered with each pained breath. "Hold on. Fight for it, Tuck. Fight."

I don't know how much time transpired, but when the tree slowly tugged off to my right, Kyle was nowhere to be found. Then, from a distance, I heard my ram air 400 revving and gravel flying. The dang kid had rigged up a towline, wrapped it around another tree for leverage, and was using my car as a tug. What other fourteen-year-old would know how to do that? And in a panic, no less? I was glad I'd left the keys in the ignition this time.

With the tree now completely off of me, the Goat went silent, but footsteps, loud ones, came fast down the hill through twigs and dried leaves. "Tuck!" Once again, he plopped down firmly into the dirt by my side. "You're going to be okay. I promise!"

"How do you know?"

"Because you *fucking are*!" Sweat dripped from his bright red face. Hair matted against his head as if he'd been swimming. He looked to be forcing himself to keep from hysterics. Nearly out of breath, he scanned the grounds left and right like he was searching for ideas and more tools to get me up with. Suddenly, he threw down the shovel and jolted upright with another idea.

As hot as it was that day, I was starting to shiver from the cold. "No!" I whispered. "No!" Inside my head, I yelled at my body to warm back up and keep hanging on. Kyle had a plan. I knew he did. "Fight for this!" I whispered again. "He's going to save me. Don't give up. Don't give up. Don't give up."

"Papa's coveralls!" He suddenly shouted and—*bam!*—he stood up fast enough to kick up a cloud of dust.

"They're still too big for you," I mumbled incoherently.

"I can make a sling with them." His eyes darted again, in idea mode, I guess. He looked up at the Goat, back over toward my camera on a stump, and then back at me, nodding like he was certain of his idea. For a kid who panicked at phone calls, he sure took charge at a crisis scene.

"A sling? For my arm? Is it broken?"

"Not that kind of sling." He had a hunting knife with him, and he started cutting through the rope rather than untie it from the log. "It's to drag you to the car on!"

"Louie's coveralls are back at the farm."

"Nope." He shouted while he turned to run over to the stump where my camera was. "I brought them with."

"Why?" I tried to yell loud enough for him to hear, but I couldn't produce much volume. Didn't matter. He'd heard.

"Just in case we found bees." He ran back to me from the stump and lifted my camera for me to see.

"Bees." I wanted to laugh but couldn't. The little fucker was making those jokes again that I wasn't sure were jokes. I shook my head in disbelief. "You're so fucking cute," I mumbled.

"I'm not that kind of girl, Tuck." He turned and ran toward the car.

The sling

Somehow, he was back already. I might have faded for a few seconds because he couldn't have gone all the way up to the car, opened the trunk, and come back down *that* fast. He knelt by my side, and before I could even figure out his next move, he'd executed it. Both hands slid beneath

The Goat Drive

my back as he bunched Louie's oversized coveralls beneath me. He was hot, sweaty, red-faced, his hair matted, and tiny…but focused and determined. Every motion and tug from his hands felt capable and experienced. "Does this hurt?"

"Everything hurts."

"I *mean* it, Tuck! I need to drag you, but…what if your back is broken!"

"I'm not trying to be funny, Kyle! Everything hurts, and I don't know if my back is broken or not."

"Fuck, I hope your back's not broken," he said, but more to himself than to me, "because I don't have a choice." He didn't stop moving. Once the coveralls were between me and the ground, he tied the legs together around his waist, like he was harnessing himself to pull a wagon. The ropes were still tied to the car, and so he hoisted himself with both arms while trudging forward with his big feet. Little tiny Kyle started dragging me uphill, head-first.

"You *tell me* if this hurts, Tucker James Taylor!" he ordered me with the command of a drill sergeant. "I don't want to move you, but I *have* to. I can't leave you here!"

The pain increased when he pulled. I still couldn't identify where it hurt the most, but a sharp burn pulsed on my right hip. Sickness overcame my gut and my eyes rolled back. I started to pass out, but I could feel my body wanting to slide off the coverall sled. "*Hang on and fight!*" I heard again, and I obeyed again. With almost no strength left in my arm at all, I grabbed a handful of cloth and squeezed it as hard as I could. "Hang on," I said to myself over and over as I started to pass out again.

"No!" he shouted. "Stay with me, Tuck! Don't fade away on me! I need you, Tuck!" Still sliding up the hill toward the Goat, I did everything in my power to keep from screaming. The hip hurt worse and worse as we moved, but God damn it, I hung on, literally *for dear life*.

"Oh, shit! You're bleeding bad, Tuck."

Instead of stopping, it felt like a second man joined in to double Kyle's speed. I fought to stay awake. I wanted to see who was helping, but when I made out shapes, no one but Kyle was there. The dove flashed to mind...almost as if it were lending some supernatural power to Kyle to grant him the strength of two men. The pain became excruciating, but I disobeyed Kyle's order and didn't shout. In fact, I think I finally, totally, and completely passed out.

Rise of expert Goat driver

I woke up in the passenger seat, curled halfway into the fetal position, facing Kyle, who was driving fast. Louie's coveralls were tied tightly around my right leg and waist. They were now a blood-soaked tourniquet.

"How the hell did you get me into this car?" I slurred like a drunk.

"It wasn't easy."

"Where are we?"

"I don't know yet." I detected a certain, contained panic in his answer.

"Where are we going?" My mouth was dry and my body was shivering like it was freezing outside.

"I'm trying to find a fucking hospital!"

I studied him as he drove. He was focused, strong, forcibly calm but scared shitless. Even his voice sounded older and in careful control of the situation. I couldn't see the speedometer, but it felt like we were doing at least eighty.

"Be careful, Kyle."

"I am, Tuck. I won't go off the road this time."

"Don't go too fast. Don't lose control. Find a gas station or something and get directions." Again, the weakness pulled me down into silence. When he saw me lose energy, I heard a "shit" and felt the car speed up.

"What are you doing?" I slurred with my last breath.

"*Ninety!*" he screamed back in a panic.

The GOAT DRIVE

I dozed off again and found myself staring into a vision of the iridescent blue eyes of the dove. I focused on it. Very peaceful. Very, very peaceful.

The positive uses for hypervigilance

"It *worked*!" he shouted. "It worked, Tuck. It *worked*! You were right! Ninety worked!"

I opened my eyes, still facing him, not sure how much time had lapsed since fading out. He was ducking and watching something in the driver's door rearview mirror. The car slowed quickly.

"What?"

"It's a cop!" He kept watching the mirror. "I went ninety…and I got caught! It worked!"

"Uh, oh." I wanted to joke with him so badly, but I could only just barely speak. "Probably gonna arrest you now," I whispered flatly.

"Stop trying to talk, Tuck. He can help us!"

With his short-but-strong arm, he held my chest to keep me upright as the car slowed to an aggressive stop. Then Kyle masterfully set the brake and shut it off. He got out slowly and stood by the driver's door. I couldn't see what was happening behind the car, but before too many seconds passed, I heard a firm voice shouting at him to stay in the car, but then I heard him confidently announce the situation.

"Help! Please help!" he shouted, "Officer, I have an emergency. Can you help us find a hospital, please?"

I knew I was in good hands with him. When I heard a man's voice exclaim, "Oh, Mother of God!" a calm settled over me. Kyle had found help. The pain worsened. Everything went dark.

Waking up

What a strange feeling to wake up again in a hospital untethered to a clock or a calendar, and completely unaware of what time or day it was. For a few minutes, I honestly believed it was 1971, and I was still a cancer patient. Today, I understand the effects of trauma well enough to know how normal that was, and that even to this day, I will never be able to visit a hospital without some part of me reliving what I went through at seventeen. Trauma sets in when the expectation of death is present. I'd once died in a hospital just like that one, and on this day in a similar environment, the reality of death was just as present as then.

"Tuck?" Kyle stood up. He'd been sitting next to me on a chair. "He's awake, Papa!"

"Oh, ya, ya. About time." Louie came into view behind Kyle. His big, strong, rugged hand lovingly and gently covered Kyle's small, but competent shoulder. "Tucker's here too, boy."

"Where is he?" I asked quietly.

"Oh, I think he's out making time with your nurse," Louie joked, which is what he always did when situations turned heavy.

I smiled and tried to laugh, but I was too drugged.

"He's sleeping on a couch in the waiting room," Kyle interjected.

Louie's big hand lifted off Kyle's shoulder and lovingly tapped at his grandson's pale, exhausted little cheek, then disappeared altogether.

"That sounds more like Grandpa," I teased.

"You scared me really bad, Tuck." Kyle's hair was a mess and his expressions heavy from what was most likely a long spell of deep emotional worry and sleeplessness.

"Sorry about that."

I felt his fingers touch my shoulder, but I was too drugged to look at them.

"We were just cutting wood a few minutes ago, Kyle. What happened?"

"That was yesterday. It's Saturday night. The tree you were sawing was holding up another tree. You weakened it and they both slid down right on top of you. The chainsaw cut you really bad."

"I'm not paying you for that," Louie joked. "You ain't done the job yet."

Trees

"Looks like I can hate trees as much as you do now," I teased.

"What was that now?" Louie stepped in closer and put the big hand back on Kyle's shoulder.

"Nothing, Papa!" Kyle's face grayed. He squeezed my shoulder. He locked eyes with me, microscopically shook his head, and mouthed the word no. Then he turned only his eyes toward his grandfather in a way that told me not to tell Louie something. I'd broached another secret.

"A private joke," I backtracked. "We, um. We were making lumberjack jokes up in the woods." I used my drugged demeanor as an excuse to change the subject. "How badly am I hurt?"

"Um." Kyle didn't respond readily. He appeared lost in his head. He shook it out as best he could and answered, "Your leg was cut open pretty deep."

"How deep? To the bone?"

"You almost bled to death." His mouth contorted and eyes watered. He stopped to compose himself, took a deep breath, and continued, "They stitched you up and gave you a whole bunch of blood. If the cop hadn't stopped me for speeding, you'd have died."

"Speeding?" I hadn't woken up enough yet to remember much. "Did you get a ticket?"

"No." He laughed once and wiped a tear off his cheek. "He was a good cop. After he saw you bleeding, he told me I did a good thing. He came by at lunchtime to check on you. His name is Rick…Schuman. He's worried about you."

"He came checkin' on *both* you boys," Louie added. "Just as worried about you too, Q-Tip."

"You would be the one to know his name." I tried to lighten his emotional load. "I told you you wouldn't go to jail for driving my car."

"He radioed for an ambulance. He's the one who saved you, not me."

"An ambulance? Phooey. You would have gotten me here in time without the cop. You could have beaten an ambulance in my hot rod car, couldn't you?"

"Turns out the hospital was the other direction, so...no."

Louie politely laughed at his grandson's response.

"Oops." Kyle chuckled and wiped another rogue tear while trying to be funny.

"Right way, wrong way...doesn't matter," I mumbled. The events of the rescue, and of being dragged, driven, and pulled over started coming back to me. With my voice low and drugged, I quietly praised Kyle while he and Louie hung on my every word. "You had the strength of two men up there. You lifted a fucking tree off me. I'm twice your size and you dragged me uphill to a car, and then God only knows how you got me in it. Then you drove me to where a cop could call for help." I smiled at him and he smiled back. "It was you I needed...or I'd have died."

"That's my boy." Louie beamed with delight and one-arm squeezed his grandson by the shoulders.

"I told you I'd have him on my team any day," I added, looking into Louie's face.

"I saved your camera too, Tuck."

"Oh, my God." I then recalled watching him retrieve it from the stump.

"I know how important it is to you."

I was dumbfounded. Recalling how laser-focused Kyle was on doing everything right to handle the crisis, it seemed that going back for something he knew was a deep part of me was an important part of his rescue measures. The bird was right; the kid loved me.

"C'mon, you guys. I just did what I had to do. That's all." Kyle's words were humble, but his tired eyes gleamed as proudly as they could.

I watched him scan the blue hospital sheets I lay beneath. I got curious about the rest of my injuries. "Is my back broken?"

"No—thank God!" He rolled his eyes in relief. "But two ribs are."

"Anything else?"

"You're not going to want to look in a mirror for a while." He put his face closer to mine to look as sympathetic as he could.

"Oh, my God!" I panicked. "Why?"

He started laughing. "Because you're still ugly."

No easy day

I teasingly shook my head and pretended to laugh also.

Kyle's laughter kept coming, and then gained a nervous shiver. Soon after that, it morphed into uncontrolled crying. It was obvious to me that the great Kyle Rickett who'd saved my life—and my most cherished possession—was now an emotional train wreck in progress.

"Oh, Kyle, Kyle, Kyle." I unsuccessfully grabbed for him with the hand closest. "C'mon, buddy. I'm going to be okay, right?"

"Yes. But…" The crying turned to mild hysterics. "You were in surgery for three hours. I didn't know-ho-ho." His mild hysterics escalated to loud bawling.

I lifted the other arm with a snarl of tubes attached to it and reached over myself.

He clasped onto it, lay his head gently across my chest, and sobbed.

Louie stretched a big hand across Kyle's back and rode out the jumping and jerking as his grandson struggled to breathe and gain control. He looked into my eyes and shook his head to express concern.

"Jesus, Kyle. You're the best friend a guy could ever have."

After a few minutes, he regained self-control and sat back up.

Time for the men to talk

"Q-Tip, I need coffee," said Louie, cutting through the solemn drama.

Kyle didn't answer immediately. He gathered his wits first and then he smiled at his grandfather. "Okay. I'll wait here." He sniffled.

"No, no, no, no. That ain't gonna work. I need *you* to get me coffee." Louie held out a quarter. "I only like it from the machine on the first floor."

"Why do I have to go all the way down to the first floor?" Kyle squinted and wrinkled his nose.

"He wants you to disappear," I interjected with a faint, tired smirk.

"Oh," Kyle responded with a sense that he understood. "Okay. How long do you want me gone for?"

"Ten minutes!" Louie boldly instructed.

"Do you want two sugars?"

"Don't care. I want you gone for ten minutes."

Kyle and I exchanged a glance. I winked at him and he smiled.

"I'll be back in ten minutes with a coffee that has two sugars in it."

"That's my boy." Louie patted his shoulder as Kyle backed out of the room, waving at me and boasting a wet, compassionate grin.

Time for a full report

"How's my face?"

"He was bein' funny. You look fine."

"Whew."

Louie rolled his eyes.

"He's an amazing young man, Louie."

"Ya, ya. Now you tell me about the trees. That comment you made. What was that about?"

"What?"

"I saw you two's faces. You know something about his trees."

"Not as much as I'd like to."

"He's a wreck." Louie sat into the chair Kyle'd occupied. "Trees mean something. What is it?" He glanced at the door, then back at me. "We been here since yesterday. He ain't been good. Not at all good."

"What do you mean?" I was groggy, but tracking okay with him.

"When he got you here, he told 'em he was your little brother. They let him stay. Took me and Tucker a couple of hours to get here. But we let 'em believe it too. He told us both what happened. Says when they cut your pants off you, he passed out. You was in surgery when we got to him."

"He passed out? Over them just cutting my clothes off?"

"Yeah, well. The nurse tells it different. Says he got crazy...tried stoppin' the doctor. They took him out and made him promise to be good before lettin' him back in the room with you."

"He lied to you?"

"I don't think so. He don't remember none of it. He believes he passed out."

"He doesn't *remember* being taken out of the room and scolded?"

"Nope."

"That's a little weird, I guess." I wanted to rub my own eyes, but I wasn't sure what parts of my own body I could touch with all the bandages and tubes in me.

"Been a whole day. He ain't slept. He walks around like a dead man. He cries when he thinks we ain't lookin'. We lose him and then find him cowering away from doctors in corners here and there. Lost in blank stares out through windows. Stammering like a drunk. Face is either pink and wet or has no color at all." He leaned in close. "Looking more like Maury all the time."

"Oh, God, Louie. He hasn't slept *at all?*"

"He dozed off once over there." He pointed toward a chair at the foot of my bed. "Woke up yellin'. We thought someone was beatin' him up. But it was a dream. A bad one. About *trees!*" He pursed his lips. "He won't tell me what the trees are about."

"Trees?" I recalled Kyle's facial message to me not to mention trees.

"I know you is on medicine and all, but I seen your eyes. You know about the trees." Louie's finger poked at my chest. "He was grabbin' at his own wrists. You tell me what that was!"

I paused. Who was I going to honor at that moment? The friend who'd asked me to get valuable information out of his closed-down grandson, or the friend who'd asked me not to tell his grandfather that he repeatedly dreamt of being tied and raped?

"That same thing happened the night before we left." I owed my honor to both friends. But keeping Kyle's secret from Louie was counterproductive. I knew it was time to be the adult and help the child I'd committed to save. "I thought he was being attacked. I grabbed his wrists and he went limp. It was a dream then too. Something about trees then too."

"Why is he doin' that? It ain't like him." His big, heavy finger pointed into my eyes. "I was right, wasn't I? My boy's not crazy, Tuck. He was grabbin' at his wrists. Someone's doin' things to him…tyin' him up maybe."

I froze in silence. I was not prepared to go there with Kyle's family, but it was glaring me in the face and I couldn't run or hide.

"Tell me what you know," Louie persisted. "Right…*now*!"

"I can't be sure, but…it kind of sounds like it." I sighed. The fact was that Louie was on our side. It was time to expose everything we could.

"Who?" His jaw tightened in anger. "Who do I gotta' pay a visit to?"

"I haven't found that out yet, but don't be too hard on his dad. I don't think it's John. But you're right about one thing. Someone's behind this. This looks more like trauma than crazy."

"Just like Maury after the war, flinchin' every time he heard a pop." The concern on Louie's face was more intense than it was the day he made me promise to help. "I know what spooked Maury. Bombs. But why is trees spookin' my boy?"

"That's how trauma works, Louie. It was a tree that brought us all here," I theorized.

"His mamma told me his bad summer started with an accident. Stitches in his leg. Says he ain't been the same since."

"An accident? Stitches?" I made fast connections with stitches in his leg and stitches in mine. "But I've seen him in shorts and there are no stitches in his legs."

The GOAT DRIVE

Louie was helping me sort this out as fast as I was helping him understand what happened. I knew that when a child has a sudden change in personality, it's often a red flag pointing to a traumatic event. Usually violent, life-threatening…or sexual.

"Says the stitches are at the top of his leg…up in his skivvies. Says Dr. Krieg saved him from bleeding to death. Gave him stitches in his private area."

"Dr. *Krieg*?" I recalled the name. Kyle hated him and said his breath *tasted like* cigarettes. "You mean his dad's friend?"

"You heard of him?"

"Kyle mentioned him. He doesn't like him at all," I noted. "Fucking hates him, in fact."

"Pumpkin's not too fond of him either. Says John gives him too much credit."

"Louie…any chance old Doc Krieg cut Kyle's clothes off him too?"

"Probably had to. What are you gettin' at?"

"Similarities. Triggers. A lot of them; tree dreams are bothering him at night; an accident cuts his leg; a doctor cuts his clothes off; he ends up getting stitches in his leg…or rather his private area. Then it happens again to me right in front of him. A tree nearly kills me and I end up getting my clothes cut off and stitches in my leg. Maybe this is like some kind of a rerun to him and he thinks he knows how it's going to end."

"You think I should take him home? This place is no good for him?"

"No, Louie. No. He needs not to be sent away again. This place is difficult for him, but sending him away will just be another trigger. He's little, but he's a man—a *real* one. And he deserves the respect of being allowed to stay. He's a part of what's going on here—in fact, he's a freaking hero because of all of it. He can't be sent away. He still needs to open up some more…. I need to know more about this Krieg character."

"So, you told me what you know? All of it?"

"All of it. I swear to god." Either the medicines were wearing off, or I was getting so focused I was overriding them. "I need to find out more about Krieg and trees now."

"Then what do I do?"

"Nothing. Just be patient with him. This place bothers *me* too. Remember, I nearly died in a hospital like this. Now being here has me squirmy too."

"You know what he's thinkin' because—"

"Because I've been here. Yes, Louie. You're right."

"Always am." He crossed his arms and smiled teasingly.

"I guess I know more about my friend than I give myself credit for."

"But he never went to no hospital. It was only a clinic."

"Probably smelled the same," I pondered. "When he comes back, leave him with me. Hopefully, I can stay awake long enough to get him to tell me what he was dreaming about."

Calming down

When Kyle returned, his smile filled the room and coaxed a mild chuckle from me. Either my painkillers were softening me up, or the bird was right and I was firmly connected by genuine affection—*love*—for the kid.

Beaming like a child, Kyle carefully held out both hands to give Louie the fresh coffee with two sugars in it. He slipped between man and boy with each motion. I pictured how mature and responsible he'd been only hours before as he took charge of a crisis and rescued me from a truly touch-and-go accident. Then I chuckled again silently as I pictured what he must have looked like when he lied to the front desk about us being brothers. Finally, I wondered if maybe to him, it wasn't so much of a lie, but a fantasy that he was pretending was true.

"You got stopped by a cop?" I asked him.

"Ninety worked. Thank God. And it's a good thing you showed me how to drive your car just before your accident." He pushed the chair back with a knee and stood beside me.

"You already knew how to drive."

"Not that fast." He smiled and began to tap out a two-fingered drum beat on my shoulder.

"You lied to the hospital." I smirked and held up a hand for a high-five as Louie left the room. "Way to go, manly man."

"I never lie." He grabbed my hand instead of slapping it.

"Yes, you did."

He chuckled quietly.

"In fact, you lied twice."

"When did I lie a second time?"

"Louie showed me a mirror. I'm still a handsome son-of-a-bitch."

He laughed aloud, but this time, he didn't break apart into hysterics.

"Have you eaten anything?" I asked.

"Not hungry."

"I've seen how you get when you don't eat, little brother."

He stopped tapping my shoulder and beamed, "It's fun pretending we're brothers. Papa didn't rat me out. Your parents are halfway here from St. Paul. Papa told them to keep pretending I'm your brother."

"My mother agreed to that?"

"Papa told them I saved you. So I guess they're okay with letting the nurses believe it's true."

"Ha! I'll play along too. In fact, I should ask the nurse for an apple or something and you can eat it when she leaves."

"My stomach can't handle food right now."

The truth, the whole truth, and nothing but the truth

Kyle let me doze for a little while. But I woke up to a nurse fiddling with my tubes and taking blood pressure while Kyle sat, nearly passed out, in the chair at the end of my bed. As she left the room, Kyle stood back up, groggily but kindly thanked her for the care, and came back to my side.

"Thank you for saving my camera, buddy." I didn't ask about that stomach ache he'd told me about before falling asleep. I didn't know the specifics, but his nervous mood swings were a telling sign that his stomach was some sort of a physical manifestation of a constant storm front living somewhere inside him. No need to discuss it now.

"You're welcome." He smiled shyly and tapped my shoulder a few more times.

"Kyle…" I paused to choose the right words, but also to digest something the dove had said during the visit in the bunk bed. I was told to disclose who I am. To open up and share myself with him. "I want to tell you something…."

"What?" He slid the chair toward himself and sat close.

"I dream about Micah…" This seemed like a great, slow, easy lead in to one of the deepest topics of who I was, "a lot."

"You called me Micah once. You said, 'Goodnight, Micah.'" He started tapping playfully on the bed rail. "I thought maybe it was a nickname for someone in your family."

"Not a nickname. Micah was my son."

"You really *are* a dad?" A stunned enthusiasm came from his face. "For real? A real dad? Can I meet him? Is he my age?"

"*Your* age?" I laughed quietly. "I was seven when you were born, Kyle." I laughed quietly a second time. "No, he'd be three now, if he'd have lived."

Kyle tightened his lips together and waited, still tapping on the bedrail. He either didn't know what to say or didn't want to embarrass me.

"He died shortly after his birth. His mom stayed in my life for just a little while longer, and then…I ended up alone." I got a lump in my throat. "Yeah. It's definitely one of the things that keeps me up at night."

"I'm sorry, Tuck." He sheepishly looked at the bedrail while speaking. "I didn't know about any of it."

"Did you hear me say that it keeps me up at night?"

He nodded, still looking at the bedrail.

"If we're going to be brothers, then I have to come clean with you. You need to know that life isn't easy for me either."

"Why do I need to know that?"

You are not alone

"Because it's important to me to tell you that you're not alone on this earth, Kyle. I can tell you sort of idolize me."

He glanced back into my eyes and gently smiled in acknowledgment.

"It's not fair to you for me to cruise around town in a hot car, wearing stylish clothes, and not tell you that I…have stomach problems too."

"Do you take antacids?" There was some excitement in his voice. I knew he didn't wish me ill; he just found energy in knowing he wasn't the only person on earth struggling to keep his head up during the day.

"Not as often as you, but I have to work at staying happy." I wanted the mood raised, so I chuckled and added, "It ain't easy being this cool all the time, you know. I have to work at it…just like you do."

"Okay." He scooted the chair even closer, until both knees were pressed snuggly to the side of my bed. "What are your dreams like about Micah?"

"I blame myself for his death."

"Oh." His look of surprise was laced with compassion, as if he were going to try and talk me out of believing such a thing.

"Kyle…I've *never* told anyone that before. You and me. This is our secret."

"Okay." He smirked again which told me he was proud to be included in one of my secrets. "I won't say anything. But…why do you blame yourself? Was it an accident?"

"No. But I was sick when Shannon and I conceived. I pulled the sympathy card to get her to sleep with me in the first place. I was on heavy medications and had no business getting her pregnant. He was born sick and only lived a few months."

"I don't see how that could be your fault. How sick were you? What kind of medicines were you on?"

Cancer scare

I quietly thought through how to tread delicately, but realized there was no delicate way to say it. "Cancer medications."

He sat up straight and startled. It was disturbing to watch.

"Kyle? You okay?"

"You have *cancer*?" His breathing turned to shallow panting. "Why didn't you tell me?" His mouth contorted again as he tried not to start crying and more pain showed in his eyes. It's possible that he was too exhausted for us to be having such a deep conversation. "Life is so *fucking* unfair!"

"*No!*" I tried to sit up also. "*Had*! I *had* cancer. It's been in remission for over three years. I don't have it anymore. I swear."

"But can't it come back?" His face was turning pinker by the second.

"No. Well...." I almost said yes, but that would have been too much for him. "*No*...I don't think so.... The doctors said I have a great chance of living a long life as long as I keep a watch on it."

He faded into his head. His eyes scanned around the room and glanced at my face several times. "So..." his voice trembled, "are you keeping a watch on it?"

"Kyle, I'm not going anywhere."

"ARE YOU KEEPING A WATCH ON IT?" he demanded.

"I.... Yes! I wasn't going to, but...."

"But *what*?" He was scolding out of anger, but scared at the same time.

"But because of *you*...."

"Me?"

"Kyle, I have a friend now. I want to make sure I'm going to be around for you. So I'm going to ask the doctors here to get my records from St. Paul and check me while I'm here."

"And?"

"And that's it. They're going to draw blood for it, and I won't know the results for a week."

He squeezed my hand and smiled, but with heavy concern.

"You're welcome," I said. "I'm going to make sure I don't croak on you."

"We just became friends." His pained words trailed off to a labored whisper. "We just became *brothers*."

"We're still brothers. We will be for a long time. If I watch it, they promise I won't get sick again." I back-pedaled, wishing I'd waited until he'd had some rest before discussing this topic, but I was in deep now and couldn't unsay any of it.

"I hope so." His nose ran, and he pulled a wadded handkerchief from his pocket to blow into. "But..." He tried to sound funny, "I'm sure not going to sleep *now*"

"I know, buddy. My sister's been trying to get me to get tested. She isn't going to sleep either."

"Not until that blood test comes back. Why did you have to wait so long?"

"Kyle, I wasn't sure I gave a shit...until now...."

"I was just starting to like you." He laughed, but sadly.

"You were *just* starting to like me?" I teased back.

"What else don't I know?" He put the cloth down in his lap, grabbed the top of his stomach, and winced in pain. "You were a dad...you had cancer...what else?"

I stared at him without speaking. I had one more thing I really wanted to experiment with. I had a story I wanted to embellish just a little. I wanted to break through all his confusion about his cousin's sexual orientation, his own battle with the nickname Homo, and any sexual abuse he may have endured at the hand of a man. I needed to bring myself into his world, and I saw my relationship with Trenton and Mark as an opportunity to open another trust bond with this kid. All I had to do was tell the truth about Mark and me, but embellish a little bit about how close I came to doing something most men would never disclose. My need for Kyle's trust was so strong that I decided to let him have something over on me.

Was this the time to dump all of it and end all the secrets once and for all? Or would it have made sense to give him bites he could digest over a little time? My mission was to teach him trust. He needed to know, before I got out of that bed, that I was 100 percent transparent to him.

"Tuck? What else don't I know?"

"I guess…we've come this far…"

"What do you mean 'we've come this far'?"

"There is one last thing." I exhaled in surrender. "Something big."

"Bigger than *cancer*?" His expressive eyes drilled holes into mine.

"For some guys, yeah. For some guys this is way bigger than cancer. Kyle, before I tell you my last little…thing…I need to know something."

"What?"

I bit at my lip. It wasn't too late to stop myself right then and there. I could easily make up a lie about one thing or another and come back to this another day. But as I stared into his eyes and thought about how he had just performed an amazing rescue and quite literally saved me from certain death, I found myself so filled with respect for him that I couldn't bring myself to let him think he was totally alone with all that had happened to him.

"Why did you tell me about Scooter being gay?" I asked. "Don't you know you're never supposed to out someone?"

"Out someone? What does that mean?"

"It means you're always supposed to let people tell that secret with their own mouths."

"Oh." He blushed like he'd just been caught murdering his cousin. "I didn't know that. But I would never tell anyone about him being…you know."

"Gay?"

"I guess." His voice jittered a bit.

"But you told me."

He shrugged

"Why?"

"Well…." He nervously shifted in his seat. "You're Tuck."

"Because I'm Tuck?"

"You're *Tuck*. I can tell you things."

"So you'll tell me things that you'll never tell anyone else?"

"Duh. I've been doing it for two days now. I trust you more than anyone else in the whole world."

"How do I *know* you aren't going to make another friend some day and tell that person about Scooter?"

"I would never tell anyone who might hurt him. Tuck, you…you would *never* hurt Scooter. I have faith…not hope."

I knew what he was trying to say. He saw me in a different light than he did anyone else. I owed him a pass for his not knowing the rules of outing a friend or relative. And when I thought back at when he'd told me, I recalled it being more a comment about him being confused about what it meant. He was unbelievably accepting of it all, too. I needed to give him some leeway.

"Now that you know you're never supposed to let out a gay person's secret, you'll probably never do it again, right?"

"No way!" he blurted. "Scooter can tell whoever he wants, but I'm never going to tell anyone."

"Okay. That's all I needed to hear."

He smiled like my forgiveness was all he needed.

"Now I have something I need to tell you."

42

Truth Be Told

> *I'd never experienced honesty to the levels Tuck went to that morning. He told me things about himself that I believed no one had ever said anywhere in all the world. As he opened up with secrets so sensitive that I could hurt him with them, I realized his trust for me was as pure as it could be. Then, just as Papa had once said would happen, my own story became crystal clear. Relief washed through me like cool water on a hot day as I—for the first time ever—was able to tell someone what it was like to be me.*

By Kyle Rickett

Tuck wasn't gay. Why was it so important for him to tell me about Mark? I guess it's important to remember that in 1974, Tuck's "close encounter" was a much bigger deal than it is today. There, in the hospital, in 1974, Tuck was the first person ever to tell me about having almost been in a relationship with another man. His confession was confusing, but not frightening. Even Scooter hadn't yet told me his secret. Poor bastard had been accused of it by my family, but that wasn't the same thing. I was used to people accusing each other of that all the time—usually as an insult to make a guy feel rejected by the crowd. Having a man openly admit it to me was a statement I didn't think anyone, anywhere, would ever say out loud.

The fact that Tuck's disclosure was private with me meant even more. He trusted me over anyone else on the earth. A month earlier, I'd have been a whole lot more freaked out than I was at this point, but that summer had torn me into shreds—figuratively and literally—like the three-sided paper. Being sent away forced me to put myself back together differently. Scooter had broken the ice. His getting caught tore a caustic trail through my family. Because it prepared me to accept Tuck, I was glad that trail had been pre-cut for me to walk on now.

Tuck told me that Trenton overreacted when he caught him and Mark in their underwear on the bed. I didn't think that was such a dark secret until Tuck confessed that ever since it had happened, he'd been sort of wishing Mark was still around. I asked Tuck why, if nothing happened, he thought it was so important to tell me about it, and he said it was because he wanted me to know he knew what it felt like to be treated how me and his gay friends were being treated. I admit now that, from that point on, knowing he'd experienced what I'd experienced really helped me feel connected to him. I'm not alone.

The bike accident wasn't such a bad thing after all. It gave my family the bang needed to shake the foundations of a tired old family tree. Getting caught in Krieg's trap woke me up. It wasn't a bad thing either because it exposed dreams about him and Christmas trees that I needed to admit were real. The summer also proved to me that my dad would side with his adult friend instead of his own young son, and that Mom would push me off to her dad instead of tell Fran to become a good person. Then Scooter getting caught opened the family up to a world we all tried to pretend didn't exist, and I saw my own family turn on him in a most disgusting way that I now knew they were capable of doing. And finally, if the cop hadn't stopped me for speeding, I'd have driven too far down the wrong road and would have ended up losing Tuck altogether. All these unwanted incidents proved that getting caught sometimes is the best thing that can ever happen to us.

Tuck was right when he said that my tolerance for pain had been too strong. It was time to let some of it go. Nothing was what it seemed anymore, and so Tuck's story of almost being in a relationship with Mark didn't blow my mind the way it would have blown anyone else's in 1974. In fact, it was an honor to have been trusted with such a delicate secret.

So it worked. I opened up and told...him...*everything*.

Gushing truth

It was surprisingly easy to tell Tuck about the bike accident and Dr. Krieg's intimidation of my mom and Kathy. I told the whole story, even that Krieg held my hands over my mouth and full-on molested me while Mom was right outside the door. Maybe it was the drugs, but Tuck didn't flinch even when I told him how many times I'd had bizarre nightmares that Krieg had molested me in Island Voyager Scouts when I was seven, eight, and nine. But he sobbed pretty hard when I told him I had dreamt there were photographs of me with Krieg and the Voyager Scouts somewhere out in the world.

While I spoke, Tuck's hand opened as an invitation for me to grab it. He gently nodded, showing me that he was absorbing every word without judging me and without telling me to "get over it." He made it so easy to talk that I was able to describe how crazy I got inside my head, and how I remembered dream-like flashbacks of Krieg—and other boys—doing it to me before.

I broke my rule of honoring family at all cost. Without first saying, "They love me, but," I openly told him that dear old Dad was not abusive, *but he was also not supportive*. I admitted that I didn't know if Mom and Dad knew what Krieg had done, but Krieg was Dad's friend and *I was to keep quiet*. I told him what Connor and I were talking about when Dad banned him. I confessed it was still about sex, but that it was not sex with a girl. I told him about Fran's taunting me when she tattled on Scooter, and how her own daughters had once really liked me, but they had begun to eye-roll and scoff at me when I talked, making it obvious that Fran insulted me behind my back to her own children, and probably to everyone else on the island.

I told him of the three-sided paper, and how important it was to me to keep all three sides separate so my family didn't come down on me hard for not being a perfect, problem-free child. I walked him through my experience trying to kill myself in St. Paul, and I gave him a detailed description of the two boy hookers I'd become so entranced by.

Tuck's reactions weren't of disbelief, nor of anger or scolding. At a few points, rogue tears appeared and fell out of one of his eyes, but he didn't say anything about it. He didn't use my reports of these actions as a chance to tell me what I was supposed to think or feel. He didn't advise or compete with me by telling stories of how his life was worse. He just listened. And cried a little. He believed me. He believed me. He *believed* me.

He trusted me, and I trusted him. It was so easy to talk. Papa was right. As soon as I trusted him, the words just came to me. *God, it felt good to get my secrets out of my head!*

Papa didn't hear any of our conversation. He stayed out of the room when he saw Tuck and me talking. A couple of times I'd looked over my shoulder to see him glancing in at us. At one point, Tuck asked me why my grandfather kept hovering at the door.

"He's not letting me leave until I either talk or we both get bloody noses."

Homeward bound

Tuck's parents arrived from St. Paul at about six-thirty Saturday evening, so both grandfathers and I went to work as a team to go back to the cabin before dark, get the equipment, and retrieve the car, which the police had impounded from the roadside rather than allow a fourteen-year-old to drive it to the hospital. Grandpa Tucker paid about forty-five dollars to get the keys from impound. He drove it home while I rode with Papa in the Fairlane.

For most of the way home, we chatted about how proud he was of me for being such a "big man" and for saving Tuck's life the way I had. I didn't have an answer for how I had managed to lift Tuck into the car, except that I had somehow just felt super-strong when I needed to. When we were about ten minutes out, Papa blurted out something that was tough for him to talk about, but it seemed important to him not to let it sit in his craw.

"Scooter called."

My breath left me. My eyes bulged. "Is he okay?"

Papa chuckled.

"What's so funny?"

"You just been through hell and back. You thought he hated you, and the first words in your mouth are askin' if *he's* okay?" He shook his head and smiled. "You got a big heart, Q-Tip."

I stared, waiting for his answer.

"He's a good boy, too. Just like you. You know that, right?" Papa checked with me.

"Of course I do. He's the best. Always has been."

"Nothing's different, Q-Tip. He's still the best."

It sounded like Papa knew what I suspected to be true. But Tuck had told me never to expose that secret for anyone. I couldn't ask Papa any questions that would lead him to find out Scooter was gay. Even if I suspected he already knew. What if I was wrong and Papa knew something different?

"You two's still Siamese twins. He told me to give you his best."

"What did you tell him back?"

"I told him the same thing I told you. That you two is still like Siamese twins."

"You made *sure* he knows that I love him?"

"I did, boy." Then he looked over at me. "He cried a bit. He said to tell you he loves you."

I fell back in the seat and exhaled a ton of relief. "You're the best, Papa."

The GOAT DRIVE

43

History in the Making

Here in the civilized world, living a life of secrets rates as the third worst thing I can think of, just beneath the threat of starvation or war. Summer wasn't completely over yet when Tuck had destroyed the boundaries that held back my secrets. He was a lot more cheerful, too, I suppose because he'd also let go of all his secrets. We got to live for several weeks side by side in a state of being that I'd never experienced before: complete open honesty.

By Tuck Taylor

On Tuesday, August 6, after only four days in the hospital, I was released into the care of my posse of two grandfathers and my new little brother. In the car, I realized two things: 1) broken ribs hurt like a mother, and 2) I had now escaped near-certain death *thrice in one lifetime*. Was I completely invincible because I kept surviving? Or was I prone to really bad luck by the way I kept almost dying? Either way, I was an anomaly, and once again, I'd beaten mortality.

Summer now smelled especially sweet beneath a sun that was particularly bright. All the way home, Kyle, whom I now loved more than ever, attended to me, repeatedly insisting that Louie slow the Fairlane down so my ribs wouldn't hurt.

Once home, the two of us brothers still had a whole month ahead of us, but our original orders, to cut and split wood, had been rescinded. I didn't sit still. Even with broken ribs, I found enough strength to putter around in the Goat, taking my new best friend to movies, beaches, burgers, and malls. It was as if we'd grown up together, never having each experienced our time of loneliness.

Kyle himself was a whole new man. It was probably my imagination, but I almost detected him growing an inch or two in height over the course of the next three weeks. A couple of times I thought I'd caught the hint of a deeper voice when he would laugh. The free spirit that our shared crisis had unleashed may have translated to a physical freedom for his body to grow a little with his spirit. In many different ways, Kyle was coming of age before my very eyes.

A lot of history was made in the next few days. On August 8, President Nixon resigned, which ended the argument our grandfathers had been keeping alive all summer. I received good news from the lab at the hospital that my blood work showed no signs of cancer, and as promised, Kyle finally began to allow me to photograph him.

And so I did. Constantly. By the third day, he had stopped wincing at the camera and began to play it up. He'd pose for pondering shots by looking off into the distance. He'd laugh on command whenever I wanted a happy summer shot. I had become his most important person on earth and was loving every second of it.

The photographers who get the most interesting shots are often those who have their cameras on them all the time because they're there and ready when life's freak opportunities appear out of thin air. One of our afternoon adventures later became historic to the two of us, when, somehow, we ended up in Duluth wandering down by the oar docks taking photos of people, waterfront scenery, ships, trains, and such. With my tripod and timer, I could snap shots of us together. One of those little freakish opportunities hangs on my wall to this day. It's a shot of the two of us posing arm in arm on the waterfront, with Kyle standing on a curb to make our shoulders the same height. The *Edmund Fitzgerald* was tied to an oar dock behind us, loading up for her next voyage across the lakes. We took the picture because we knew she was the largest ship on the Great Lakes, but unknown to us at the time, she was only a year or so from making history by sinking in a November storm and becoming the object of a Gordon Lightfoot ballad, one of the most famous ballads of the 1970s.

But still, the most noticeable change in my life, even more than my post-surgery limp and constant grunting at rib pain, was that the dove had not visited me even once since I had woken up in the hospital. I had done everything the dove had instructed. I'd held on. I'd fought. And here we were: Brothers.

Preparing for the event

On Saturday, August 31, our day to recreate the gazebo event came with enough excitement to overshadow the sadness of summer's end. Kyle's beautiful white hair was longer than ever, so on Friday, the day before the event, I took him into town and bought him his first professional haircut and style. The kid looked so different from when I'd met him only five weeks prior that it seemed he wasn't the same person at all. The haircut aged him another five years. It was 1974, and feathering was the style. His white locks were thick like a rock star's. A curved wave of bangs fell heavily over his left eye. He got to where he did my famous four-finger comb-back several times an hour, but now he had the hair to do it with. He usually didn't notice, but wherever we went together in the car, we got a lot more second looks than I ever got when alone.

Louie had devoted a full week to building up the event. He began with inviting the two of us to sit on stools behind him while he played accordion on his local TV spot. He announced the event as if it were going to be Kyle's performance, not his. Then we all spent the full week putting up flyers all over town. By this time—the final days of August—my four-week-old limp was only detectable after I'd been walking for a ways, and my ribs only hurt when I laughed hard or bumped into something.

The photo-shoot

Louie had managed to get the band back together. The crowd was thin, but I had ways of angling the camera and clustering people to make the photos look as crowded as Woodstock. An inordinate number of young people showed up, possibly because an especially flattering picture of sexy, longer-haired Kyle was on the posters all over town, making him appear to be a bigger star than he really was.

During the event, a thin crowd mulled around on the dry grass. Being less of a festival, more of a picnic, the event had led to a neighborly softball game organizing itself on the north field.

My fantasy was fulfilled when Kyle and Louie played, giving me a variety of musical action shots. In some, they stood side by side. In others, Kyle hovered behind Louie, while still in others, the opposite. I'd gotten from them what I felt I needed in order to present an artistic visual display of ageless/timeless festivals, bridged through multiple generations by the old man and the young grandson, both sporting white hair and sparkling eyes.

My favorite of all the shots ended up being one of white-haired Kyle, sweat dripping, eyes cinched tightly, blasting the most difficult piece of his song on the accordion while his equally white-haired grandfather fingered the keys of his own accordion while chuckling at him from behind. Because of the traditional Bavarian attire and the wooded backdrop, the photo could have taken place in the 1800s, were it not for a watch on Kyle's wrist. That masterpiece broke through time barriers to generations of cultural celebration, and would one day make its way onto the front cover of a nationally marketed travel brochure.

After the music, the crowd stayed for a picnic hosted by the senior center and the local TV show producers. Brats, beer, and kraut, just like before, filled the senses. Through the blistering August heat, Kyle wandered about in his lederhosen, soaking in the attention more than I'd ever seen a kid do. His personality had completely blossomed. The spark and the joy on his face attracted people from all ages to want photos with him. So I set them up on one of Louie's homemade horse buggies and charged four dollars each to give the locals their portraits; some with Kyle, others with their own families. As I took their money, I realized I'd become a professional photographer right then and there.

The GOAT DRIVE

Kyle's walk had changed as well. He didn't look toward the ground anymore, but kept eyes attentively focused on the faces around him. His smile never seemed to fade as he nodded and greeted everyone he saw.

He was a particularly attractive young man, and it was about time his body movements showed he could own that. But at the same time, his empathetic DNA and heritage of childhood abuse and isolation tempered his ego and kept him from expressing arrogance. He looked into people, not at them. He made eye contact and smiled as if he knew each person he saw. I sensed his joy at being accepted in ways he'd not yet experienced. I'd never seen anyone who could just be so genuinely likeable.

As the crowd thinned after lunch, two particularly cute young girls, only slightly older than him, asked for a photo, so I posed them to his left and right, each beneath one of his Bavarian musician's arms across their shoulders. When I hit the final shutter, I shouted, "Now kiss him!"

Both giggling girls kissed a cheek. The surprise on his face lit up the whole shot. As promised, that photo never made it to Washington State, but with Kyle's permission, it became the poster for Railroad Riding Days Events for the next *eleven* seasons!

Heading back to the ranch

Louie and Tucker towed the wagon home on a flatbed trailer behind Tucker's pickup while Kyle and I drove the Goat home in our own time.

"What's in that bag?" Kyle asked of a grocery sack I'd tried to hide behind his seat.

"What bag?"

"It's on the floor behind me."

"Jeez, Kyle! I can't get away with *anything* around you."

"When did you go shopping?" he teased with a big grin. "I never said you could go shopping without me."

"None of your business!" I jokingly scolded, then changed the subject. "How'd you like your first kiss with two girls at once?"

He blushed but smiled brightly.

"Those girls seemed pretty smitten with you."

"I…can't believe it, Tuck."

"Oh, come on."

"No, really! I can't believe people *like* me."

"Why not? I've been telling you all along that you're a real catch."

"I just…this isn't what life is like back home."

I gave a polite smile, but I didn't know what to say.

"I have to go back there in two fucking days."

"Maybe it won't be so bad this time."

"Yes, it will. I know it. I hate it there. I hate it so bad. It's going to be just like it was. Nothing's going to change."

"Don't you miss your mom?"

"Sometimes. But I also think she's going to cut my hair short again and make me wear hand-me-downs that went out of style when Daniel was my age."

"Wow." I had helped Kyle come to terms with who he was there in Minnesota, but his toxic life back home was waiting for him just as he'd left it. Suddenly, it hit me that tonight Kyle was a lifesaving local hero, who gave his autograph a dozen times, and got an article written about him in the local paper. In a few days, he would likely be playing with small cars on the floor of his bedroom, trying to hide from a family that would, again, be treating him like a pet.

"I want to stay here." He finger-combed his longer hair as it blew in the wind, bangs slapping his eyes.

"I don't blame you," I responded politely.

"No, Tuck. I mean it. Do you think you could talk Papa into…?"

I looked over to see a boy who was not kidding, and who was glaring into my eyes in hopes I would give a real answer.

"Kyle, I can't…. Louie can't…."

"Are you sure?"

"Well…you didn't know this, but Louie and I have already talked about it," I admitted. "A lot. He wishes he could keep you, but he knows John and Marie will come after him with cops if he tries it."

"I know." He deflated. "I just thought I'd ask."

I gently slapped at his shoulder with my knuckles.

"Will you move to the island with me?" He livened up as if he'd been planning to ask this for a long time.

"I…uh…" I was surprised, and not surprised at the same time. "I'll think about it. How's that?"

44

Coming of Age Ceremony

Our society has lost a powerful tradition by not performing a coming-of-age ceremony for boys who've proven they are no longer children. Tuck gave me the most amazing gift of the summer when he let me open the bag he'd been protecting.

By Kyle Rickett

On our last night together, I cooked dinner for the grandfathers and Tuck, who still hadn't committed to moving to Torano Island with me.

After dinner, we went to the living room to watch the five o'clock news with the grandfathers. I made sure to press up against Tuck on the sofa as if he were my natural-born brother. He seemed to have started to like when I did that.

A few minutes into the news, Tuck leaned toward me to say something he'd been holding on to for the whole day. I could feel his excitement.

"Let's camp out tonight," he whispered.

"Where?"

"Down by the creek. Where you and Scooter used to play. I've already put together a firepit and everything."

"When did you do that?"

"This morning before you got up."

I stared at him, mouth open. "You're sneaky!"

He laughed.

"Okay. A campout would be fun, especially since you ruined our last one by almost dying."

He laughed some more. "Yeah. I'm a real selfish jerk sometimes."

"Ha!" I chuckled back and then tried to get my grandfather's attention. "Papa!"

"I already know," Papa grumbled. "Your brother there borrowed my tent this mornin'." Then he waved his hand toward the door. "Go on—git. I'm watchin' the news."

Tuck and I both chuckled at his response while we walked out the door. But Tuck surprised me by walking toward his car rather than to the trailhead.

"We're not going to drive, are we?"

"Do you know where the sack is that I hid from you?"

"Is it still in the backseat of the Goat?" I excitedly asked.

He nodded.

I ran on ahead and he followed me the rest of the way to the car. I smiled from ear to ear as I pulled it through the open window. He asked if I'd peeked into it even once since it was put there.

"No way!" I responded, "I love surprises!" I paused and locked eyes with him.

"Well, don't peek yet! It's for the campout."

The GOAT DRIVE

"What is it? I want to know."

"It's our dessert."

The dark truth

We chatted energetically on the walk to the creek-side campsite. There, I saw that Tuck had already set up Papa's tent, laid out two sleeping bags, gotten the firepit ready to light, and even brought marshmallows, graham crackers, and chocolate bars. This was as official as any campout I'd ever seen.

"Oh, my God!" I laughed so hard I almost dropped the sack when I found Papa's smaller accordion—the one I always played—sitting on a campstool next to the firepit.

"Yes," he said over my childish laughing. "I *am* planning to polka with bears tonight."

"All right. You asked for it. Polka by the campfire." I held up the bag. "Now, what's for dessert?"

"Eh-eh!" He grabbed it from me. "In due time, my boy. In due time."

We lit the fire and let it smolder until it would become hot enough to roast marshmallows. While Tuck puttered around gathering more twigs, I gently played single notes and partial songs on the accordion. If I didn't get too loud with it, I admit it actually sounded kind of nice with the babbling creek in the background.

"Tuck?" I stopped playing and looked up at him.

"Yeah?"

"So, you really think I'm ready to go back to Torano alone?"

"No." He sat down and put a marshmallow on a stick and hovered it over the crackling fire. "But I can help you can make it work anyway. You don't have a choice. Fran's always going to be Fran. Andreo, Chad, Krieg. They're all the same people they were."

"How am I going to get ready for that? I couldn't deal with them before, and they're still the same."

"Because *you're* different. They're going to be in your brain forever, but *this summer's going to be in your brain forever too*."

"Torano Island sucks."

"You know what?" He reached behind himself and then handed me the bag. "Now's the perfect time for dessert."

"Oh, good! I finally get to see what you got me!" I unrolled the bag and stared inside. Then I put it down on my lap and looked at him with a comical, overly exaggerated look of confusion.

"What? That's quality stuff right there."

"It's beer."

"It's dessert."

"It's *beer*."

"And…" He grabbed the bag from me and reached in excitedly. Then after fishing for only a second or two, he pulled out two cellophane wrapped tubes, "a cigar!"

Sometimes a cigar

"But I don't smoke cigars!"

"You didn't when you were a boy. You do tonight."

"Why?"

"Because, my good *man*…" He held up the cigar as if it were a flag, "you rebuilt a *tractor*!"

"Oh, God! I haven't heard you say that in hours."

"Your dad owed this to you, but I'm the lucky son-of-a-bitch who gets to give it to you. Say it for me right now…I'm a…."

"I'm a manly man." I giggled at first. But his eyes were penetrating mine and a wave of some sort of pride wafted through my chest and face. I stopped giggling and said it in a way that showed that for once, I finally believed it. "I'm a man, Tuck. And because of you I know that now."

"Almost." His smile lit up his whole face. "You have to smoke the cigar to make it official."

The GOAT DRIVE

The whole summer flashed before my eyes, beginning with the first time we'd talked on this trail, the beekeeper's suit he'd helped me make, the fact that I'd hated him when we met, and finally, the lonely train station in St. Paul and how angry I was at the man who had pulled me out of my jump. Tuck was still smirking in his fun, but I lost my smile and puffed up with emotion.

"Kyle Rickett," Tuck declared, "is not leaving Minnesota until he's celebrated us *both* being alive." He stopped all movements and stared for a few seconds squarely into my eyes. "We're strong together, Kyle. It's time you had your first beer and cigar. You, my friend, have earned them."

"You helped." I still couldn't take a compliment without giving one back in exchange. "So I'm the one who should be buying you gifts."

"Yeah, well, you saved me in more ways than you know. I've been half-dead for years." He patted me firmly on the back. "Hell, I might start dating real girls again! I feel horny for the first time since Shannon left."

I laughed at his comment.

He looked, again, into my eyes and hesitated until I finally looked up from the bag and into his again. "I'm definitely the one who should thank *you*."

I smiled. I knew what he meant. He was undeniably happier and more energetic than he had been when we met.

"Dad and my uncles did this for me on a snowmobile trip when I was exactly your age. And it really did change me," he said while unwrapping the cigars. "I'm damn proud to be the man who gets to pass this on to you this summer."

I cringed a little at the sight of the unwrapped dessert.

As if in a movie, I watched my own hand reach up and accept it. I'd never once even thought about smoking a cigar, but no part of me was going to turn this one down on this night. He ran one slowly beneath his nose to enjoy the aroma. I copied him. It did smell nice. Then he broke into a speech that sounded rehearsed.

"Kyle Rickett, with this cigar..." he said, dubbing me on the left shoulder, "I hereby declare thee..." then he lifted and dropped the cigar slowly onto my right shoulder, "a manly man."

"This is crazy." I didn't know what else to say.

"This is the good kind of crazy, Kyle." He drew back his arm and added, "This has been the best summer of my life." He grabbed two beers out of the six pack and offered me one.

As daylight faded, the fire's reflection in the glass beer bottles brought them to life. Tuck pulled a bottle opener from the bag, spritzed his open, and handed the device over. When mine popped and fizzed, he held his up and we bumped them together. They foamed like volcanoes and soaked our hands. It felt amazing.

"Here's to the coolest woodcutting buddy ever!" He nodded at me.

"Agreed." Not knowing what to expect, I sipped and closed my eyes tightly. The beer was warm from sitting in the car all day. It was *awful*! "Mmm. That's good," I lied.

"It's an acquired taste." He laughed. "Next time we do this, I promise they'll be ice cold." Then he pulled matches out of his pocket and struck one on a rock; it burst in a microscopic explosion. He held it to the end of his cigar, puffed, then held the flame toward me. "See if you like this any better."

I stuck the stogie in my mouth and leaned in toward him.

"Do *not* inhale," he instructed. "Just puff it in your mouth and blow it out. Or you'll turn green again."

There was a look of pure happiness, or perhaps immense pride, in his eyes. I stared into them while I puffed the cigar. It lit. It tasted fruity. I coughed. The flame reflected in his eyes. I saw, for the first time, how engaging a flickering eye could be. I wanted to grasp the importance of this moment so I could force it to my memory and enjoy it as much as he seemed to.

Time slowed to a crawl. The rich smoke overpowered all my taste buds, triggering a couple of deep coughs laced with chuckles, but not as many as you'd expect. Not inhaling helped. The world beyond the campsite vanished as I started to feel what Tuck was feeling. This moment was what I had come to the earth to live for.

"This brings me back to the night my dad and uncles did this for me." He pointed at me with his cigar. "If you're like me, young man, you'll never be the same after tonight."

"I hope I'm like you," I said with certainty. "That'd be cool."

As the most magical night of my life-so-far went on, we laughed and talked and danced to only two accordion songs, which proved to Tuck that it wasn't the best instrument for a campsite. Then when I tried to put the instrument down, he teasingly wrestled with me as if he wanted me to keep wearing it. But I got it off my neck and we sat back down to talk some more like adults.

During much of the conversation, when Tuck was lounging against the log with a stogie flopping in one hand and a beer in the other, I didn't even register the words being said between us. I just listened and laughed and soaked up the experience. We'd been passing a bottle of mosquito repellent back and forth, coating our arms, legs, necks, and faces, and now the world around us smelled of a blend of cigars, campfire, and repellent. An aroma I'll never, *ever* forget. During the course of the evening, Tuck used a full role of film capturing it all. I was giddy and excited to be permanently documented in his camera without posing. They were shots of real life in play. A stump became a tripod, and his timer captured a few poses of us arm-in-arm, with our stogies and our beers. In the final shot, with the campfire behind us, we raised our middle fingers in defiance to the outside world while he held me in an elbow lock around my neck. This was nothing like those fake smiles with my siblings' hands on my shoulders. This was how brothers are *supposed* to interact.

In the end, I'd really only smoked half the cigar and drank three quarters of one beer, but I laughed and hooted like a drunken sailor all the way to bedtime. I'd never released shouts and yelps like that—ever in my life. But Tuck somehow liberated the jungle-man in me. My drunkenness was mostly from being who I was now as the young man who had rebuilt a tractor, driven the world's most beautiful car, saved a life, and celebrated my initiation into manhood at the campfire of the great Tucker James Taylor. Blood may be thicker than water, but it didn't matter—*he was my big brother now.*

Late that night, in the tent

Later, in the musty, green canvas tent, we had been lying next to each other for nearly a half hour, each in our own sleeping bag, when my tormenting thoughts got to be too much to deal with alone. My vacation was over. Visions of going back to the island were sickening me. I'd never experienced this before. I'd never wanted a long time away from home and family to stay that way. This time, my homesickness was from knowing I had to leave Duluth. It was clear to me that Minnesota was my home now. In my brain, I'd moved. Tuck was my family. And just like my trip here, I was about to be put on an outbound train, away from it all, against my will. Again.

"Tuck?" I whispered into the darkness, over the rhythm and music of the crickets.

"Yeah?"

"Are you awake?"

I heard nothing at first. But then the nylon of his sleeping bag swooshed. The direction of his voice shifted like his mouth was pointed directly at my ear. "No."

I laughed.

"What's on your mind?"

"Thank you."

"What for?" His hoarseness got worse. Then he yawned loudly.

"For everything. Absolutely *everything*."

"I could say the same to you, buddy."

I let a minute pass, but I still had more to say.

"Tuck?"

"Still asleep."

I chuckled again.

"What's the matter, Kyle? Can't you sleep?"

"I don't want to."

Without words, he asked why. A long, slow breath told me he cared enough for me to go on.

"This is fucked. As soon as I fall asleep, the last day in Minnesota is over. When I wake up, I have to go back."

Tuck sighed.

The GOAT DRIVE

"I didn't want to come here. I fucking tried to kill myself so I wouldn't have to come here."

"I know."

"And now I don't want to leave. How stupid is that?"

"It's not stupid at all. You made friends here."

We listened to crickets again for a while.

"Kyle?"

"I'm sleeping." I tried not to laugh, but my own jokes always cracked me up.

"This wasn't *just* a good time for me, you know. It was a whole lot more. I made a friend too. A *real* friend. For life. Somehow this summer was supposed to happen just how it did—for both of us."

"It *was* kind of a miracle for me."

"For me too, Kyle. You have no idea how you've changed my life." His hand found mine resting on my chest. Over the sleeping bag, he wiggled me gently. "I'm going to miss all this too. When you go home, I have to start looking for work. This was a *vacation* for both of us."

"I wish it was permanent."

"Vacations end. Eventually, real life finds you again."

"I wish I could go with you, back to *your* real life instead of mine."

"You will someday. I know you can survive the island, Kyle. I survived my teen years, and you're twice the man I was at your age."

I thought about his unbelievable story, the one that had taken him so long to tell me about—an entire life that he had lived between my age and his. At seven, he had gotten a scar and watched his friend's dad die. At fourteen, his dad and uncles had given him his beer and cigar party. Then at sixteen, he had found out he had cancer. *He* had died. He had come back to life, had a baby, had the baby die, and the mom leave him. Then he had gone to college and hated it. All his friends had left him. He was completely alone and lost at only twenty-one. And then he met me and everything got better for him. I started to smile at how honored that made me feel.

We listened to the crickets again for a while. Something shuffled about in the bushes outside the tent. Probably a rabbit.

"Do you really think I'm twice the man you were?" I broke the silence.

If a person could hear a smile, I heard his. A gentle chuckle over the crickets' chirp. "I have never, ever met a fourteen-year-old with so much life as what you have in just your little pinky. Kyle, what I went through at your age made me into someone smart enough to see what a prize you are. The shit you've had to deal with your whole life is making you into a better man too. If you read enough biographies, you'll start to see that really *good* people seldom had easy, spoiled childhoods."

"I hope when I'm your age, I'm as nice a guy as you are."

"You'll be better. Way better."

"All I have to do is live through one more fucking year at St. Tiberius's."

"You can do it. I taught you how to sucker-punch a bigger boy."

"There's a dozen bigger boys."

"You'll only have to punch one."

"Andreo?"

"Probably not him. He's a sociopath. They're chicken. They trick their flying monkeys into doing all their dirty work."

"Flying monkeys?"

"Their followers. Like in the Land of Oz. The flying monkeys do the dirty work for their wicked leader. They're like puppets. Andreo tricks them into doing his dirty work and then hides behind them. He'll never get within arm's distance of you. He'll see it in your eyes, that you're ready to take him on, and he'll hide behind his allies."

"His allies are my bullies."

"For now. Bullies and allies are actually the same people. They can change teams like you do socks. You show them, just one time, that you aren't their little bitch anymore, and those bullies will start to act like *your* allies again. They're puppets. Pawns. Flying monkeys. All of Andreo's power is in his words, getting the pawns to believe him is his only, only defense. You show them he's wrong, and they'll turn on him as fast as they turned on you."

"All of them?"

"Enough will. And enough is enough. Once you're not alone, you're not alone. Once you have one friend, you are no longer alone. Just one ally is 99 percent of the whole solution to loneliness."

I didn't have a response. The chill in the night air wasn't enough to cool me down inside the warm sleeping bag, and since the mosquitos were all safely outside the tent, I slid it off my chest, down to my waistline to cool off. Neither of us spoke for a moment.

"Kyle, you can do this." This time he was the one to break the silence.

"I guess."

"No guess!" Tuck imitated Papa. "Do!"

I laughed.

His hand found mine on my chest again, but this time we were skin-on-skin. The warmth of his touch on the back of my hand still had a magic in it that felt like he was truly a blood relative and that he truly cared about me.

"Trust," I said loudly.

"Trust?" He pulled his hand off me. "The safe word? Did I do something wrong?"

"Not you." I reached around in the dark air until I found his hand. I put it back how it was on mine. "It's always going to be my safe word. When I go home, when Fran starts lying about me to mom and she believes it…*trust*."

"I'm not sure that's how a safe word works. It's a contract you have with me, not her. She's not going to stop."

"Oh. I guess you're right."

"I have a better word for you. Tractoooor."

I laughed again. "You haven't said that word in almost an hour."

"I use it a lot, don't I? You need to start using it now."

"How will that help?"

"What does it mean? When I say it, what does it remind you of?"

"That I rebuilt the tractor when I was only twelve and thirteen. And that I didn't realize how big a deal that was, but you keep telling me it's something other guys can't do, and it makes me manly."

"Does it remind you of anything else?"

"Yeah." I smiled, really, really big, as his idea started to make sense to me. "If I say it on the island, it'll remind me of you."

"And?"

"And Papa, and Grandpa Tucker..." I started brainstorming my summer memories out loud, "aaaand saving your life in the woods, and the newspaper article calling me a hero."

"Another fourteen-year-old couldn't have gotten me into that car, and then driven it like a fucking professional driver, which, by the way, *saved my life*!"

"It seems like anyone could do those things if they had to. You left the keys in the ignition again. Anyone can use a car to save someone."

"Well, you're wrong. They can't. They can't cook like you either. Or play the accordion. Jesus, Kyle, you were the star of a summer event that was organized just for you."

A smile overpowered me.

"You've hardly practiced, and still you could hold your own for a crowd."

"Papa's letting me take the accordion home with me tomorrow, so I can get better at it."

"Really? And you're okay with that? You're not going to hide it under your bed?"

"I'm going to play it, Tuck. A lot. Papa said I'm the only grandkid who has fun playing it, and it needs to breathe, so he *wants* me to take it home. He *wants* me to play it. So I'm going to. I'm going to fucking play it!" I started to cry, quite by accident. "I can't believe I let them take that away from me for so long. I gave up what I wanted because I was worried a bunch of flying monkey *assholes* would laugh. But I get to play music now! And I'm not going to lie about it. Not even to Fran."

"My God, you've come a long way in a short time."

We listened to more crickets while I calmed down and started a whole new train of thought. For me, the best part of sleepovers with friends like Connor, Scooter, and now Tuck was the long list of thoughtful and quiet conversations we'd have while staring into the silent darkness of a night that we seemed to own for a little while.

"Tuck?"

"Kyle?"

"Remember when we met? And you asked me what kind of car was my favorite?"

"You said you liked lots of cars."

"I sort of lied."

He laughed quietly. "So I'm guessing you didn't want to tell me you liked Goats."

"Gold ones. When I saw your gold GTO, it almost blew my freaking mind." With both hands, I imitated an explosion emanating from my head. "Bam!"

"Is that why you knew so much about it? The gear ratio? The engine size? Even that the color was named *signet* gold?"

"Yes. I have watercolor paintings at home that I've made of that exact car. A signet gold 1967 GTO has always been my single, most favorite car in the world. And then you *drive up in one*." I made the same hand gesture, exploding from my head again. "Bam!"

"Hmm." He chuckled at my exploding head demo. He couldn't see it, but he could feel my hands bumping him. "I guess that would freak me out, too. But why did you lie about it?"

"I don't know. Jealousy? I guess I didn't want you to know I liked what you had."

"I get that. Also, you didn't trust me yet."

"And the truth sounded more like a lie than the lie did. If I told you that I liked gold GTOs just like yours, you might have thought I was just saying it to be nice or something."

"That's Fran's work. Hypervigilance. You've been attacked so many times for what you say that you nervously try to guess how others are going to call you a liar, no matter how true it is, every time you plan to open your mouth."

We listened to more crickets as I thought about everything he'd just said.

"Fuck, Fran," I blurted out. "It really *is* my favorite car in the whole world. And I've never been the same since you let me drive it. That was the coolest day ever. It changed me."

"You wanna hear a confession?"

"Yeah."

"That's why I did it."

"To change me?"

"Not to change *you*. But to change your perspective. To make you see yourself how I saw you. I wanted you to trust me, so I wanted to prove I trusted you too. I know I told you this already, but since the day my parents bought it for me, no one else has ever driven it. *Ever*."

We listened again to the crickets for a minute or so. I had a grin on my face that he couldn't see in the dark.

"I can do this, Tuck. I'm going to go back to that stupid, fucking island, and that stupid, fucking Catholic school, and I'm going to be different." Manly, fearless energy swelled in my chest. In fact, all of a sudden, I actually wanted to go back to the island and take them all on—Fran, Andreo, the Catholic-school-flying-monkey-pawns. This was going to be my time to soar. My war to win.

"When you get back there, you won't be alone. You remember this summer, okay? I'll be on the phone to you every Thursday. Because Louie and I both know your parents and Fran have a way of isolating you from your friends, Louie's never going to tell them about me. They can't make you stop talking to me, like they did Scooter, if they don't know I exist. Your family thinks you spent the summer with Louie and my grandfather."

"I know. Papa told me that last week. He hasn't mentioned your name even once to my mom."

"He knows what he's doing. Every Thursday, just before the five o'clock news, he's going to sneak a phone call in and hand the receiver to me after your mom gives the phone to you. While she's in the other room watching the news, I'll use that call to help you remember all the amazing things you've done, and can still do. You can give me progress reports and I can coach you with the words you need to go another week. You're not alone anymore, Kyle. Not by a long shot."

"I'm ready."

"No, you're not. Not quite."

Tuck's sleeping bag swooshed again. I felt him leave my side. Pretty soon a flashlight brightened the tent. He moved over to his pants folded neatly by the door. He dug something from the pocket and twisted back toward me.

"I still have one more gift for you," he said while walking on his knees toward me. "I wasn't going to give this to you until you were getting on the train tomorrow. But there will never be a more perfect moment than now."

I smirked with excitement. I held my palm out and he dropped a key into it.

"Put this on your key ring."

"What is it to?"

"That's the original spare key for the Goat."

Chills exploded throughout my entire body. All my skin tingled. "My own key?"

"You've earned it, Kyle. Just like I did. That car was given to me as a gift when I lived through cancer and lost my son. My parents bought it off a neighbor. They knew I'd always admired it. They told me I needed something beautiful in my life. A celebratory symbol of leaving a sad childhood for a strong manhood. Ever since that day, that car has only had two drivers. Now each of those two has his own key."

"That car's your best friend. You told me yourself."

"Not anymore."

I smiled at him.

"Now I'm going to share it with you. I don't want you going back to the place that almost killed you, feeling like all you have are empty memories of a fun summer with a guy you hope is thinking about you."

"This really works? It's a real Goat key? To *your* Goat?"

"It's real. Every new car comes with two keys. Even the neighbor who bought it new had never used it. No one in history has ever gotten to use that one…not yet. It's yours now. And you will use it in the future."

"There's a future? I'll see you again?"

"That's the stupidest question I've ever heard, Kyle." He slapped at my shoulder with the back of his hand. "There's no way in hell you and I are never going to see each other again. And that key is proof." He tapped the key while I held it. "Now you can go back to the island with a real, true functioning item in your pocket that you know isn't just a fantasy memory."

"I'm really going to be okay." I held the key up and examined it from every angle. "Aren't I, Tuck?"

"Yes, Kyle. As long as you don't forget what you are right now. You were a disaster-in-the-making when we met. But you, me, and our grandfathers have changed your direction. You're not headed to the streets or bus stations anymore. These past five weeks were real. You *really* lived them. If you don't let yourself forget about these five weeks, you can go home and have them as a better past now—and that will set you on course for a brighter future. All you have to do to survive your next four years on that fucking 'disaster island' of yours is remember Duluth was real. When the sociopaths in your world try to convince you that you are someone to torment, all you have to do is put *your* hand in *your* pocket and jingle *your* keys to remember who you really are."

I lurched toward him and bear-hugged him around his neck.

"You're my best friend now, Kyle. That's who you *really* are."

"I'm going to make it. I'm really going to get through this."

"You're still the cutest little shit I've ever met, but, God damn it, Kyle James Rickett, you're also a man above men."

"I just realized…I haven't daydreamed that I was someone else, even once, ever since your accident." I thought for a second, then added, "Tuck, I haven't even imagined myself floating out in space, away from everyone."

"So, Pinocchio, you're a real boy now?"

"I'm not a boy," I teased, "just small for my age."

"I haven't heard you say that in over a month, either." He laughed.

"I guess I haven't needed to."

"Wait 'til they get a load of you, little brother." He leaned in and squeezed me this time, tightly around my shoulders. "Wait 'til they get a fucking load of you. They're in for the shock of their lives."

"I'm not their little bitch anymore, am I, Tuck?"

"Not by a long shot. You've proven it six ways from Sunday."

"I really do make a difference, don't I, Tuck? I can do real things." As I said these words, I realized that for the first time in my life, I actually, truly *believed* them.

"That you can, Kyle James Rickett. You thought you were nothing. But it turns out you are something, just like the rest of us."

"Damn right I am." I pulled away from him and held the key between us. Visions of him letting me drive the GTO, and of not getting mad at me when I almost crashed it, rolled across my mind. Then more visions came, like when I used it to pull the tree off his lungs, and when I came up with the idea to drive ninety miles an hour so a cop would stop us and save his life. I bubbled with pride I'd never felt before. "I'm not what Andreo says I am. Or what Fran says I am. I'm Kyle James Rickett."

"A manly man, if ever there was one."

I proudly held up the key I'd earned by being who I am and not what anyone said I was.

"I am the *Goat Driver*."

ABOUT THE AUTHOR

James F. Johnson is the author of the *Bullies & Allies* series, consisting of *Disaster Island, The Goat Driver*, and *The Puzzled*, and he is a contributor to the Richer Fuller Life project. He has spent years working with people in crisis, most commonly, adult survivors of childhood sexual abuse. He's worked on crisis intervention hotlines and worked with law enforcement and hospital emergency room staffs to advocate for victims of sexual assault. He has been hosted as guest speaker in various community outreach programs, colleges, and professional development seminars, and is a former amateur standup comedian. In his writing, James expertly captures the experiences he's shared with his many clients and peers who have helped him to understand the feelings and pitfalls of living with the lifelong emotional effects of childhood trauma.

James's studies have led him through years of research on PTSD, Complex-PTSD, gaslighting, and sociopathy. He readily shares his knowledge and insight into these topics in his public presentations, private conversations, novels, blog articles, and at his website, www.jamesfjohnson.com. He posts suggested reading lists, showing others how to find the same research that has enlightened him on how to identify and stand up to the many sociopaths who cross our paths. James believes that by teaching others how to identify and handle sociopaths, people have a chance of becoming free from their grips and power, and ultimately, of turning our society into a better, safer place for all of us.

JAMES F JOHNSON

NEXT IN THE SERIES:

Be sure to read the whole Bullies & Allies series to experience Kyle's adventures as he learns about the sociopaths in his life, and that Post-Traumatic Stress Disorder (PTSD) can be managed, trust can be learned, friendships can be made, and a long, happy life can still be lived, even when the traumas of childhood remain hidden in the background.

The Bullies & Allies story is told in the 1970s. Now, forty-plus years later, our hairstyles have changed and our cars, phones, and electronics have advanced in ways we could not have predicted. Our social and human challenges, however, remain unmoved. Bullying, abuse, isolation, PTSD, withdrawal, and even suicide, are still prevalent in far too many lives. These problems not only cause the same grief as before, but they are also driven by the same reasons they were then.

In *Disaster Island*, the first book, we traveled into Kyle's isolation with him. In the second book, *The Goat Driver*, we saw the amazing and glorious healing power of friendship and trust. Trust is the bonding ingredient that makes us strong together. In the third book, *The Puzzled*, Kyle will learn that the effects of trauma can be challenging and far-reaching, but that there is always a productive future worth living for, and while he will always be an adult survivor of childhood abuse, his capacity for true happiness will be far greater than it would have been had his childhood been easier.

Kyle's past is with him for life. He will never *not* be the survivor of aggressive isolationism (mob-bullying), but Kyle will learn that plenty can be done to enjoy life despite a difficult and unforgettable past.

Bullies & Allies Book 1: Disaster Island

The story begins with a summertime bicycle accident that disrupts thirteen-year-old Kyle Rickett's illusion of living a perfect life. Dr. Krieg, the pedophilic family friend who stitches him up, unlocks PTSD-driven, repressed memories of horrific events that Kyle used to think were dreams. Unable to shake the fear that they really happened, Kyle finds that the event tips the first domino in a long series of unrelated, individual problems, each of which he had thought he was handling. But now, the whole picture becomes far too overwhelming for him to handle alone.

Kyle's been surviving mob-bullying at school, and his sociopathic older sister is cruel beyond words at home. His dysfunctional family is no help. The Ricketts are led by his father, whose own military PTSD makes the family live on eggshells, nervously keeping him calm by hiding or ignoring all problems.

As Kyle learns he will always be alone with his memories, and unsupported by his family, he fades from the real world into emotional withdrawal. His life loses all meaning. He can't make sense of his complicated, dreamlike past, and he loses any belief in having a future. He begins to plan his escape, to run to the streets, and to make money doing whatever a blond boy can do for it. If that doesn't work, suicide is always an option.

There is a person who can save him, a young man with a similar past, but who is thousands of miles away and a stranger. Tuck Taylor's depression is eating him alive in Texas. When things seem their most hopeless for both, luck sends them to a new place. By the end of July, both end up somehow on the road to Duluth where their grandfathers just happen to be best friends. Kyle is sent against his will to sit out the rest of summer in hopes that whatever's eating at him back in Washington State will heal itself before school starts again in the fall. Tuck drives to Duluth in hopes his own grandfather will help pull him out of his funk. Now if they can find each other in time, they both might find a second chance at a happy and perfect life.

Bullies & Allies Book 2: The Goat Driver

Now distant from his family's dysfunction in Washington, Kyle arrives in Minnesota to spend the summer with his grandfather, Papa Louie. But Louie sees withdrawn vacancy in Kyle's eyes, and after having lost a friend named Maury to suicide, Louie comes to believe his grandson is following the same path. When withdrawn and secretive Kyle won't talk to him, Louie rallies the support of his young neighbor,

Tuck Taylor, to intervene. Tuck, a trustworthy, but somewhat lost soul, quickly takes a liking to the boy and then makes a promise to Louie that he'll never let Kyle jump like Maury did. Through Tuck, Kyle is able to learn, for the first time, how to trust someone. What happens over those few weeks surprises even Tuck when, by the end of the summer, he discovers and experiences the great power of friendship, and that by saving Kyle, he has brought meaning to his own life. By saving another, he has saved himself.

Bullies & Allies Book 3: The Puzzled

Fourteen-year-old Kyle returns to Torano Island to resume the path he once struggled to survive, but this time not alone. He has a long-distance alliance with Tuck in the shadows as his secret mentor. But only if Tuck remains a secret, will he have the power to help. Things improve when Dr. Krieg's pedophilic attacks are stopped once and for all, and a change of schools gives a whole new start to a social life. Kyle now seems to have what he needs to survive the last four years of childhood. Or does he?

Kyle has become a funny, happy, well-loved, well-connected kid, but unfortunately, trauma lingers and Kyle's traumas have left invisible scars and triggers, which act as dangerously hidden emotional booby-traps. His life is now a complicated puzzle with too many pieces to name. When a key member of the family dies and cousin Scooter vanishes and is presumed dead, Tuck's long-distance advice isn't enough, and best friend Connor becomes the only stable grip to remain in Kyle's life. But Connor is just a boy, and even he becomes frustrated by Kyle's self-destructive episodes.

Kyle has survived his enemies, but now he must learn to survive himself. Before Kyle turns eighteen, the final blow comes when his secret friendship with Tuck, his knowledge of Scooter's whereabouts, and his past sexual abuse at the hands of Dr. Krieg are all exposed once and for all. His family isn't equipped to know how to handle him, so Kyle feels more alone than ever before and unsure how to survive his personal shame or his family's dysfunction. Some say God never gives a person more than he can handle, but Kyle discovers that is not true. If he wants a chance at any happiness at all, he has to make the most difficult choice of his entire life, and no matter which way he chooses to go, someone's going to get hurt.

SNEAK PEAK AT:

The Puzzled

By JAMES F JOHNSON

In the following excerpt, Connor has spotted Kyle returning home to Torano Island from his mysterious trip to Duluth. The two best friends are now in Kyle's bedroom, unpacking Kyle's suitcase.

4

Obvious Changes

By Kyle Rickett

"Well, you're right about one thing; you're not the same person you used to be." Connor's straight brown bangs had grown to cover his entire forehead until they blended with his dark frame glasses, which were now riding high on his crinkled, smirking nose. He'd finally shaved off that fur that had been growing above his lip, but at the same time, more zits had formed around his mouth and chin than earlier that summer. What little of his face I could see looked oily. His voice was even deeper than when I'd left. His smile was the same, but he looked different. It was like I'd been gone years instead of weeks.

We were still in my room, and I was now unpacking the blue suitcase, hanging new jeans and stylish shirts in my closet. The window was open, letting in a fresh, sweet-smelling breeze. Connor's exuberance helped me enjoy the slight hint of fall, which was my favorite Pacific coastal weather.

"How can you tell?" I asked. I poked at his shoulder with one of my shirt hangers.

"'Cause you got nice clothes now. And you're taller!"

"Taller? That's it? I'm *taller*? That's how you think I've changed?"

"No, there's more."

"Damn straight there is!" I paused and waited for him to say that I was more self-assured. More confident. Manlier.

"Your blonder than blond hair is so *pretty*." He comically ran his fingers through the left side of my scalp, making me cringe and bat his arm away. "Oh, my God! Did you *blow dry* it?"

"That's not what I meant!" I laughed. "But yeah." I shook my head enthusiastically to show off the long hair. "I finally joined the 1970s! Papa Louie got me an actual, real-life, professional haircut a week ago."

"And your mom's letting you keep it?"

"I just got home. She hasn't threatened to shave it off yet. So I hope she never does."

"She'd be crazy to."

"Yeah, well," I leaned in like I had a secret, "she's crazy, so…." I waved my hand slowly.

"Well, I hope she lets you keep it. It looks awesome!"

"And Papa Louie bought me a blow dryer." I pushed Connor aside, lifted my duffle bag from the floor to the bed, put it next to the open suitcase, unzipped it, and pulled out a shiny white blow dryer with the cord wrapped tightly around it. I pointed it at him to pretend it was a pistol. "Pow! Pow! Pow-pa-pow!"

"Aaahhh!" He grabbed his chest and fell dead on the bed, laughing.

I'd met Connor when we were both ten. I'd always been secretive about Catholic school, but I had never once outright lied to him—until now. It felt *horrible*. But life was unmanageably complicated now, and I had even more new life-or-death secrets than ever that I needed to protect. Connor could not know that it was Tuck who had purchased all the new clothes for me, and who put me in the salon chair, and that it was Tuck who gave me the dryer and showed me how to use it. This mysterious Tuck had even shown me how to dress so I didn't look like a dork. He was the only person in the world willing to teach me how to stand up to my family. If anyone on Torano found out he existed, my family would cut the lifeline and I'd be right where I once had been.

"It's a powerful dryer. I used it on the train this morning before I got into the Everett station."

"Ah," he teased as he stood back up, "did you pretty yourself up for me?" He started rifling through my duffle bag. His eyes caught my black case still on the floor. "What's that thing?"

"That's my accordion."

"For real? I've never seen one in real life. Is that the one from the picture?" He pointed at my desk photo of me and Papa and cousin Scooter in our lederhosen. Then he lifted the case onto the bed and started opening it up.

"Yup. Papa told me I was the only person in the family who wanted it, so he gave it to me."

"Did you get *me* anything?" He pulled the accordion out, but he couldn't figure out how to wear it. So he put it back in the case and changed over to rifling through my blue suitcase instead.

"No, I didn't *get* you anything." I slapped at his shoulder. This was my next lie, but it was for an acceptable reason. In the suitcase's zippered lid, an inch away from his prodding fingers, were his birthday gifts; the new Neil Diamond album he'd been saving for; and a pair of eagle pendants we were each going to get one of.

"Well," He stood up straight and looked me in the eye, "I got *you* something." Then he smiled with a goofy, proud grin.

"I know. You told me on the phone. *Disaster Island*, issues forty-two and forty-three." Sadly, once lying begins, it can take on a life of its own. Along with the Neil Diamond album, I had hidden two pristine, brand new issues, forty-two and forty-three. Tuck had bought them for me in Duluth on the same days Connor was buying them for me here, and I didn't want to make any references of any kind to spark any interest in who my friends were while I was away. It felt like I was cheating on him. Were the lies necessary? Probably not, but like I said, the complication was unmanageable and, *once we practice to deceive....*

"And the world's most perfect birthday present." His voice raised an octave with excitement. "You're going to love it!"

I had to force myself to keep laughing.

"What?" he asked, obviously able to tell I'd lost my joy.

"I hate that we missed each other's birthdays."

"I know." He stopped smiling too.

"Since you moved here, we've never missed each other's birthdays before...*ever*."

"It wasn't our fault." He put a brotherly hand on my shoulder. "As soon as you admit you got me a birthday present too, we'll schedule our own private party." He chuckled.

"Ha!" I laughed with him and covered my ongoing lie. "I still have to get you one."

We paused and stared at each other for a moment. Emotions too complicated to figure out welled up in me. I think my sinking feeling was because of the lies I was telling. They seemed to be building quickly. One was leading to the next. Where was this going to end? Or maybe it was from the anger I was feeling that my parents had ruined our birthday celebrations. Or worse. That everything between the two of us may have changed this summer and he just didn't know it yet. Probably, my sinking feeling was all of the above.

For whatever reason, I could feel a wall going up between us. And even though *I* was the one building it, it hurt. Bad.

Up and out

"I have to get out of the *fucking* house." From out of nowhere, my mood shifted. I threw the hair dryer onto the soft bed and headed for the door like the room was on fire.

"Whoa, Kyle!" Connor followed me into the hall. "Where are we going?"

To be continued.

The GOAT DRIVE

JAMES F JOHNSON

www.ingramcontent.com/pod-product-compliance
Lightning Source LLC
LaVergne TN
LVHW020925090426
835512LV00020B/3198